RIDLEY.

TREATISES

AND

LETTERS

OF

DR. NICHOLAS RIDLEY,

BISHOP OF LONDON, AND MARTYR, 1555.

Eugene, Oregon

Wipf and Stock Publishers
199 W 8th Ave, Suite 3
Eugene, OR 97401

Treatises and Letters of Dr. Nicholas Ridley
By Ridley, Nicholas
ISBN: 1-59752-200-7
Publication date 5/17/2005
Previously published by The Religious Tract Society, 1830

BRIEF ACCOUNT

OF

DR. NICHOLAS RIDLEY,

Bishop of London, and Martyr, 1555.

Dr. Nicholas Ridley was born in the beginning of the sixteenth century, at Willemonstwick, a town in Northumberland, near the borders of Scotland. His father was the third son of an ancient and respectable family who had long resided in that country. After being educated at Newcastle on Tyne, he was removed to Pembroke-hall, in Cambridge, about the year 1518, just at the time when Luther's opposition to the pope's bulls respecting indulgences began to excite general attention. He applied studiously to acquire the learning then most in repute, and, as his biographer states, 'his character at that time, appears to have been that of an ingenious, virtuous, zealous papist.'

After some years passed at Cambridge, Ridley visited France, and studied at the universities of Paris and Louvain. On his return (about 1529), he pursued his theological studies with much earnestness, in particular committing to memory the greater part of the epistles in the original Greek, and his mind appears to have been enlightened by the study of the scriptures. In 1534, he took an active part in the public discussions relative to the pope's supremacy, and, in 1537, archbishop Cranmer appointed him one of his chaplains.

In 1538, Ridley was collated to the vicarage of Herne, in Kent, where the people for many miles round crowded to attend his preaching; and he diligently instructed his charge in the doctrines of the gospel, although on the point of transubstantiation, he was not as yet fully emancipated from popish errors. When the act of the six articles came out, Ridley bore public testimony against it, but being unmarried, and as yet in error as to the Sacrament of the altar, he did not fall within its penalties.

In October, 1540, Ridley was appointed to the mastership of Pembroke-hall, which was then remarked for the learning and scriptural knowledge of its members, and, in the following year, he was nominated one of the prebendaries of Canterbury, where he preached so strongly against the abuses of popery, as to excite some of the bigoted ecclesiastics to accuse him of having offended against the laws then in force; but their malice was disappointed. He particularly contended that prayer should be made in a language which the people could understand.

Ridley passed a great part of the year 1545 at Herne, when he was induced to examine more particularly respecting the Sacrament; the arguments and sufferings of those who opposed the popish errors upon this subject having made a strong impression upon his mind. The effect of this investigation, was to remove the error under which he had laboured, and, communicating his views to Cranmer, they examined the doctrines of the church of Rome as to transubstantiation, and those of the Lutheran church respecting consubstantiation. After a full investigation of the scriptures, and the writings of the Fathers of the primitive church, they were enabled to discern the truths which had been till then obscured and concealed from their view.

On the accession of Edward VI., Ridley was appointed one of the preachers at court, and forwarded the Reformation to the utmost of his power. In 1547, he was made bishop of Rochester, and, in 1549, we find him bearing a prominent part in a public disputation, with the Romanists at Cambridge, on the subject of the Sacrament of the Lord's Supper, the particulars of which are fully stated in Fox's Acts and Monuments.

In April, 1550, Ridley was appointed to the see of London; this important office he discharged with much faithfulness, and in a very exemplary manner. He behaved with much kindness to Bonner, who was removed from that bishopric on account of his obstinate attachment to popery, and was particularly careful that he should suffer as little pecuniary loss as possible from his removal. When at Fulham, he always, at dinner and supper, sent for Bonner's mother and sister, who resided near, and constantly placed the former at his right hand, alleviating her misfortunes to the utmost of his power.*

Fox thus speaks of Ridley's discharge of his episcopal duties. "He so laboured and occupied himself in preaching and teaching the true and wholesome doctrine of Christ, that a good child never was more loved by his dear parents, than he was by his flock and diocese. Every Sunday and holy day, he preached in some place or other, unless hindered by weighty business. To these sermons the people resorted, swarming about him like bees, and coveting the sweet flowers and wholesome juice of the fruitful doctrine, which he not only preached, but showed the same by his life as a shining light, in such pure order; that even his very adversaries could not reprove him in any one jot thereof." His ordinary course of life at that time, is thus described by the same writer. "He, using all ways to mortify himself, was given to much prayer and contemplation. For early every morning so soon as his apparel was upon him, he prayed on his knees half an hour, which being done, immediately he went to his study, if there came no other business to interrupt him, where he continued till ten o'clock, and then came to common prayer daily used in his house. The prayers being done, he went to dinner,† where he talked little, and then it was sober, discreet, and wise, and sometimes merry, as the cause required. The dinner being over, which was not very long, he used to sit an hour or thereabouts talking, or playing at chess. That done, he returned to his study, and continued there until five o'clock, unless suitors or business abroad prevented. He then came to common prayer, which being finished, he went to supper. After supper he recreated himself an hour, and then returned to his study, continuing there till eleven o'clock, which was his common hour to go to bed, then saying his prayers upon his knees as in the morning when he rose. When at Fulham, he read a lecture to his family every day at the common prayer, beginning at the Acts, and so going through all the epistles, giving a New Testament to every man that could read, and hiring them

* When Bonner was restored, he acted in a very different manner, not only treating Ridley's relations with much harshness and severity, but even depriving them of property to which they were legally entitled, and endeavouring to procure the death of Ridley's brother-in-law.

† At that period, it was usual for the nobility and gentry to dine at eleven o'clock.

with money to learn by heart certain principal chapters, but especially Acts xiii. He often read to his household the 101st psalm, being very careful over his family, that they might be an example of all virtue and honesty to others. To be short, as he was godly and virtuous himself, so nothing but godliness and virtue reigned in his house, he feeding them with the food of our Saviour Jesus Christ."

Much of Ridley's time, during the reign of Edward VI., was occupied in discharging the public duties of his office, which were neither few nor small, and during the prevalence of a pestilential distemper in London, called the sweating sickness,* he continued to reside among his flock. In his pastoral duties, he was ably assisted by Bradford and Grindal, two of his chaplains.

In the beginning of 1553, the king's health was evidently in a declining state, when, by Ridley's means, the noble foundation of Christ's Hospital, and those of St. Bartholomew, Bridewell, and Bethlehem were established.

The particulars of the last days of Edward VI., and the brief reign of Lady Jane Grey need not be given in this place. Ridley does not appear to have taken a prominent part in those events, if we except a sermon preached by him at Paul's Cross, by order of the council, on one of the two Sundays between the death of king Edward, and the entrance of queen Mary into London. On that occasion, he strongly urged the evils which must ensue from Mary's attachment to popery, if she obtained the crown. This was not forgotten by his enemies, and as soon as Mary's authority was established, Ridley was committed to the tower, and Bonner was again established as bishop of London—of the wide difference between his conduct and that of Ridley, both in private life and public affairs, the reader doubtless is fully aware.

Ridley continued in the tower several months. During the greater part of the time he had Cranmer and Latimer for his fellow-prisoners;—the result of their conferences will be found in the following pages. In April, 1554, these venerable Fathers of the English church were sent to Oxford, to dispute publicly

* The 15th of April, 1551, the infectious sweating sickness began at Shrewsbury. What number died cannot be well accounted, but certain it is, that in London in a few days 960 gave up the ghost.- *Stowe's Annals.*

with a number of the Romish doctors on the subject of the mass and the Sacrament of the Lord's Supper. The particulars of this disputation were recorded by Jewel, and are given at length in Fox's Acts and Monuments:—the manner in which it was conducted is noticed in a subsequent page of this work: we may, however, observe that Ridley's knowledge of the Greek language, and his being versed in the writings of the Fathers, enabled him to correct many attempts to pervert the meaning of the ancient writers.* After these disputations were concluded, the three bishops were condemned as heretics, when Ridley replied, " Although I be not of your company, yet, I doubt not, but that my name is written in another place, whither this sentence will send us sooner than we should have come by the course of nature."

They were not put to death at that time, but were closely confined at Oxford during the next eighteen months. Though kept from scenes of active usefulness, they were not idle. Latimer, weak and enfeebled through age, could do little but read his Testament; and that, as he afterwards declared, he read over diligently seven times during his confinement. Cranmer reviewed, and added to, his writings on the Sacrament. Ridley was strictly watched, deprived of most of his books, and denied the use of pen, ink, and paper; but he snatched every opportunity; and when his scanty supplies of materials for writing failed him, he cut the lead from his prison-windows, and wrote in the margins of the few books he possessed.

In the letters given in the following pages, the reader will find many interesting notices of this irksome period of Ridley's confinement. It was particularly severe with regard to him; while in the tower he had been more favourably treated than many others but when the papists found he could not be wrought upon by all their blandishments they changed their measures, and acted towards him with much severity.

At length, in October, 1555, Ridley and his companions were called before commissioners appointed to examine and condemn them. After some discussions, which chiefly related to

* Latimer was not well skilled in Greek, having been far advanced in life before that language was much taught. Of this the Romanists took advantage, and when arguing with him, actually falsified a quotation from the New Testament!

the usurped authority of the popes, Ridley was condemned, and also his fellow-prisoners. His life was spared a fortnight longer, during which he wrote some farewell letters and admonitions. On the 15th of October he was degraded by the Romish commissioners, and the next morning he was led forth to the place where he and Latimer were to be burned. Ridley arrived there first, and as soon as his fellow-sufferer came, Ridley kissed him, saying, " Be of good heart, brother, for God will either assuage the fury of the flame, or else strengthen us to abide it." The latter was his experience. Dr. Smith preached a sermon, in which he asserted many falsities respecting the martyrs and their doctrines, to which Ridley wished to reply, but was not permitted : " Well," said he, " so long as the breath is in my body, I will never deny my Lord Christ and his known truth."

They were then fastened to the stake. Ridley lifted up his hands towards heaven and prayed. " O heavenly Father, I give thee most hearty thanks that thou hast called me to be a professor of thee even unto death. I beseech thee, Lord God, have mercy upon the realm of England, and deliver her from all her enemies." Ridley then addressed himself to lord Williams, who was appointed to superintend the execution, and besought him to plead with the queen in behalf of his poor relatives, and others who were unlawfully deprived by Bonner of the leases they had agreed for with Ridley while he possessed the see of London.

The fire was lighted—when Ridley saw it flaming up towards him, he cried out with a loud voice, " Into thy hands, O Lord, I commend my spirit. O Lord, receive my spirit." Latimer soon died, apparently with little or no pain ; but on Ridley's side the fire was kept down, owing to the bad management of those that had built up the fagots, so that it only burned beneath. When Ridley felt this, he intreated them, for Christ's sake, to let the fire come to him. His brother-in-law, desiring to relieve his pain, but misunderstanding his wishes, heaped on more fagots, which kept the fire down still longer, and it burned all his lower parts without touching the upper. He repeated his desire to have the fire suffered to come unto him, and after his legs were consumed, the spectators saw one side of his body shirt and all, untouched with the flame. But his confident expectation was granted; for although the torment was indeed dreadful, " he was strengthened to abide it." He frequently exclaimed, " O Lord, have mercy upon me," and requested that they would let the fire come to him. At last he was understood; one of the bystanders pulled off the upper fagots—the flame arose, and when the tortured martyr saw the fire, he leaned towards it. After the flame reached the gunpowder affixed to him and it had exploded, he stirred no more; but his legs being wholly consumed, the upper part of his body turned over the chain, and fell at Latimer's feet.—These horrifying details are given from Fox, not needlessly to wound the reader's feelings, but for the striking picture they present of the constancy of this faithful martyr of Christ.

Let us briefly contrast the last hours of Ridley with those of his cruel persecutor, bishop Gardiner, which occurred immediately afterwards. On the day of Ridley and Latimer's martyrdom, he waited with impatience for the account of their burning, having arranged that messengers should be despatched to inform him as soon as the pile was set on fire. He delayed sitting down to his dinner till he received the desired intelligence. About four o'clock an express arrived with the welcome news, and Gardiner sat down to dinner. He " was not disappointed of his lust, but while the meat was yet in his mouth the heavy wrath of God came upon him." While at table he felt the first attacks of a mortal disease, the effect of vices in which he had long indulged; and though, for some days afterwards, he was able to go out and attend the parliament, his illness rapidly increased, until, as was stated by one of his contemporaries, he became so offensive, " that it was scarcely possible to get any one to come near him." The sufferings of his mind were not less painful than those of his body. He frequently exclaimed, " I have sinned like Peter, but I have not wept like him." Dr. Day, the bishop of Chichester, seeing Gardiner's dreadful state, and knowing that the juggleries of popery could not afford any support at such an hour, endeavoured to comfort him with the offers of free justification through the blood of Christ made in the scripture. Gardiner convinced, but not changed, showed the natural enmity of the heart of man against the doctrines of grace, exclaiming, " What, my lord, will you open that gap now? Then farewell all together. To me, and such other in my case, indeed you may speak it; but open this window to the people, and then fare well all together." He endured these protracted torments longer than Ridley had suffered, lingering in this state till the 13th of November, during which time it is recorded, that " he spake little but blasphemy and filthiness, and gave up the ghost with curses in his mouth, in terrible and unexpressible torments." What were Ridley's sufferings when compared with these? Surely every reader will exclaim, " Let me die the death of the righteous, and let my last end be like his."

The writings of bishop Ridley are not numerous, some few have been lost, among them a treatise on Predestination, which is much regretted; and it is also to be lamented that some, at least, of his sermons, have not been preserved, for he excelled as a preacher, and devoted much of his studies to preparation for the pulpit. His treatise on the Lord's Supper is the most important of his works; his other pieces, however, are valuable additions to the Writings of the British Reformers. In the present publication, his letters are collected from Fox, Coverdale, and Burnet, and are arranged in the order adopted in Dr. Gloucester Ridley's valuable life of his ancestor; and various references are made to that work, and other sources, which are explanatory of their contents.

It is also to be noticed, that the writings of Bishop Ridley have not yet (1830) been printed in a complete or collected form. A few pieces have been, from time to time, reprinted; but the different editions vary very much from each other, even more so than is usual with the different editions of books printed in the sixteenth century. There does not appear to have been any design in these variations; but they will be found very numerous, and difficult to be accounted for, by those who compare the Black Letter editions. These variations, however, do not materially affect the sense, or meaning of the author.

TREATISES

OF

BISHOP RIDLEY.

A TREATISE

OF

M. NICHOLAS RIDLEY,

IN THE NAME, AS IT APPEARS, OF THE WHOLE CLERGY,

ADDRESSED TO KING EDWARD THE SIXTH,

CONCERNING IMAGES;

THAT THEY ARE NOT TO BE SET UP, NOR WORSHIPPED IN CHURCHES.

ABRIDGED.

Certain reasons which move us that we cannot, with safe consciences, give our assent that the Images of Christ &c., should be placed and erected in churches.

FIRST, the words of the commandment, Exod. xx. "Thou shalt not make to thyself any graven image," &c. And the same is repeated more plainly, Deut. xxvii. "Cursed is the man which maketh a graven or a molten Image, &c., and setteth it in a secret place, and all the people shall say, Amen."

In the first place, these words are to be noted, "Thou shalt not make to thyself," that is, to any use of religion.

In the latter place, these words: "And setteth it in a secret place:" for no man then durst commit idolatry openly. So that, comparing the places, it evidently appears that Images, both for use of religion, and in place of peril* for idolatry, are forbidden.

God, knowing the inclination of man to idolatry, showeth the reason why he made this general prohibition, "Lest peradventure thou being deceived, shouldst bow down to them and worship them."†

In Deuteronomy iv. God gives a special charge to avoid Images. "Beware that thou forget not the covenant of the Lord thy God which he made with thee, and so make to thyself any graven Image of anything which the Lord

---

* Placed where there is danger of their being worshipped.

† Reference is here made, in the original, to the cases of the marriage of Moses with the daughter of Jethro, and that of Boaz with Ruth, as showing there are examples of those not hurt by union with idolaters; but these cases are not applicable to the argument used, and therefore are omitted. This treatise, it will be observed, is abridged. Some think it was not written by Ridley, but Fox states he was the author It is here given in a somewhat abridged form.

hath forbidden thee, for the Lord thy God is a consuming fire, and a jealous God. If thou have children and nephews, and do dwell in the land, and being deceived, make to yourselves any graven Image, doing evil before the Lord your God, and provoke him to anger, I do this day call heaven and earth to witness, that you shall quickly perish out of the land which you shall possess, you shall not dwell in it any longer, but the Lord will destroy you and scatter you amongst all nations."

Note what a solemn obtestation God useth, and what grievous punishments he threatens to the breakers of the second commandment.

In the tabernacle and temple of God, no Image was by God appointed to be set openly, nor by practice afterwards used or permitted, so long as religion was purely observed; so that the use and execution of the law, is a good interpreter of the true meaning of the same.

If, by virtue of the second commandment, Images were not lawful in the temple of the Jews, then, by the same commandment, they are not lawful in the churches of the christians. For being a moral commandment and not ceremonial, for, by consent of writers, only a part of the precept of observing the sabbath is ceremonial, it is a perpetual commandment, and binds us as well as the Jews.

The Jews by no means would consent to Herod, Pilate, or Petronius, that Images should be placed in the temple at Jerusalem, but rather offered themselves to death than assent unto it. Who, besides that they are commended by Josephus for observing the meaning of the law, would not have endangered themselves so far, if they had thought Images had been indifferent in the temple of God: for as St. Paul saith: 2 Cor. vi. "What hath the temple of God to do with Idols?" See Joseph. Antiq. lib. xvii. 8. lib. xviii. 5, et 15.

God's scripture in no place commends the use of Images, but in a great number of places doth disallow and condemn them.

[And] they are called in the book of Wisdom, the trap and snare of the feet of the ignorant.

It is said the invention of them was the beginning of spiritual fornication. And that they were not from the beginning, neither shall they continue to the end. In the same book it is said, "their pictures are a worthless labour." And again, they are worthy of death that put their trust in them, that make them, that love them, and that worship them.

The psalms and prophets are full of like sentences; and how then can we praise that which God's Spirit doth always dispraise.

Furthermore, an Image made by a father, as appears in the same book, for the memorial of his son departed, was the first invention of Images, and occasion of idolatry.*

How much more then shall an Image made in the memory of Christ, and set up in the place of religion, occasion the same offence? Euseb. Eccles. Hist., lib. vii. cap. 18. Images have their beginning from the heathen, and of no good ground, therefore they cannot be profitable to Christians. Whereunto Athanasius agrees, when writing of Images against the gentiles: "The invention of Images came of no good but of evil, and whatsoever hath an evil beginning can never in any thing be judged good, seeing it is wholly naught."

St. John saith, "My little children beware of Images;" but to set them in the churches, which are places dedicated to the service and invocation of God, and that over the Lord's table, being the highest and most honourable place, where most danger of abuse both is, and ever hath been, is not to beware of them, nor to flee from them, but rather to embrace and receive them. Tertullian expounding the same words, writeth thus, "Little children keep yourselves from the shape itself, or form of them."

Images in the church either serve to edify or to destroy. If they edify, then is there a kind of edification which the scriptures neither teach nor command, but always disallow. If they destroy, they are not to be used; for in the church of God all things ought to be done to edify.

The commandment of God is, Thou shalt not lay a stumbling-block or a stone before the blind: and Cursed is he that maketh the blind to wander in his way.

The simple and unlearned people who have been so long under blind guides, are blind in matters of religion, and inclined to error and idolatry. Therefore, to set

---

* "Thus some parent mourning bitterly for a son who hath been taken from him, makes an Image of his child; and him who before had been to his family as a dead man, they now begin to worship as a God, rites and sacrifices being instituted to be observed by his dependents."—Book of Wisdom. xiv. The reader will bear in mind that the reformers did not quote the Apocryphal books as holy scripture.

Images before them to stumble at, for they are snares and traps for the feet of the ignorant, or to lead them out of the true way, is not only against the commandment of God, but deserves also the curse of God.

The use of Images is to the learned and confirmed in knowledge, neither necessary nor profitable. To the superstitious, it is a confirmation in error. To the simple and weak, an occasion to fall, and very offensive and wounding to their consciences: and, therefore, very dangerous. For St. Paul saith (1 Cor. ix.), offending the brethren, and wounding their weak consciences, they sin against Christ. And (Matt. xviii.) "Woe be to him by whom offence or occasion of falling cometh; it were better that a millstone were tied about his neck and he cast into the sea, than to offend one of the little ones that believe in Christ." And where an objection may be made that such offence may be taken away by sincere doctrine and preaching, it is to be answered, that is not sufficient; and although it should be admitted as true, yet it should follow that sincere doctrine and preaching should always, and in all places, continue as well as Images: and so that wheresoever an Image were erected to offend, there should also, of reason, be a godly and sincere preacher continually maintained: for it is reason that the remedy be as large as the offence, the medicine as general as the poison; but that is not possible in the realm of England if Images should be generally allowed.

It is not expedient to allow and admit that which is hurtful to the greatest number, and in all churches and commonwealths the ignorant and weak are the greatest number, to whom Images are hurtful and not profitable.

And, whereas, it is commonly alleged that Images in churches stir up the mind to devotion, it may be answered, that contrariwise, they rather distract the mind from prayer, hearing of God's word, and other godly meditations, as we read that, in the council chamber of the Lacedæmonians, no Picture or Image was suffered, lest in consultation of weighty matters of the commonweal, their minds, by the sight of the outward Image, might be occasioned to withdraw or to wander from the matter.

The experience of this present time declares that those parts of the realm which think, and are persuaded, that God is not offended by doing outward reverence to an Image, most desire the restitution of Images, and have been most diligent to set them up again. Restitution, therefore, of them by common authority shall confirm them more in their error to the danger of their souls, than ever they were before. For, as one man writeth, "Nothing is more certain or sure than that which of doubtful, is made certain."

The profit of Images is uncertain; the peril, by experience of all ages and states of the church, is most certain. The benefit to be obtained by them, if there be any, is very small: the danger in seeing of them, which is the danger of idolatry, is the greatest of all other. Now, to allow a most certain peril for an uncertain profit, and the greatest danger for the smallest benefit, in matters of faith and religion, is tempting God, and a grievous offence.

Probations out of the fathers, councils, and histories.

First, it is manifest that, in the primitive church, Images were not commonly used in churches, oratories and places of assembly for religion: but they were generally detested and abhorred, so that the want of Imagery was objected to the christians by the heathen as a crime.

Origen relates that Celsus objected the lack of Images.

Arnobius saith also, that the heathens accused the christians that they had neither altars nor Images.

Zephirus, in his commentary upon the apology of Tertullian, gathers thus of Tertullian's words: "That place of persuasion were very cold, and to no purpose at all, except we hold that christians in those days, did hate most of all Images with their trim-decking and ornaments."

Irenæus, lib i. cap. 24, reproves the heretics, called Gnostics, because that they carried about the Image of Christ made in Pilate's time after his own proportion,* which were much more to be esteemed than any that can be made now, using also, for declaration of their affection towards it, to set garlands upon the head of it.

Lactantius affirms plainly, Divin. Instit. ii. cap. 19: " It is not to be doubted that there is no religion where ever there is any Image." If christians had then used Images, he would not have made his proposition so large.

St. Augustine, De civitate Dei., lib. iv. cap. 31, com-

* Made like to the actual bodily form and proportion in which Christ appeared upon earth.

mends Varro, the Roman, in these words: "Since Varro thought religion might be kept more purely without Images, who does not see how near he came to the truth?" so that not only by Varro's judgment, but also by St. Augustine's approbation, the most pure and chaste observation of religion, and the nearest the truth, is to be without Images.

The same St. Augustine, in Psalm 113, hath these words: "Images have more force to bow down and crook the silly soul than to teach it."

And upon the same Psalm he moves this question: "Every child, yea, every beast, knows that it is not God which they see, why then does the Holy Ghost so often give warning to beware of that which all do know?" St. Augustine answers: "When they are set in churches, and begin to be worshipped of the multitude or common people, straightway springs up a most filthy affection of error."

This place of St. Augustine well opens how weak a reason it is to say Images are a thing indifferent in chambers and in churches. For the alteration of the place, manner, and other circumstances, oftentimes alters the nature of the thing. It is lawful to buy and sell in the market, but not so in churches. It is lawful to eat and drink, but not so in churches. And therefore, saith St. Paul, "Have you not houses to eat and drink in? Do you contemn the church of God?"

Many other actions there are which are lawful and honest in private places, which are neither comely nor honest, not only in churches, but also in other assemblies of honest people.

Tertullian saith, he used sometimes to burn frankincense in his chamber, which was then used by idolaters, and is so still in the Romish churches, but he joineth with all: "But not after such a rite or ceremony, nor after such a manner and fashion, nor with such preparation or sumptuousness, as it is done before the Idols."

So that Images placed in churches, and set in an honourable place of estimation, as St. Augustine saith, and especially over the Lord's table, which is done "after the same manner and fashion" which the papists used, especially after so long continuance of abuse of Images, and so many being blinded with superstitious opinion towards them, cannot be counted indifferent, but a most certain ruin of many souls.

Epiphanius, in his epistle to John, bishop of Jerusalem, (which epistle was translated out of the Greek by St. Jerome, showing that it is likely that Jerome misliked not the doctrine of the same,) writes a fact of his own, which most clearly declares the judgment of that notable learned bishop concerning the use of Images: his words are these: "When I came to a village called Anablatha, and saw there, as I passed by, a candle burning, and inquiring what place it was, and learning that it was a church, had entered into the same to pray; I found there a veil or cloth hanging at the door of the same church, dyed and painted, having on it the Image of Christ as it were, or of some saint, for I remember not well whose it was. Then when I saw that in the church of Christ, against the authority of the scriptures, the Image of a man was hung up, I cut it in pieces," &c. And a little after: "And commanded that such manner of veils or cloths, which are contrary to our religion, be not hanged in the church of Christ."

Out of this place of Epiphanius, observe

First, that by the judgment of this ancient father, to permit Images in churches, is against the authority of the scriptures, meaning against the second commandment, "Thou shalt not make to thyself any graven Image," &c.

Secondly, that Epiphanius rejects not only graven and molten, but also painted Images: for he cut in pieces the Image painted on a veil hanging at the church-door; what would he have done if he had found it over the Lord's table?

Thirdly, that he spareth not the Image of Christ, for no doubt that Image is the most perilous in the church.

Fourthly, that he did not only remove it, but with vehemency of zeal cut it in pieces, following the example of the good king Hezekiah, who broke the brazen serpent, and burnt it to ashes.

Last of all, that Epiphanius thinks it the duty of vigilant bishops to be careful that no such kind of painted Images are permitted in the church.

Serenus, bishop of Massilia, broke down Images, and destroyed them when he saw them begin to be worshipped.

Experience of the times since has declared whether of the two sentences were better. For since Gregory's time, the Images standing in the western churches, they have been overflowed with idolatry, notwithstanding his or other men's doctrine: whereas, if Serenus' judgment had universally taken place, no such thing had happened. For if no Images had been suffered, none could have been worshipped, and, consequently, no idolatry committed by them.

To recite the proceedings in Histories and Councils about the matter of Images, would require a long discourse, but it shall be sufficient here briefly to touch a few.

It is manifest to them that read histories, that not only emperors, but also divers and sundry councils in the eastern church have condemned and abolished Images both by decrees and examples.

Peter Crinitus in his book of Honest Discipline, the 9th book, the 9th chapter, wrote out of the emperor's books these words. " Valens and Theodosius, the emperors, wrote to the pretorian prefect, in this sort. ' Whereas we are very careful that the religion of almighty God should be kept in all things, we permit no man to cast, grave, or paint the Image of our Saviour Christ, either in colours, stone, or other matter: but, wheresoever it be found, we command it to be taken away, punishing them most grievously that shall attempt anything contrary to our decrees and empire.' "

Leo the third, a man commended in histories for his excellent virtues and godliness, by public authority commanded abolishing of Images, and in Constantinople caused all the Images to be gathered together on a heap, and burned them to ashes.

Constantine the fifth, his son, assembled a council of the bishops of the eastern church, in which council it was decreed as follows. " It is not lawful for them that believe in God through Jesus Christ, to have any Images either of the Creator, or of any creatures set up in temples to be worshipped, but rather that all images by the law of God, and for the avoiding of offence, ought to be taken out of churches." Which decree was executed in all places where any Images were, either in Greece or in Asia. But in all these times, the bishops of Rome rather maintaining the authority of Gregory, than considering the peril of the church, always in their assemblies allowed Images.

Not long after, the bishop of Rome practising with Tarasius, patriarch of Constantinople, obtained of Irene the empress, her son Constantine the sixth being then young, that a council should be called at Nice, in which the pope's legates were presidents, which appeared by their fruits: for in that council it was decreed, that Images should not only be permitted in churches, but also worshipped, which council was confuted by a book written by Charlemagne, the emperor.

To be short, there never was anything that made more division, or brought more mischief into the church, than the controversy of Images: by reason whereof, not only the eastern church was divided from the western, and never since perfectly reconciled, but also the empire was cut asunder and divided, and the gate opened to the Saracens and Turks to enter and overcome a great part of Christendom. The fault whereof most justly is to be ascribed to the patrons of Images, who could not be contented with the example of the primitive church, being most simple and sincere, and most agreeable to the scripture. For as Tertullian saith: " What is the first, that is true, and that which is later is counterfeit." But with all extremity, they maintained the use of Images in churches, whereof no profit nor advantage ever grew to the church of God. For it is evident, that infinite millions of souls have been cast into eternal damnation by the occasion of Images used in place of religion; and no history can record that ever any one soul was won unto Christ by having of Images. But lest it might appear that the western church had always generally retained and commended Images, it is to be noted, that in a council holden in Spain, called the Eliberian Council, the use of Images in churches was clearly prohibited in these words: " We decree that pictures ought not to be in churches, lest that which is painted upon the walls be worshipped or adored."

But notwithstanding this, experience has declared, that neither assembling in councils, neither writings, preachings, decrees, making of laws, prescribing of punishments, have holpen against Images, to which idolatry has been committed, nor against idolatry whilst Images stood. For these blind books and dumb schoolmasters, which they call laymen's books, have more prevailed by their carved and painted preaching of idolatry, than all written books and preachings in teaching the truth and horror of that vice.

Having thus declared unto your highness a few causes, out of many, which move our consciences in this matter, we beseech your highness most humbly not to strain us any further, but to consider that God's word threatens a terrible judgment unto us, if we, being pastors and ministers in his church, should assent unto that thing which, in our learning and conscience, we are persuaded tends to the confirmation of error, superstition, and idolatry, and finally, to the ruin of the souls committed to our charge, for which we must give an account to the Prince of Pastors at the last day. Heb. xiii., 1st Pet. v. We pray your majesty also not to be offended with this our plainness and liberty, which all good and christian princes have ever taken in good part at the hands of the godly bishops.

St. Ambrose, writing to Theodosius, the emperor, says, " Neither is it the part of an emperor to deny free liberty of speaking, nor yet the duty of a priest not to speak what he thinks." And again, " In God's cause whom wilt thou hear, if thou wilt not hear the priest to whose great peril the fault should be committed? Who dare say the truth unto thee, if the priest dare not?" These and such like speeches of St. Ambrose, Theodosius and Valentinianus the emperors, always took in good part; and we doubt not but your grace will do the like, not only of whose clemency, but also beneficence, we have largely tasted.

We beseech your majesty, also, in these and such like controversies of religion, to refer the discussion and deciding of them to a synod of your bishops and other godly learned men, according to the example of Constantine the great, and other christian emperors, that the reasons on both parts being examined by them, the judgment may be given uprightly in all doubtful matters.

And to return to this present matter, we most humbly beseech your majesty to consider, that besides weighty causes in policy, which we leave to the wisdom of your honourable counsellors, the establishment of Images by your authority, shall not only utterly discredit our ministers as builders up of the things which we have destroyed, but also blemish the fame of your most godly father, and also of such notable fathers as have given their life for the testimony of God's truth, who by public law removed all Images.

The almighty and everliving God plentifully endue your majesty with his Spirit and heavenly wisdom, and long preserve your most gracious reign and prosperous government over us, to the advancement of his glory, to the overthrow of superstition, and to the benefit and comfort of all your highness' loving subjects.

BRIEF TREATISE

UPON

THE LORD'S SUPPER,

BY

DR. NICHOLAS RIDLEY,

BISHOP AND MARTYR.

WRITTEN A LITTLE BEFORE HIS DEATH.

In the year 1544, Luther had written with great warmth against the opinions of the Helvetian divines, to which they replied in the following year, explaining their doctrine and faith. The latter work inclined Ridley to give the question a fair examination, he having hitherto held the doctrine of transubstantiation. He also procured a little treatise written seven hundred years before, by Ratramus or Bertram, a monk of Corbie, at the request of the emperor Charles the Bald, about A.D. 840.

From this book Ridley learned that the determination of the church in favour of transubstantiation had not been so early or so general as he had supposed, for it showed that Bertram, a catholic doctor, held contrary to the present decrees, and that the faithful at that time were divided in their opinions upon the subject, without either party being condemned as heretics. This fact at once destroyed that foundation of *the authority of the church* on which Ridley had depended, and left him open to consider the reasonings of Bertram, who establishes his doctrine of the figurative and mysterious body and blood by the evidence of the senses, and the nature and analogy of Sacraments, and does not require the belief of the monstrous absurdity of the change of a piece of bread into flesh and blood, (to say nothing of the whole body of Christ, and his soul also, as the Romish doctrine asserts,) considering that the things *seen* and the things *believed* are not all one ; as *seen*, they feed the corruptible body being themselves corruptible ; as *believed*, they feed our immortal souls being themselves immortal. Bertram confirmed that doctrine by scripture and observes,—Think not so grossly, as that the actual flesh and blood of Christ were given to be eaten and drunk, for that shall ascend up to heaven, and even could you actually eat and drink this flesh and blood, it would be of no benefit, " for the flesh profiteth nothing," but you shall eat and drink it in the mystery, in virtue, power, and efficacy ;—" It is the Spirit that giveth life." He also showed that the Fathers of the church before him understood respecting this Sacrament in the same manner. See *Gloucester Ridley's Life of Ridley*, p. 165, &c.

Ridley was thus induced fully to examine the subject, and the result was, that the main doctrine of popery no longer influenced the mind of Cranmer or himself. In April, 1554, he was called upon to dispute publicly at Oxford, respecting the doctrine of transubstantiation, on which occasion he produced a protest in the Latin language, containing his views upon the subject drawn up in a close and logical manner. Subsequently, while in prison and waiting his martyrdom, he stated nearly the same arguments in a more popular form in the treatise here given.

The following Treatise is here reprinted from the edition of A.D. 1574, which has usually been followed in the reprints of it; but there is an edition of 1556 which has many verbal differences throughout, though, for the most part, not of material import. Some of the principal variations and corrections have been noted, or inserted.

ON

THE LORD'S SUPPER.

MANY things confound a weak memory; a few places well weighed and perceived, lighten the understanding. Truth is to be searched for where it is certain to be had. Though God speaks the truth by man, yet man's word which God has not revealed to be his, a man may doubt, without mistrust in God. Christ is the truth of God revealed unto man from heaven by God himself; and therefore in his word the truth is to be found, which is to be embraced by all that are his. Christ bids us to ask, and we shall have; to search, and we shall find; to knock, and it shall be opened unto us.

Therefore, O heavenly Father, the author and fountain of all truth, the unfathomable sea of all understanding; send down, we beseech thee, thy Holy Spirit into our hearts, and lighten our understandings with the beams of thy heavenly grace. We ask thee this, O merciful Father, not in respect of our deserts, but for thy dear Son, our Saviour Jesus Christ's sake. Thou knowest, O heavenly Father, that the controversy about the Sacrament of the blessed body and blood of thy dear Son, our Saviour Jesus Christ, has not only of late troubled the church of England, France, Germany, and Italy, but also many years ago. The fault is ours, no doubt thereof, for we have deserved thy plague.

But, O Lord, be merciful, and relieve our misery with some light of grace. Thou knowest, O Lord, how this wicked world rolleth up and down, and reeleth to and fro, and careth not what thy will is, so it may abide in wealth. If truth have wealth, then who are so stout to defend the truth as they! But if Christ's cross be laid on truth's back, then they vanish away straight, as wax before the fire. But these are not they, O heavenly Father, for whom I make my greatest moan, but for those silly* ones, O Lord, which have a zeal unto thee; those, I mean, who would and wish to know thy will, and yet are

* Ignorant, weak.

hindered, holden back, and blinded, by the subtleties of satan and his ministers, the wickedness of this wretched world, and the sinful lusts and affections of the flesh.

Alas! Lord, thou knowest we are of ourselves but flesh, wherein there dwelleth nothing that is good. How then is it possible for man without thee, O Lord, to understand thy truth indeed? Can the natural man perceive the will of God? O Lord, to whom thou givest a zeal for thee, give them also, we beseech thee, the knowledge of thy blessed will. Suffer not them, O Lord, blindly to be led to strive against thee, as thou didst those, alas! that cru cified thine own dear Son; forgive them, O Lord, for thy dear Son's sake, for they know not what they do. Alas! O Lord, for lack of knowledge, they think that they do unto thee good service, even when they most cruelly rage against thee. Remember, O Lord, we beseech thee, for whom thy martyr Stephen did pray, and whom thine holy apostle Paul did so truly and earnestly love, that for their salvation, he wished himself accursed for them.* Remember, O heavenly Father, the prayer of thy dear Son our Saviour Christ upon the cross, when he said unto thee: " O Father, forgive them, they know not what they do." With this forgiveness, O good Lord, give me, I beseech thee, thy grace, here briefly to set forth the sayings of thy Son, our Saviour Christ, of his evangelists, and of his apostles, that, in this controversy, the light of the truth, by the lantern of thy word, may shine unto all that love thee.

Of the Lord's last Supper, the evangelists Matthew, Mark, and Luke speak expressly; but none more plainly, nor more fully declares the same, than St. Paul, partly in the tenth, but especially in the eleventh chapter of the first epistle to the Corinthians. As Matthew and Mark agree much in words, so likewise Luke and St. Paul; but all four, no doubt, as they were all taught in one school, and inspired with one Spirit, so they all taught one truth. God grant us to understand it well. Amen.

Matthew sets forth Christ's Supper thus:

" When even was come, he sat down with the twelve, &c. As they did eat, Jesus took bread, and gave thanks, brake it, and gave it to his disciples, and said: ' Take, eat, this is my body.' And he took the cup, gave thanks, and gave it to them, saying: ' Drink ye all of it, for this is my blood of the new testament, that is shed for many for the remission of sins. I say unto you, I will not drink

* From thee, Ed. 1555.

On the Lord's Supper.

henceforth of this fruit of the vine-tree until the day when I shall drink it new in my Father's kingdom. And when they had said grace, they went out, &c."

Now Mark speaks of it thus:—

"And as they did eat, Jesus took bread, blessed and brake, and gave to them, and said: 'Take, eat, this is my body.' And he took the cup, gave thanks, and gave it to them, and they all drank of it. And he said unto them: 'This is my blood of the new testament, which is shed for many. Verily, I say unto you, I will drink no more of the fruit of the vine until that day that I drink it new in the kingdom of God.'"

Here Matthew and Mark agree, not only in the matter, but also almost in the form of words, except, that for those words in Matthew, "gave thanks," Mark has one word, "blessed;" which signifies in this place the same. And where Matthew saith, "Drink ye all of this," Mark saith, "they all drank of it." And where Matthew saith, "of this fruit of the vine," Mark leaveth out the word "this," and saith, "of the fruit of the vine."

Now likewise let us see what agreement in form or words there is between St. Luke and St. Paul. Luke writes thus:

"He took bread, gave thanks, brake it, and gave it to them; saying: 'This is my body, which is given for you. This do in remembrance of me.' Likewise also when they had supped, he took the cup, saying: 'This cup is the new testament in my blood, which is shed for you.'"

St. Paul sets forth the Lord's Supper thus:

"The Lord Jesus, the same night in which he was betrayed, took bread, and gave thanks, and brake, and said: 'Take, eat, this is my body, which is broken for you. This do in remembrance of me.' After the same manner he took the cup, when supper was done, saying: 'This cup is the new testament in my blood. This do, as often as ye drink it, in the remembrance of me. For as often as ye shall eat this bread, and drink this cup, ye show the Lord's death, until he come.'"

Here, where Luke saith, "which is given," Paul saith, "which is broken." And as Luke adds to the words of Paul spoken of the cup, "which is shed for you:" so likewise Paul adds to the words thereof, "This do, as often as ye shall drink it, in the remembrance of me." The rest that follows in St. Paul, both there and in the tenth chapter, pertains unto the right use and doctrine of the Lord's Supper.

Thus the evangelists and St. Paul have rehearsed the words and work of Christ, whereby he instituted and ordained this holy Sacrament of his body and blood, to be a perpetual remembrance until his coming again of himself, that is, of his body given for us, and of his blood shed for the remission of sins.

But this remembrance, which is thus ordained, as the author thereof is Christ. both God and man, so by the almighty power of God it far passes all kinds of remembrances that any other man is able to make, either of himself, or of any other thing; for whosoever receives this holy Sacrament thus ordained in remembrance of Christ, he receives therewith either death or life. In this, I trust, we all agree. For St. Paul saith of the godly receivers in the tenth chapter of his first epistle unto the Corinthians: " The cup of blessing which we bless, is it not the partaking or fellowship of Christ's blood?" And also he saith: " The bread which we break (and he means at the Lord's table), is it not the partaking or fellowship of Christ's body?"

Now the partaking of Christ's body and of his blood unto the faithful and godly, is the partaking or fellowship of life and immortality. And again, of the bad and ungodly receivers, St. Paul plainly saith thus: " He that eateth of this bread, and drinketh of this cup, unworthily, is guilty of the body and blood of the Lord." Oh! how necessary then is it, if we love life and would eschew* death, to try and examine ourselves before we eat of this bread and drink of this cup; for else, assuredly, he that eateth and drinketh thereof unworthily, eateth and drinketh his own damnation, because he esteemeth not the Lord's body; that is, he reverences not the Lord's body with the honour that is due unto him. And by that which was said, that with the receiving of the holy Sacrament of the blessed body and blood of Christ, there is received by every one, good or bad, either life or death, it is not meant that they, which are dead before God, may hereby receive life; or that the living before God can hereby receive death. For as no one is fit to receive natural food, whereby the natural life is nourished, except he is born and live before; so no man can feed by receiving this holy

Sacrament, upon the food of eternal life, except he be regenerated and born of God before: and, on the other hand, no man here receives damnation, who is not dead before.

Thus hitherto, without all doubt, God is my witness; I say, so far as I know, there is no controversy among them that are learned among the church of England, concerning the matter of this Sacrament, but all agree, whether they are new or old; and to speak plain, and as some of them odiously call each other, whether they are Protestants, Papists, Pharisees, or Gospellers.

And as all agree hitherto in the aforesaid doctrine, so all detest, abhor, and condemn the wicked heresy of the Messalians, who otherwise are called Eutichites,* who said, that the holy Sacrament can neither do good nor harm.

Also all do condemn those wicked men,† who put no difference between the Lord's table and the Lord's meat, and their own; and because charity would that we should, if it be possible, and so far as we may with the safeguard of a good conscience, and maintenance of the truth, agree with all men; therefore, methinks, it is not charitably done, to burden any man, either new or old, as they call them, further than such declare themselves to dissent from that we are persuaded to be the truth, and pretend there are controversies, where none such are indeed; and so multiply debate, which, the more it increases, the further it departs from the unity which the true christian should desire.

And again, this is true, that the truth neither needeth, nor will be maintained with lies. It is also a true common proverb, "that it is even sin to lie against the devil;" for though by thy lie thou dost seem ever so much to speak against the devil, yet in that thou liest, indeed thou workest the devil's work; thou dost him service, and takest the devil's part.

Now then, do they act godly and charitably, who either by their pen in writing, or by their words in preaching, tell the simple people, that those who thus teach and believe, go about to make the holy Sacrament ordained by Christ himself, a thing no better than a piece of common bread? or who say, that such make the holy Sacrament of the blessed body and blood of Christ nothing else, but a bare sign, or a figure, to represent Christ, no otherwise

---

* A sect of heretics in the fourth century.—See Mosheim.
† The original has Anabaptists, referring to the followers of Munzer in Germany

than the ivy-bush represents the wine in a tavern; or as a vile person gorgeously apparelled, may represent a king or a prince in a play? Alas! let us leave lying and speak the truth every man, not only *to* his neighbour, but also *of* his neighbour;. for we are members one of another, saith St. Paul.

The controversy, no doubt, which at this day troubles the church, wherein any moderately learned man, either old or new, doth stand in, is not, whether or no the holy Sacrament of the body and blood of Christ is no better than a piece of common bread; or whether the Lord's table is no more to be regarded, than the table of any earthly man; or whether it is but a bare sign or figure of Christ, and nothing else. For all grant, that St. Paul's words require, that the bread which we break is the partaking of the body of Christ: and all also grant that he who eateth of that bread, or drinketh of that cup unworthily, is guilty of the Lord's death, and eats and drinks his own condemnation, because he esteems not the Lord's body. All grant that these words of St. Paul, when he saith, "if we eat, it advantages us nothing; or if we eat not, we want nothing thereby," are not spoken of the Lord's table, but of other common meats.

Thus then hitherto we all still agree. But now let us see wherein the dissension doth stand. The understanding of that wherein it chiefly stands, is a step to the true searching forth of the truth. For who can well seek a remedy, if he know not first the disease?

It is neither to be denied nor dissembled, that in the matter of this Sacrament there are divers points, wherein men counted to be learned cannot agree: as, Whether there is any transubstantiation* of the bread, or not? Any corporeal and carnal presence of Christ's substance, or not? Whether the adoration, only due unto God, is to be done to the Sacrament, or not? And whether Christ's body is there offered indeed unto the heavenly Father by the priest, or not? Or whether the evil man receives the natural body of Christ, or not?

Yet, nevertheless, as in a man diseased in divers parts, commonly the original cause of such divers diseases, which are spread abroad in the body, comes from some one chief member, as from the stomach, or from the head: even so, all the five aforesaid points chiefly hang upon this one

* Change of the substance.

question, which is, What is the matter of the Sacrament;
—is it the natural substance of bread, or the natural substance of Christ's own body?

The truth of this question, truly tried out and agreed upon, no doubt will end the controversy of all the rest. For if it be Christ's own natural body, born of the virgin, then assuredly, seeing that all learned men in England, so far as I know, both new and old, grant there is but one substance, then, I say, they must needs grant transubstantiation, that is, a change of the substance of bread into the substance of Christ's body: then also they must grant the carnal and corporeal presence of Christ's body: then must the Sacrament be adored with the honour due unto Christ himself, for the unity of the two natures in one person: then if the priest offers the Sacrament, he offers indeed Christ himself: and, finally, the murderer, the adulterer, or wicked man, receiving the Sacrament, must needs then receive also the natural substance of Christ's own blessed body, both flesh and blood.

Now, on the other side, if after the truth shall be truly tried out, it is found, that the substance of bread is the natural* substance of the Sacrament, although for the change of the use, office, and dignity of the bread, the bread indeed is sacramentally changed into the body of Christ, as the water in baptism is sacramentally changed into the fountain of regeneration, and yet the natural* substance remains the same as it was before—If, I say, the true solution of that former question, whereupon all these controversies depend, is, that the natural substance of bread is the material substance in the Sacrament of Christ's blessed body, then must it needs follow from the former proposition, which is confessed of all that are said to be learned, so far as I know in England, that there is but one material substance in the Sacrament of the body, and one only likewise in the Sacrament of the blood: so that there is no such thing indeed and in truth, as that which they call transubstantiation, for the substance of bread remains still in the Sacrament of the body. Then also the natural substance of Christ's human nature, which he took of the virgin Mary, is in heaven, where it now reigneth in glory, and is not here inclosed under the form of bread. Then that godly honour, which is only due unto God the Creator, and may not be done unto the creature

* Material. 1556.

without idolatry and sacrilege, is not to be done unto the holy Sacrament. Then also the wicked, I mean the impenitent, murderers, adulterers, or such like, do not receive the natural substance of the blessed body and blood of Christ, Finally, then it follows that Christ's blessed body and blood, which was once only offered and shed upon the cross, being available for the sins of all the whole world, is offered up no more in the natural substance thereof, neither by the priest, nor any other thing.

But here, before we go any further to search in this matter, and to wade, as it were, to search and try out as we can the truth hereof in the scripture, we shall do well, by the way, to know whether they, that thus make answer and solution unto the former principal question, do take away simply and absolutely the presence of Christ's body and blood from the Sacrament, ordained by Christ, and duly ministered according to his holy ordinance and institution of the same. Undoubtedly, they deny that utterly, either so to say, or so to mean. Hereof, if a man do or will doubt, the books which are written already in this matter by those who thus answer, will make the matter plain.

Now, then, you will say, what kind of presence do they grant, and what do they deny? Briefly, they deny the presence of Christ's body in the natural substance of his human and assumed nature, and they grant the presence of the same by grace: that is, they affirm and say, that the substance of the natural body and blood of Christ is only remaining in heaven, and so shall be until the latter day, when he shall come again in glory, accompanied with the angels of heaven, to judge both the quick and the dead.

And the same natural substance of the very body and blood of Christ, because it is united in the divine nature in Christ, the second Person of the Trinity, therefore, hath not only life in itself, but is also able to give, and doth give life unto as many as are, or shall be partakers thereof. That is, to all that believe on his name,—which are not born of blood, as St. John saith, or of the will of the flesh, or of the will of man, but are born of God,—though the self-same substance abide still in heaven, and they, for the time, of their pilgrimage, dwell here upon earth. By grace, I say, that is, by the gift of this life, mentioned in John, and the properties of the same suitable for our pilgrimage here upon earth; the same body of Christ is here present with us. Even as, for example, we say, the same sun which, in substance, never removes from his place out of the heavens, is yet present here by his beams, light, and natural influence, where it shines upon the earth. For God's word and his sacraments are, as it were, the beams of Christ, who is "Sol justitiæ," the Sun of righteousness.

Thus hast thou heard, of what sort or sect soever thou art, wherein stands the principal state and chief point of all the controversies which properly pertain unto the nature of this Sacrament. As for the use thereof, I grant there are many other things whereof here I have spoken nothing at all.

And now, lest thou mayest justly complain and say, that I have, in opening of this matter, done nothing else but digged a pit, and have not shut it up again;* or opened the book, and have not closed it again; or else call me as thou listest, as neutral dissembler, or whatsoever else thy lust or learning shall serve to name me worse, therefore, here now I will, by God's grace, not only shortly, but also as clearly and plainly as I can, make thee now to know which of the aforesaid two answers to the former principal state and chief point pleases me best. Yea, and also I will hold all those accursed, who in this matter that now so troubles the church of Christ, have of God received the key of knowledge, and yet go about to shut up the doors, so that they themselves will not enter in, nor suffer others that would.

And, for my own part, I consider, both of late what a charge and cure of souls has been committed unto me, whereof God knows how soon I shall be called to give account; and also now, in this world, what peril and danger of the laws, concerning my life, I am now in at this present time; what folly were it then for me now to dissemble with God, of whom assuredly I look and hope by Christ to have everlasting life! Seeing that such charge and danger, both before God and man, compass me in round about on every side; therefore, God willing, I will frankly and freely utter my mind, and though my body be captive, yet my tongue and my pen, as long as I may, shall freely set forth that which undoubtedly I am persuaded is the truth of God's word. And yet I will do it

* Here is added, Or broken a gap, and have not made it up again. 1556.

under this protestation,—call me a protestant who list, I pass* not thereof.

My protestation shall be this: that my mind is and ever shall be (God willing) to set forth sincerely the true sense and meaning, to the best of my understanding, of God's most holy word, and not decline from the same, either for fear of worldly danger, or else for hope of gain. I do protest also due obedience and submission of my judgment in this my writing, and in all mine other affairs, unto those of Christ's church, who are truly learned in God's holy word, gathered in Christ's name, and guided by his Spirit. After this protestation, I plainly affirm and say, that the second answer, made unto the chief question and principal point, I am persuaded is the very true meaning and sense of God's holy word; that is, that the natural substance of bread and wine is the true material substance of the holy Sacrament of the blessed body and blood of our Saviour Christ; and that the places of scripture whereupon this my faith is grounded are these, both concerning the Sacrament of the body, and also of the blood.

First, let us repeat the beginning of the institution of the Lord's Supper, wherein all the three evangelists and St. Paul, almost in words, do agree, saying, that "Jesus took bread, gave thanks, brake, and gave to the disciples, saying, 'Take, eat, this is my body.'" Here it appears plainly, that Christ calls very bread,† his body. For that which he took, was very bread, in this all men do agree,— and that which he took, after he had given thanks, he brake,—and that which he took and brake, he gave to his disciples,—and that which he took, brake, and gave to his disciples, he himself said of it: "This is my body." So it appears plainly that Christ called very bread his body. But very bread cannot be his body in very substance: therefore it must needs have another meaning, which meaning appears plainly by the next sentence that follows, both in Luke and in Paul, and that is this; "Do this in remembrance of me."

Whereupon it seems to me to be evident that Christ took bread, and called it his body, for that he would institute thereby a perpetual remembrance of his body, especially of that singular benefit of our redemption, which he would then procure and purchase unto us by his body upon the cross. But bread, retaining still its own very

* Care.   † Real bread, mere bread.

natural substance, may thus, by grace, and in a sacramental signification, be his body: whereas else the very bread which he took, brake, and gave them, could not be in any wise his natural body, for that were confusion of substances. And therefore the very words of Christ, joined with the next sentence following, both enforce us to confess that the very bread remains still, and also open unto us how that bread may be, and is, thus, by his divine power, his body which was given for us.

But here I remember, I have read in some writers, of the contrary opinion, who deny that Christ brake that which he did take. For, say they, after his taking, he blessed it, as Mark relates, and by his blessing he changed the natural substance of the bread into the natural substance of his body: and so, although he took the bread and blessed it, yet because in blessing he changed the substance of it, he brake not the bread, which then was not there, but only the form thereof.

Unto this objection I have two plain answers, both grounded upon God's word. The one I will rehearse; the other answer I will defer until I speak of the Sacrament of the blood. Mine answer here is taken out of the plain words of St. Paul, which manifestly confound this fantastical invention, first invented by pope Innocent,* and afterwards confirmed by the subtle sophister Duns, and now lately renewed in our days, with an eloquent style and much fineness of wit. But what can crafty invention, subtlety in sophisms, eloquence or fineness of wit, prevail against the infallible word of God?

What need have we to strive and contend what it is we break? For Paul saith, speaking undoubtedly of the Lord's table: "The bread, saith he, which we break, is it not the partaking or fellowship of the Lord's body?" Whereupon follows, that after the thanksgiving it is bread which we break. And how often, in the Acts of the apostles, is the Lord's Supper signified by breaking of bread? "They persevered," saith St. Luke, "in the apostles' doctrine, communion, and breaking of bread." And, "They brake bread in every house." And again, in another place, "When they were come together to break bread," &c. St. Paul, who sets forth most fully in his writings both the doctrine and the right use of the Lord's Supper, and the sacramental eating and drinking

* In the fourth Lateran council, A. D. 1215.

of Christ's body and blood, called it five times, 'bread,' 'bread,' 'bread,' 'bread,' 'bread.'

The sacramental bread is the mystical body, and so it is called in scripture (1 Cor x.), as it is called the natural body of Christ. But Christ's mystical body is the congregation of Christians; now no man was ever so fond* as to say, that the sacramental bread is transubstantiated and changed into the substance of the congregation. Wherefore, no man should think or say that the bread is transubstantiated and changed into the natural substance of Christ's human nature.

But my mind is not here to write what may be gathered out of scriptures for this purpose, but only to note here, briefly, those which seem to me to be the plainest places. Therefore, contented to have spoken thus much of the sacramental bread, I will now speak a little of the Lord's cup.

And this shall be my third argument, grounded upon Christ's own words. The natural substance of the sacramental wine remains still, and is the material substance of the Sacrament of the blood of Christ: therefore it is likewise so in the sacramental bread. I know that he, who is of a contrary opinion, will deny the former part of my argument: but I will prove it thus by the plain words of Christ himself, both in Matthew and in Mark. Christ's words are these, after the words said upon the cup: " I say unto you, I will not drink henceforth of this fruit of the vine-tree, until I shall drink it new in my Father's kingdom." Here note, how Christ plainly calls his cup the fruit of the vine-tree. But the fruit of the vine-tree is very natural wine; wherefore the natural substance of the wine still remains in the Sacrament of Christ's blood.

And here, in speaking of the Lord's cup, comes unto my remembrance the vanity of Innocent's fantastical invention, which, by Paul's words, I confuted before, and promised to speak of more fully; and that is this: if the transubstantiation be made by the word "blessed" in Mark, said upon the bread, as Innocent, that pope, did say; then surely, seeing that word is not said by Christ, neither in any of the evangelists, nor in St. Paul, upon the cup, there is no transubstantiation of the wine at all. For, where the cause doth fail, there the effect cannot follow. But the sacramental bread, and the sacramental

* Foolish.

wine, both remain in their natural substance alike; and if the one is not changed, as of the sacramental wine, it appears evident that there is not any such transubstantiation in either of them.

All that put and affirm this change of the substance of bread and wine into the substance of Christ's body and blood, called transubstantiation, also say and affirm this change is made by a certain prescribed form of words, and no other. But what they are that make the change either of the one or of the other, undoubtedly even they that write most finely in these our days almost plainly confess that they cannot tell. For, although they grant to certain of the old doctors, as Chrysostom and Ambrose, that these words, "This is my body," are the words of consecration of the Sacrament of the body, "yet," say they, "these words may well be so called, because they assure us of the consecration thereof, whether it is done before these words be spoken, or not." But as for this their doubt, concerning the Sacrament of the body, I let it pass.

Let us now consider the words which pertain to the cup. This is first evident, that as Matthew much agrees with Mark, and likewise Luke with Paul, herein in the form of words, so the form of words in Matthew and Mark is diverse from that which is in Luke and Paul. The old authors mostly rehearse the form of words in Matthew and Mark, because, I suppose, they seemed most clear to them. But here I would know, whether it is credible or not, that Luke and Paul, when they celebrated the Lord's Supper with their congregations, did not use the same form of words at the Lord's table which they wrote, Luke in his gospel, and Paul in his epistle. Of Luke, because he was a physician, I cannot tell whether some will grant that he was a priest or not, and was able to receive the order of priesthood, which they say is given by virtue of these words said by the bishop; "Take thou authority to sacrifice for the quick and the dead."—But if they should be so strait upon Luke, either for his craft, or else for lack of such power given him by virtue of the aforesaid words, then both Peter and Paul are in danger to be deposed from their priesthood; for the craft of fishing which was Peter's, or making of tents which was Paul's, were more vile than the science of physic. And as for those sacramental words of the order of priesthood, to have authority to sacrifice both for the quick and the dead, I think that Peter and Paul, if they both were alive, were not able to prove that Christ ever gave them such authority, or ever said any such words unto them. But I will let Luke go, and because Paul speaks more for himself, I will rehearse his words:—

"That, saith Paul, which I received of the Lord, I gave unto you: for the Lord Jesus," &c. and so he sets forth the whole institution and right use of the Lord's Supper. Now, seeing that Paul here said, that which he had received of the Lord he had given them, and that which he had received and given them before by word of mouth he now rehearses and writes the same in his epistle; is it credible that Paul would never use this form of words upon the Lord's cup, which, as he saith, he received of the Lord, which he had given them before, and now rehearses in his epistle? I trust no man is so far from all reason but he will grant me that this is not likely to be.

Now, then, if you grant me that Paul used the form of words which he writes, let us then rehearse and consider Paul's words, which he saith Christ spake thus upon the cup; "This cup is the new testament in my blood; this do as often as ye shall drink it in the remembrance of me." Here I would know, whether Christ's words spoken upon the cup were not as mighty in work, and as effectual in signification, to all intents, constructions, and purposes, as those that were spoken upon the bread?

If this be granted, which, I think no man can deny, then, further, I reason thus.—But the word 'is' in the words spoken upon the Lord's bread, mightily signifies, say they, the change of the substance of that which goes before it into the substance of that which follows after; that is, of the substance of bread into the substance of Christ's body, when Christ saith, "This is my body." Now, then, if Christ's words, which are spoken upon the cup, which Paul here rehearses, are of the same might and power, both in working and signifying, then must this word 'is,' when Christ saith, "This cup is the new testament," &c. turn the substance of the cup into the substance of the new testament.

And if you say, that this word 'is' neither makes nor signifies any such change of the cup; and although it is said of Christ, that this cup is the new testament, yet Christ meant no such change as that—truly, sir, even so say I,—when Christ said of the bread which he took, and after giving thanks, brake, and gave to them, saying: "Take, eat, this is my body;" he meant no more any such change of the substance of bread into the substance of his natural body, than he meant the change and transubstantiation of the cup into the substance of the new testament.

And if you say, that the word 'cup' here in Christ's words does not signify the cup itself, but the wine, or thing contained in the cup, by a figure called metonymy, for that Christ's words meant, and must needs be taken so; you say very well. But, I pray you, by the way, here note two things: first, that this word 'is' hath no such strength and signification in the Lord's words, to make or to signify any transubstantiation; and, secondly, that in the Lord's words, whereby he instituted the Sacrament of his blood, he used a figurative speech.

How vain, then, is it, that some so earnestly say, as if it were an infallible rule, that in doctrine and in the institution of the Sacraments, Christ used no figures, but all his words are to be strained to their proper signification; when here, whatsoever you say was in the cup, neither that, nor the cup itself, taking every word in its proper signification, was the new testament; but to understand that which was in the cup, by the cup, that is a figurative speech. Yea, and also, whether you say it was wine or Christ's blood, you cannot verify, or truly say that was the new testament, without a figure also. Thus, in one sentence, spoken by Christ in the institution of the Sacrament of his blood, the figure must help us twice; so untrue is that which some write, that Christ uses no figure in the doctrine of faith, nor in the institution of his Sacraments. But some say, if we thus admit figures in doctrine, then all the articles of our faith, by figures and allegories, will shortly be transformed and unloosed. I say, it is a like fault, and even the same, to deny the figure where the place so requires to be understood, as vainly to make that a figurative speech, which is to be understood in its proper signification.

Of the rules whereby the speech is known, when it is figurative, and when it is not, St. Augustin, in his book called "Of Christian Doctrine," gives divers learned lessons, very necessary to be known by the student in God's word. Of which I will rehearse one, which is this: "If," saith he, "the scripture seems to command a thing which is wicked and ungodly, or to forbid a thing that charity requires, then know thou, saith he, that the speech is figurative." And for example he brings the saying of Christ in the sixth chapter of St. John: "Except ye eat the flesh of the Son of man, and drink his blood, ye cannot have life in you." It seems to command a wicked or an ungodly thing; wherefore it is a figurative speech, commanding to have communion and fellowship with Christ's passion, and devoutly and wholesomely to lay up in memory that his flesh was crucified and wounded for us.

And here I cannot but marvel at some men, of excellent fineness of wit, and of great eloquence, who are not ashamed to write and say, that this aforesaid saying of Christ is (according to St. Augustin) a figurative speech indeed; but not unto the learned, but unto the unlearned. Here let any man that indifferently understands the Latin tongue, read the place in St. Augustin, and if he perceive not clearly St. Augustin's words and mind not to be the contrary, let me abide the rebuke thereof.

This lesson of St. Augustin I have, therefore, the rather set forth, because as it teaches us to understand that place in John figuratively, even so surely the same lesson, with the example of St. Augustin's exposition thereof, teaches us, not only by the same to understand Christ's words in the institution of the Sacrament, both of his body and of his blood, figuratively, but, also, the very true meaning and understanding of the same. For, if to command to eat the flesh of the Son of man, and to drink his blood, seems to command an inconvenience and an ungodliness, and is even so indeed, if it be understood as the words stand in their proper signification; and, therefore, must be understood figuratively and spiritually, as St. Augustin godly and learnedly interprets them; then, surely, Christ, commanding his disciples in his Last Supper to eat his body and to drink his blood, seems to command, in sound of words, as great and even the same inconvenience and ungodliness, as his words do in the sixth chapter of St. John; and, therefore, they must, even by the same reason, be likewise understood, and expounded figuratively and spiritually, as St. Augustin did the other. Whereunto that exposition of St. Augustin may seem to be the more suitable, for Christ in his Supper, to the commandment of eating and drinking his body and blood, adds, "Do this in the remembrance of me." Which words, surely, were the key that opened and revealed this spiritual and godly exposition unto St. Augustin.

But I have tarried longer in setting forth the form of Christ's words upon the Lord's cup, written by Paul and Luke, than I intended. And yet in speaking of the form of Christ's words, spoken upon his cup, the form of words used in the Latin mass upon the Lord's cup now comes to my remembrance. Whereof I not a little marvel what should be the cause, seeing the Latin mass agrees with the evangelists and Paul in the form of words said upon the bread; why, in the words upon the Lord's cup, should it differ from them all? Yea, and it adds to the words of Christ, spoken upon the cup, these words, "the mystery of faith," which are not read as being attributed unto the Sacrament of Christ's blood, neither in the evangelists, nor in Paul, nor, so far as I know, in any other place of holy scripture. Yea, and if it may have some good exposition, yet, surely, I do not see the mystery, why it should not be as well added unto the words of Christ upon his bread, as upon his cup.

And I see in the use of the Latin mass the Sacrament of the blood abused, when it is denied unto the lay people, contrary unto God's most certain word. For why, I do beseech you, should the Sacrament of Christ's blood be denied unto the lay christians, more than to the priest? Did not Christ shed his blood for the godly layman as well as for the godly priest? If you will say, "Yes, he did so; but yet the Sacrament of the blood is not to be received without the offering up and sacrificing thereof unto God the Father, both for the quick and for the dead; and no man may make oblation of Christ's blood unto God but a priest, and, therefore, the priest alone, and that in his mass only, may receive the Sacrament of the blood." And call you this, my masters, the mystery of faith? Alas! alas! I fear me, this is, before God, the mystery of iniquity, such as Paul speaks of in his epistle to the Thessalonians. The Lord be merciful unto us, and bless us, and lighten his countenance upon us, and be merciful unto us; that we may know thy way upon earth, and among all people thy salvation. This kind of oblation stands upon transubstantiation, its cousin german, and grow both upon one ground. May the Lord weed out of his vineyard shortly, that bitter root, if it be his will and pleasure!

To speak of this oblation, how injurious it is unto Christ's passion, how it cannot, but with high blasphemy, and heinous arrogance, and intolerable pride, be claimed of any man, other than of Christ himself—how much and how plainly it opposes the manifest words,* and the true sense and meaning of holy scripture in many places, especially in the epistle to the Hebrews; the matter is so long, and others have written of it so at large, that I intend not now to treat thereof any further.

For in this my scribbling I intended only to search out and set forth by the scriptures, according to God's gracious gift of my poor knowledge, whether the true sense and meaning of Christ's words in the institution of his holy Supper do require any transubstantiation, as they call it, or that the very substance of bread and wine do remain still in the Lord's Supper, and are the material substance of the holy Sacrament of Christ our Saviour's blessed body and blood. Yet there remains one vain quiddity of Duns in this matter, the which, because some that write now seem to like it so well, that they have stripped it out of Duns' dusty and dark terms, and pricked him and painted him in fresh colours of an eloquent style, may therefore deceive the more, except the error be warily eschewed.

Duns saith on these words of Christ, "This is my body," "If you would know what this pronoun demonstrative, meaning the word 'this,' shows or demonstrates, whether the bread, that Christ took or no, he answers, no; but it points only one thing in substance; the nature and name whereof it does not tell, but leaves that to be determined and told by that which follows the word, 'is,' that is, by the predicatum, as the logician speaks." Therefore he calls the pronoun demonstrative 'this,' an 'individuum vagum,' that is, a wandering proper name, whereby we may point out and show anything in substance, whatsoever it be.

That this imagination is vain and untruly applied unto those words of Christ, "This is my body," may appear plainly, by the words of Luke and Paul, said upon the cup, when compared with the form of words spoken upon the cup in Matthew and Mark. For, as upon the bread it is said of all the evangelists, "This is my body;" so of Matthew and Mark is said of the cup, "This is my blood."

* The plain acceptation of the words.

Then if in the words, "This is my body," the word 'this' be, as Duns calls it, a 'wandering name,' to appoint and show forth any one thing, the name and nature whereof it does not tell, so must it be likewise in these words of Matthew and Mark upon the Lord's cup, "This is my blood." But in the words of Matthew and Mark it signifies and points out the same that it does in the Lord's words upon the cup, in Luke and Paul, where it is said, "This cup is the new testament in my blood," &c. Therefore, in Matthew and Mark, the pronoun demonstrative 'this' does not wander to point out only one thing in substance, not showing what it is, but tells plainly what it is no less in Matthew and Mark unto the eye, than is done in Luke and Paul, by putting this word 'cup' both unto the eye and to the ear.

For, taking the cup, and demonstrating or showing it unto his disciples by the pronoun demonstrative 'this,' and saying unto them: "Drink ye all of this," it was then all one to say, "This is my blood;" as to say, "This cup is my blood," meaning by this cup, as the nature of the speech requires, the thing contained in the cup. So likewise, without all doubt, when Christ had taken bread, given thanks, and broken it, and giving it to his disciples, said, "Take;" and so demonstrating and showing that bread which he had in his hands, to say then, "This is my body," and to have said, "This bread is my body," had been the same. As it were all one, if a man, lacking a knife, and going to his oysters, would say to another, whom he saw to have two knives, "Sir, I pray you lend me one of your knives:" were it not now all one to answer him: "Sir, hold, I will lend you this to eat your meat, but not to open oysters withal:" and "Hold, I will lend you this knife to eat your meat, but not to open oysters?"

This similitude serves but for this purpose, to declare the nature of speech, where the thing that is demonstrated and showed, is evidently perceived, and openly known to the eye. But, O good Lord, what a wonderful thing is it to see, how some men labour to teach, what is demonstrated and showed by the pronoun demonstrative 'this,' in Christ's words, when he saith, "This is my body:" —"this is my blood:" how they labour, I say, to teach what that word 'this' was then indeed; when Christ spake in the beginning of the sentence the word 'this, before he had pronounced the rest of the words that followed in the same sentence; so that their doctrine may agree with their transubstantiation; which, indeed, is the very foundation wherein all their erroneous doctrine does stand.

And here the transubstantiators do not agree among themselves, no more than they do in the words which wrought the transubstantiation, when Christ first instituted his Sacrament. Wherein Innocent, bishop of Rome, of the latter days, and Duns, as was before noted, attribute the work unto the word "benedixit, he blessed;" but the rest for the most part to "hoc est corpus meum, this is my body." Duns, therefore, with his sect, because he puts the change before, must needs say, that when Christ spake 'this' in the beginning of the sentence, it was, indeed, Christ's body. For in the change the substance of bread departed, and he saith that the change was done in 'benedixit,' that went before. Therefore, according to him and his, that 'this' was then, indeed, Christ's body, though the word did not then import so much, but only one thing in substance, which substance, according to Duns, the bread being gone, must needs be the substance of Christ's body.

But they that put their transubstantiation to be wrought by these words of Christ, "This is my body," and say, that when the whole sentence was finished, then this change was perfected, and not before; they cannot say, but yet Christ's 'this' in the beginning of the sentence before the other words were fully pronounced, was bread indeed. For as yet the change was not done, and so long the bread must needs remain; and so long as the substance of bread remains, so long, with the universal consent of all transubstantiators, the natural substance of Christ's body cannot come, and, therefore, must their 'this' of necessity demonstrate and show the substance, which was as yet at the pronouncing of the first word 'this' by Christ, but bread.

But how can they make and verify Christ's words to be true, demonstrating the substance, which, in the demonstration, is but bread, and say thereof, "This is my body," that is, as they say, the natural substance of Christ's body? except they would say, that the verb 'is' signifies 'is made,' or 'is changed into:' and so then, if the same verb 'is' be of the same effect in Christ's words spoken upon the cup, and rehearsed by Luke and Paul; the cup, or the wine in the cup, must be made or turned into the new testament, as was declared before.

There are some among the transubstantiators who walk so wilily and so warily betwixt these two aforesaid opinions, allowing them both, and holding plainly neither of them both, that methinks they may be called neutrals, ambidexters, or rather such as can shift on both sides. They play on both parts; for with the latter they all allow the doctrine of the last syllable, which is, that transubstantiation is done by miracle in an instant, at the sound of the last syllable, ' um,' in this sentence, hoc est corpus meum. And they allow Duns' fantastical imagination of ' individuum vagum,' which demonstrates, as he teaches, in Christ's words one thing in substance, then being, according to his mind, the substance of the body of Christ.

It is a marvellous thing how any man can agree with both these two, they being so contrary the one to the other.* For the one saith the word ' this' demonstrates the substance of bread, and the other saith, " No, not so; the bread is gone, an' it demonstrates a substance which is Christ's body."—' Tush," saith the third man, " you understand nothing t all: they agree well enough in the chief point, which is the ground of all; that is, both agree and bear witness that there is transubstantiation."

They agree, indeed, in that conclusion. I grant; but their proofs and doctrine thereof agree together as well, as did the false witnesses before Annas and Caiaphas against Christ, or the two wicked judges against Susanna. For against Christ the false witnesses agreed, no doubt, to speak all against him. And the wicked judges were both agreed to condemn poor Susanna: but on examination of their witnesses they dissented so far, that all was found false that they went about; both that wherein they agreed, and also those things which they brought for proofs.

Thus much have I spoken in searching out a solution for this principal question, which was, What is the material substance of the holy Sacrament in the Lord's Supper?

Now, lest I should seem to set by my own conceit more than is right; or to regard the doctrine of the old

* Here and in other places Ridley refers to Gardiner.

ecclesiastical writers less than is convenient for a man of
my poor learning and simple wit to do; and because, also,
I am indeed persuaded, that the old ecclesiastical writers
understood the true meaning of Christ in this matter; and
have both so truly and so plainly set it forth in certain
places of their writings, that no man, who will vouchsafe
to read them, and without prejudice of a corrupt judgment
will indifferently weigh them, and construe their minds
none otherwise than they declare themselves to have
meant; I am persuaded, I say, that in reading of them
thus, no man can be ignorant in this matter, but he that
will shut up his own eyes, and blindfold himself.

When I speak of ecclesiastical writers, I mean such as
were before the wicked usurpation of the see of Rome
was grown so unmeasurably great, that not only with
tyrannical power, but also with corrupt doctrine, it
began to subvert Christ's gospel, and to turn the state,
that Christ and his apostles set in the church, upside
down.

For the causes aforesaid, I will rehearse certain of their
sayings; and yet, because I take them only as witnesses
and expounders of this doctrine, and not as authors of the
same; and also that I may not be tedious, I will rehearse
but few; that is, three old writers of the Greek church,
and other three of the Latin church, which seem to me to
be most plain in this matter: the Greek authors are
Origen, Chrysostom, and Theodoret; the Latin are Tertullian, St. Augustin, and Gelasius.*

I know there can be nothing spoken so plainly, but that
crafty wit, furnished with eloquence, can darken it, and
wrest it quite from the true meaning to a contrary sense.
And I know also that eloquence, craft, and fineness of
wit, have gone about to blear men's eyes, and to stop
their ears in the aforenamed writers, that men should neither hear nor see what those authors both write and teach
so plainly, that except men should be made both stark
blind and deaf, they cannot but of necessity, if they will
read and weigh them indifferently, hear and see what they
mean, even when eloquence, craft, and fineness of wit,

* Origen was born about A. D. 185, and died A. D. 252. Chrysostom was born A. D. 347, and died A. D. 407. Theodoret was
born A. D. 386, and died A. D. 457. Tertullian flourished from
about A. D. 194 to A. D. 216. Augustin was born A. D. 354, and
died A. D. 430. Gelasius was chosen to be pope A D. 492.—
Dupin.

have done all they can. Now let us hear the old writers of the Greek church.

Origen, who lived above twelve hundred and fifty years ago; a man, for the excellency of his learning, so highly esteemed in Christ's church, that he was counted and judged the singular teacher, in his time, of Christ's religion, the confounder of heresies, the schoolmaster of many godly matters, and an opener of the high mysteries in scripture: he, writing upon the 15th chapter of St. Matthew's gospel, saith thus:

"But if any thing enter into the mouth, it goeth away into the belly, and is voided into the draught. Yea, and that meat which is sanctified by the word of God and prayer, concerning the matter thereof, it goeth away into the belly, and is voided into the draught. But, for the prayer which is added unto it, according to the proportion of faith, it is made profitable, making the mind able to perceive, and to see that which is profitable. For it is not the material substance of bread, but the word, which is spoken upon it, that is profitable to the man that eateth it not unworthily. And this I mean of the typical and symbolical (that is, sacramental) body."

Thus far go the words of Origen, where it is plain, first, that Origen, speaking here of the Sacrament of the Lord's Supper, as the last words do plainly signify, doth mean and teach, that the material substance thereof is received, digested, and voided, as the material substance of other bread and meats; which could not be if there were no material substance of bread at all, as the fantastical opinion of transubstantiation alleges. It is a world[*] to see the answer of the papists to this place of Origen! In the disputations, which were in this matter in the parliament house, and in both the universities of Cambridge and Oxford, they that defended transubstantiation said, that this part of Origen was only set forth of late by Erasmus, and therefore is to be suspected. But how vain this their answer is, it plainly appears. For so may all the good old authors, which lay in old libraries, and are set forth of late, be by this reason rejected: as Clemens Alexandrinus, Theodoretus, Justinus, Ecclesiastica Historia Nicephori, and such others.

Another answer they had, saying, that Origen is noted to have erred in some points, and therefore faith is not to

[*] Worth while.

be given in this matter unto him. But this answer, well
weighed, ministers good matter to the clear confutation of
itself. For indeed we grant that in some points Origen
did err But those errors are gathered out and noted
both by St. Jerome and Epiphanius, so that his works,
those errors excepted, are now so much the more of authority, that such great learned men took pains to take
out of him whatsoever they thought in him was written
amiss. But, as concerning the matter of the Lord's Supper, neither they nor any other ancient author, ever said
that Origen did err.

Now because these two answers have been of late so
confuted and confounded, that it is well perceived, that
they will take no place; therefore some, who have written
since that time, have forged two other answers, even of
the same mould. The former is, that Origen in this place
spake not of the Sacrament of bread or wine of the Lord's
table, but of another mystical meat; which St. Augustin
mentions was given unto them, that were taught the faith,
before they were baptized. But Origen's own words in
two sentences before rehearsed, being put together, prove
this answer untrue. For he saith, that " he meaneth that
figurative and mystical body, which profiteth them that do
receive it worthily:" alluding so plainly unto St. Paul's
words, spoken of the Lord's Supper, that it is a shame for
any learned man once to open his mouth to assert the
contrary. And as to that bread which St. Augustin speaks
of, he cannot prove that any such thing was used in Origen's time. Yea, and though that could be proved, yet
there never was bread at any time called a sacramental
body except the sacramental bread of the Lord's table,
which is called by Origen, the typical and symbolical body
of Christ.

The second of the two new-found answers is yet more
monstrous, it is this: " But let us grant, say they, that
Origen spake of the Lord's Supper, and by the matter
thereof was understood the material substance of bread
and wine; what then?" say they, " For though the material substance was once gone and departed by reason of
transubstantiation, whilst the forms of the bread and wine
remained; yet it is no inconvenience to say, that as the
material substance departed at the entering in of Christ's
body under the aforesaid forms, so when the said forms
are destroyed and do not remain, then the substance of

bread and wine comes again. And this," say they, " is very right in this mystery, that that which began with a miracle, shall end in a miracle."*

If I had not read this fantasy, I would scarcely have believed, that any learned man ever would have set forth such a foolish fantasy; which not only lacketh all ground either of God's word, reason, or of any ancient writer, but is also wholly contrary to the common rule of school divinity: which is, that no miracle is to be affirmed and put without necessity. And although, for their former miracle, which is their transubstantiation, they have some colour, though it is but vain, saying, it is done by the power and virtue of these words of Christ, " This is my body;" yet to make this second miracle, of the material substance returning again, they have no colour at all. Or else, I pray them to show me, by what words of Christ is that second miracle wrought? Thus you may see, that the sleights and shifts, which craft and wit can invent, to wrest the true sense of Origen, cannot take place. But now let us hear one other place of Origen.

Origen, in the seventh Homily on Leviticus, says, That there is in the four gospels, and not only in the Old Testament, a letter, meaning a literal sense, which killeth: " For if thou follow," saith he, " the letter in that saying, ' Except ye eat the flesh of the Son of man, and drink his blood,' &c. this letter doth kill." If in that place the letter doth kill, wherein is commanded the eating of Christ's flesh, then surely in those words of Christ, wherein Christ commands us to eat his body, the literal sense likewise does kill. For it is no less a crime, but even the same and all one in the literal sense, to eat Christ's body, and to eat Christ's flesh. Wherefore, if the one do kill, except it be understood figuratively and spiritually; then the other surely kills likewise. But that to eat Christ's flesh so understood, does kill, Origen affirms plainly in his words above rehearsed; wherefore, it cannot be justly denied, that to eat Christ's body, literally understood, must needs according to him, kill likewise.

The answer that is made to this place of Origen by the papists is so foolish, that it betrays itself without any further confutation. It is the same, that they make to a place of St. Augustin, in his book " Of Christian Doctrine," whereas St. Augustin speaks in effect the same that

* This and the preceding objections were urged by Gardiner

Origen does here. The papists' answer is this—'To the carnal man the literal sense is hurtful, but not so to the spiritual.' As though to understand in its proper sense, that which ought to be taken figuratively, were to the carnal man a dangerous peril, but to the spiritual man none at all!

Now to Chrysostom, whom I bring for the second writer in the Greek church. He, speaking of the unholy using of man's body, which, according to St. Paul, ought to be kept pure and holy, as the very temple of the Holy Ghost, saith thus: "If it be a fault to translate the holy vessels, in which is not contained the true body of Christ, but the mystery of the body, to private uses; how much more offence is it to abuse and defile the vessels of our body?" These are the words of Chrysostom: but there are many foul shifts devised to defeat this place. "The author," saith one, "is suspected." I answer, that in this place fault never was found with him until these our days. And whether the author were John Chrysostom himself, the archbishop of Constantinople, or not, that is not the matter: for of all it is granted, that he was a writer of that age, and a man of learning. So that it is manifest, that this which he writes was the received opinion of learned men in his days, or else undoubtedly in such a matter his saying should have been impugned by some that wrote in his time, or near unto the same. "Nay," saith another, "if this solution will not serve, we may say, that Chrysostom did not speak of the vessels of the Lord's cup, or such as were then used at the Lord's table, but of the vessels used in the temple of the old law."

This answer will serve no more than the other. For here Chrysostom speaks of vessels, wherein was that which was called the body of Christ, although it was not the true body, saith he, of Christ, but the mystery of Christ's body. Now of the vessels of the old law, the writers use no such manner of phrase; for their sacrifices were not called Christ's body; for then Christ was not, except in shadows and figures, and not revealed by the Sacrament of his body. Erasmus, who was a man that could understand the words and sense of the writer, although he would not be seen to speak against this error of transubstantiation, because he durst not; yet in his[*]time declares plainly, that this saying of this writer is not to be understood otherwise.

[*] This. Ed. 1556.

"Yet can I," saith a third papist, "find out a fine and subtle solution for this place, and grant all that yet is said, both allowing here the writer, and also that he meant the vessels of the Lord's table. For, saith he, the body of Christ is not contained in them, at the Lord's table, as in a place, but as in a mystery." Is not this a pretty shift, and a mystical solution? But by the same solution then Christ's body is not in the Lord's table, nor in the priest's hand, nor in the pix, and so he is no where here. For they will not say, that he is either here or there, as in a place. This answer pleases the maker so well, that he himself, after he had played with it a little while, and showed the fineness of his wit and eloquence therein, is content to give it over and say; "But it is not to be thought, that Chrysostom would speak after this fineness or subtlety:" and therefore he returns again unto the second answer for his sheet anchor, which is sufficiently confuted before.

Another short place of Chrysostom I will rehearse, which, if any thing may be heard impartially, in plain terms sets forth the truth of this matter. "Before the bread," saith Chrysostom, writing to Cæsarius, "be hallowed, we call it bread, but the grace of God sanctifying it by the means of the priest, it is delivered now from the name of bread, and esteemed worthy to be called Christ's body, although the nature of bread tarry in it still." These are Chrysostom's words, wherein I pray you, what can be said or thought more plain against this error of transubstantiation, than to declare, that the bread abides so still? And yet some are not ashamed shamefully to elude this very plain place, saying: "We grant the nature of bread remains still thus, for it may be seen, felt, and tasted; and yet the corporeal substance of the bread is gone; lest two bodies should be confused together, and Christ should be thought impanate."*

What contradiction and falsehood is in this answer, the simple man may easily perceive. Is it not plain contradiction, to grant that the nature of bread remains so still, that it may be seen, felt, and tasted, and yet to say that the corporeal substance is gone, to avoid the absurdity of Christ's impanation? And what manifest falsehood is this, to say or mean, that if the bread should remain still, then

---

* Become united to, or made a part of the substance of the bread.

must follow the inconveniency of impanation ? As though the very bread could not be a Sacrament of Christ's body, as water is of baptism, except Christ should unite the nature of bread to his nature, in unity of person, and make of the bread, God.

Now let us hear Theodoret, who is the last of the three Greek authors. He writes in his dialogue, against Eutyches: " He that called his natural body corn and bread, and also named himself a vine tree ; even he, the same, has honoured the symbols, that is, the sacramental signs, with the names of his body and blood, not changing indeed the nature itself, but adding grace unto the nature." What can be more plainly said than what this old writer saith ? Although the Sacraments bear the name of the body and blood of Christ, yet their nature is not changed, but abides still. And where is then the papists' transubstantiation ?

The same writer, in the second dialogue of the same work against the aforesaid heretic Eutyches, writes yet more plainly against this error of transubstantiation, if any thing can be said to be more plain. For he makes the heretic speak thus against him that defends the true doctrine, whom he calls Orthodoxus: " As the Sacraments of the body and blood of our Lord are one thing before the invocation, and after the invocation they are changed, and are made another; so likewise the Lord's body, saith the heretic, is, after the assumption or ascension into heaven, turned into the substance of God ;" the heretic meaning thereby, that Christ, after his ascension, remained no more a man.

To this Orthodoxus answers thus, and saith to the heretic: " Thou art taken in thine own snare ; for those mystical symbols or Sacraments, after the sanctification, do not go out of their own nature, but they tarry and abide still in their substance, figure, and shape ; yea, and are sensibly seen, and handled to be the same they were before,' &c. At these words the papists are startled ; and, to say the truth, these words are so plain, so full, and so clear, that they cannot tell what to say; but yet will not cease to go about to play the cuttles,* and cast their colours over them, that the truth, which is so plainly told, should not have place. " This author wrote," say they,

---

* The cuttle fish, which, when pursued by an enemy, emits a dark liquor, which blackens the water around, and so conceals itself

"before the determination of the church."* As who would say, whatsoever that wicked man Innocent, the pope of Rome, determined in his congregations with his monks and friars, that it must needs be holden for an article, and of the substance of our faith, for so Duns saith.†

Some charge Theodoret, that he was suspected to be a Nestorian, which was tried in the council of Chalcedon, and proved to be false. But the foulest shift of all, and yet the best that they can find in this matter, when none other will serve, is, to say, that Theodoret understands by the word substance, accidents,‡ and not substance indeed. The gloss is like a gloss of a lawyer upon a decree, the text whereof began thus: "We decree." The gloss of the lawyer there after many other pretty shifts,|| which he thinks will not well serve to his purpose, and therefore at last, to clear the matter, he saith thus: "we do decree—that is, we do abrogate or disannul." Is not this a worthy and goodly gloss? Who will not say, but he is worthy to be retained of counsel in the law, that can gloss so well, and find in a matter of difficulty such fine shifts; and yet this is the law, or at the least the gloss of the law. And therefore who can tell what peril a man may incur to speak against it, except he were a lawyer indeed, who can keep himself out of the briers, whatsoever wind may blow?

Hitherto you have heard the writers of the Greek church,—not all that they say, for that were a labour too great for me to gather, and too tedious for the reader,—but one or two places of each. The which how plain, and how full and clear they are against the error of transubstantiation, I refer to the judgment of the indifferent§ reader. And now I will likewise rehearse the sayings of three ancient writers of the Latin church, and so make an end. And first I will begin with Tertullian, whom Cyprian, the holy martyr, so highly esteemed, that whensoever he would have his book, he was wont to say, "Give me the master."

This old writer, in his fourth book against Marcion, the heretic, saith thus: "Jesus made the bread, which he

* Before the church had determined the subject.
† Pope Innocent III., in the fourth Lateran Council, held A.D.1215, and attended by an extraordinary number of ecclesiastics, for the first time established the doctrine of transubstantiation, and then decreed the use of that term.
‡ Or appearances. || There set forth, Ed. 1556 § Impartial.

took and distributed to his disciples, his body, saying, 'This is my body,' that is to say, saith Tertullian, a figure of my body." In this place it is plain, that according to Tertullian's exposition, Christ meant not, by calling the bread his body, and the wine his blood, that either the bread was his natural body, or the wine his natural blood, but he called them his body and blood, because he would institute them to be unto us Sacraments; that is, holy tokens and signs of his body and of his blood: so that by them remembering, and firmly believing the benefits procured to us by his body, which was torn and crucified for us, and of his blood which was shed for us upon the cross, and so with thanks receiving these holy Sacraments, according to Christ's institution, we might by the same be spiritually nourished and fed to the increase of all godliness in us, here, in our pilgrimage and journey, wherein we walk unto everlasting life.

This was undoubtedly Christ our Saviour's mind, and this is Tertullian's exposition. The wrangling that the papists make to elude this saying of Tertullian, is so far out of frame, that it even wearies me to think on it. "Tertullian writes here, say they, as none had done before him, neither yet any other catholic man after him."

This saying is manifestly false: for Origen, Hilary, Ambrose, Basil, Gregory Nazianzen, St. Augustin, and other old authors likewise, call the Sacrament a figure of Christ's body. And where they say, that Tertullian wrote this when in a heat of disputation with a heretic, coveting by all means to overthrow his adversary; as if they should say, he would not take heed what he did say, and especially what he would write in so high a matter, so that he might have the better hand of his adversary; is this credible to be true in any godly wise man? How much less then is it worthy to be thought or credited in a man of such great understanding, learning, and excellency as Tertullian is worthily esteemed to have been?

Likewise, this author, in his first book against the same heretic Marcion, writes thus: " God did not reject bread, which is his creature: for by it he has made a representation of his body.'' Now I pray you, what is it to say, that Christ has made a representation (by bread) of his body, but that Christ had instituted and ordained bread to be a Sacrament, to represent unto us his body? Now, whether the representation of one thing by another requires the corporeal presence of the thing which is so re presented or no, every man that has understanding is able in this point, the matter is so clear of itself, to be a sufficient judge.

The second doctor and writer of the Latin church, whose saying I promised to set forth, is St. Augustin: of whose learning and estimation I need not speak. For all the church of Christ both has and ever has had him, for a man of most singular learning, understanding, and diligence, both in setting forth the true doctrine of Christ's religion, and also in defence of the same against heretics.

This author, as he has written most plenteously, on other matters of our faith, so likewise on this argument he has written at large in many of his works so plainly against this error of transubstantiation, that the papists love less to hear of him than of any other writer; partly for his authority, and partly because he opens the matter more fully than any other. Therefore I will rehearse more places from him, than I have done of the others.

And first, what can be more plain, than that which he writes upon the 89th Psalm, speaking of the Sacrament of the Lord's body and blood; and rehearsing, as it were, Christ's words to his disciples, after this manner: " It is not this body, which ye do see, which ye shall eat, neither shall ye drink this blood, which the soldiers that crucify me shall spill or shed.—I commend unto you a mystery, or a Sacrament, which spiritually understood shall give you life." Now if Christ had no more natural and corporeal bodies, but that one which they then presently both heard and saw, nor other natural blood, but that which was in the same body, and which the soldiers afterwards cruelly shed upon the cross: and neither his body nor this blood was, by this declaration of St. Augustin, either to be eaten or drunken, but the mystery thereof spiritually to be understood: then I conclude, if this saying and exposition of St. Augustin be true, that the mystery which the disciples should eat, was not the natural body of Christ, but a mystery of the same, spiritually to be understood.

For as St. Augustin saith, in his 20th book against Faustus, " Christ's flesh and blood in the old testament were promised by similitudes and signs of their sacrifices, and were exhibited in deed and in truth upon the cross, but the same is celebrated by a Sacrament of remembrance upon the altar." And in his book of Faith to Peter, cap. 19, he saith, that "In these sacrifices, (meaning of the old law,) is figuratively signified what was then to be given: but in this sacrifice, what is already given is evidently signified, understanding in the sacrifice upon the altar, the remembrance and thanksgiving for the flesh, which he offered for us, and for the blood which he shed for us upon the cross:" as in the same place evidently appears.

Another evident and clear place, wherein it appears, that by the sacramental bread, which Christ called his body, he meant, "a figure of his body," is upon the third Psalm, where St. Augustin speaks thus in plain terms: "Christ admitted Judas unto the feast, in which he commended unto his disciples *the figure* of his body*." This was Christ's last Supper before his passion, wherein he ordained the Sacrament of his body, as all learned men agree.

St. Augustin also, in his 23d epistle to Boniface, teaches how Sacraments bear the names of the things whereof they are Sacraments, both in baptism and in the Lord's table; even as we call every Good Friday, the day of Christ's passion; and every Easter Day, the day of Christ's resurrection; when in very deed there was but one day wherein he suffered, and but one day wherein he rose. And why do we then call them so, which are not so indeed, but because they are in like time and course of the year, as those days were, wherein those things were done?

"Was Christ," saith St. Augustin, "offered more than once? And he offered himself. And yet in a Sacrament or representation he is offered, not only every solemn feast of Easter, but also every day to the people. So that he does not lie, that saith, "He is offered every day." For if Sacraments had not some similitude or likeness of those things whereof they are Sacraments, they could in no wise be Sacraments; and for their similitudes and likeness commonly they have the name of the things whereof they are Sacraments. Therefore, as after a certain manner of speech, the Sacrament of Christ's body is Christ's body, the Sacrament of Christ's blood is Christ's blood; so likewise the Sacrament of faith is faith."

After this manner of speech, as St. Augustin teaches in his question upon Leviticus and against Adamantus, "it is said in Scripture, that seven ears of corn are seven

* Sign or representation.

years, seven kine are seven years, and 'the rock was Christ;' and blood is the soul:" which last saying, saith St. Augustin is understood to be spoken in a sign or figure, for the Lord himself did not hesitate to say, 'This is my body,' when he gave the sign of his body."—" For we must not consider in Sacraments," saith St. Augustin in another place, " what they are, but what they signify. For they are signs of things, being one thing in themselves, and yet signifying another."—" For the heavenly bread, saith he, speaking of the sacramental bread, by some manner of speech is called Christ's body, when in very deed it is the Sacrament of his body," &c.

What can be more plain or clearly spoken, than these places of St. Augustin before rehearsed, if men were not obstinately bent to maintain an untruth, and to receive nothing, whosoever sets it forth? Yet one place more of St. Augustin I will allege, which is very clear to this purpose, that Christ's natural body is in heaven, and not here corporeally in the Sacrament, and so let him depart.

In his 50th treatise, which he writes upon John, he teaches plainly and clearly, how Christ, being both God and man, is both here, after a certain manner, and yet in heaven, and not here in his natural body and substance which he took of the blessed virgin Mary; speaking thus of Christ, and saying, " By his divine majesty, by his providence, by his unspeakable and invisible grace, that is fulfilled which he spake: ' Behold, I am with you to the end of the world.' But, as concerning his flesh which he took in his incarnation; as touching that which was born of the virgin; as concerning that which was apprehended by the Jews, and crucified upon a tree, and taken down from the cross, wrapped in linen clothes, and buried, and rose again, and appeared after his resurrection—as concerning that flesh, he said, ' Ye shall not ever have me with you.' Why so? Because concerning his flesh, he was conversant with his disciples forty days, and they accompanying, seeing, and not following him, he went up into heaven, and is not here. By the presence of his divine majesty, he did not depart; as concerning the presence of his divine majesty, we have Christ ever with us, but, as concerning the presence of his flesh, he said truly to his disciples; ' Ye shall not ever have me with you.' For, as concerning the presence of his flesh, the church had him but a few days; now it holdeth him by faith, though it see him not."

Thus much St. Augustin speaks, repeating one thing so often; and all to declare and teach how we should understand the manner of Christ's being here with us, which is by his grace, by his providence, and by his Divine nature; and how he is absent by his natural body which was born of the virgin Mary, died, and rose for us, and is ascended into heaven, and there sitteth, as it is in the articles of our faith, on the right hand of God, and thence, and from no other place, saith St. Augustin, he shall come on the latter day, to judge the quick and the dead. At the which day the righteous shall lift up their heads, and the light of God's truth shall so shine, that falsehood and errors shall be put to perpetual confusion. Righteousness shall have the upper hand, and truth that day shall bear away the victory; and all the enemies thereof be quite overthrown, to be trodden under foot for evermore. O Lord, I beseech thee, hasten this day. Then shalt thou be glorified with the glory due unto thy holy name, and unto thy Divine majesty: and we shall sing unto thee in all joy and felicity, laud and praise for evermore. Amen.

Here now I would make an end: for methinks St. Augustin is so full and plain in this matter, and of such authority, that it should not need, after this his declaration, being so firmly grounded upon God's word, and so well agreeing with other ancient authors, to bring in any more for the confirmation of this matter. And yet I said I would allege three of the Latin church, to testify the truth in this cause. Now, therefore, the last of all shall be Gelasius, who was a bishop of Rome: but one that was bishop of that see, before the wicked usurpation and tyranny thereof spread and burst out into all the world. For this man was before Boniface, yea, and Gregory the first; in whose days corruption of doctrine and tyrannical usurpation chiefly grew, and had the upper hand.

Gelasius, in an epistle of the two natures of Christ, against Eutyches, writes thus: "The Sacraments of the body and blood of Christ, which we receive, are godly things, whereby, and by the same, we are made partakers of the divine nature; and yet nevertheless the substance or nature of the bread and wine does not depart or go away.' Note these words, I beseech you, and consider whether any thing can be more plainly spoken, than these words against the error of transubstantiation; which is the ground and bitter root whereupon spring all the horrible errors before rehearsed.

Wherefore, seeing, that the falsehood hereof appears so manifestly, and by so many ways, so plainly, so clearly, and so fully, that no man needs to be deceived, but he that will not see, or will not understand; let us all that love the truth embrace it, and forsake the falsehood. For he that loveth the truth is of God: and the lack of the love thereof is the cause why God suffers men to fall into errors, and to perish therein; yea, and as St. Paul saith, why he sends unto them illusions, that they believe lies, unto their own condemnation: "because, saith he, they love not the truth"

This truth, no doubt, is God's word: for Christ himself saith unto his Father: "Thy word is truth." The love and light whereof Almighty God, our heavenly Father, give us, and lighten it in our hearts by his Holy Spirit, through Jesus Christ our Lord. Amen.

Vincit Veritas

CONFERENCES.

Doctor Ridley being had from Framlingham to the tower; where, being in durance, and invited to the lieutenant's table, he had certain talk or conference with secretary Bourn, Master Fecknam, and others, concerning the controversies in religion; the sum whereof, as it was penned with his own hand, here follows.—*Fox.*

The sum and effect of the communication between Dr Ridley, and secretary Bourn, with others, at the lieutenant's table in the tower.

MASTER THOMAS BRIDGES said at his brother Master Lieutenant's board; "I pray you, Master Doctors, for my learning, tell me what a heretic is." Master Secretary Bourn said, "I will tell you who is a heretic; whoso stubbornly and stiffly maintaineth an untruth, he is a heretic."

"You mean, sir," said I, "an untruth in matters of religion, and concerning our faith." "Yea, that is true," said he; "and in this we are soon agreed."

Then said Master Fecknam, whom they called Dean of Paul's, sitting at the upper end of the table: "I will tell you by St. Augustine who is a heretic: 'He who, to flatter princes or for the sake of gain, invents or follows false opinions, he is a heretic.'" "Sir," said I, "I ween St. Augustine adds a third member, which is, 'or for vain glory.'" "You say even true, Master Doctor," said he: and thus far we agreed all three.

Master Fecknam began again to say, "Whoso does not believe what the scripture affirms, but obstinately maintains the contrary, he is a heretic. As in the sacrament of the altar, Matthew affirms there is Christ's body: Mark affirms it, Luke affirms it, Paul affirms it, and none deny it: therefore to hold the contrary, is heresy. It is the same body and flesh that was born of the Virgin: and this is confirmed by unity, antiquity, and universality.

For none before Berengarius did ever doubt of this, and he was a heretic, as Master Doctor there knows full well; I testify his own conscience."

"Marry, sir," said Master Secretary, "Master Fecknam has spoken well. These are great matters, unity, antiquity, and universality. Do you not think so, master Doctor?" said he to me.

Here, while I strained courtesy, and pretended not to talk, one of the commissioners said: "Peradventure Master Ridley agrees with Master Fecknam, and then there needs not much debating of the matter."

"Sir," said I, "in some things I do and shall agree with him, and in some things which he has spoken, to be plain, I do not agree with him at all. Masters," said I, "you are, as I understand, the queen's commissioners here, and if you have commission to examine me in these matters, I shall declare unto you plainly my faith; if you have not, then I shall pray you either to give me leave to speak my mind freely, or else to hold my peace."

"There is none here," said Master Secretary, "that doth not favour you." And then every man showed what favour they bore towards me, and how glad they would be of an agreement.

But as I strained to have a license of them in plain words to speak my mind, so methought they granted me it, but scarcely and unwillingly. Well, at the last I was content to take it for a license, and so I began to talk.

To Master Fecknam's arguments of the manifold affirmation where there was no denial, I answered; "Where is a multitude of affirmations in scripture, and where is one affirmation, all is one concerning the truth of the matter; for what any one of the evangelists spake, inspired by the Holy Ghost, was as true as that which is spoken of them all. What John saith of Christ; 'I am the door of the sheep,' is as true as if all had said it. For it is not in scripture as in the witness of men, where a number are credited more than one, because it is uncertain of whose spirit he speaks.—And where Master Fecknam spake of so many affirming without any negation, &c., Sir, said I, they all affirm the thing which they meant. Now, if you take their words and leave their meaning, then they affirm what you take, but not what they meant. Sir, said I, if in talk with you, I should so utter my mind in words, that you, by the same, may plainly perceive my meaning, and could, if you would be captious, cavil at my words, and writhe them to another sense, I should think you were no gentle companion to talk with, except you would take my words as you perceived that I meant."

"Marry," said Master Secretary, "we should else do you plain injury and wrong."

Master Fecknam perceiving whereunto my talk went: "Why," said he, "what circumstances can you show me that should move to think of any other sense, than as the words plainly say: 'This is my body which shall be betrayed for you.'"

"Sir," said I, "even the next sentence that follows: 'Do this in my remembrance.' And also by what reason you say the bread is turned into Christ's carnal body; by the same I may say, that it is turned into his mystical body. For as that saith of it, 'This is my body which shall be delivered for you:' so Paul, who spake by Christ's Spirit, saith: 'We being many are all but one bread, and one body, inasmuch as we are partakers of one bread.'"

"Here he called one loaf, one bread," said Master Secretary.

"Yea," said I, "one loaf, or one bread, it is the same with me."

"But what say you," quoth Master Secretary, "of the universality, antiquity, and unity, that Master Fecknam spoke of."

"I ensure you," said I," "I think them weighty matters, and to be well considered. As for unity, the truth is, before God, I do believe it and embrace it, so it be with verity, and joined to our head Christ, and such one as Paul speaketh of, saying: 'One faith, one God, one baptism.' And for antiquity, I am also persuaded to be true that Iræneus saith: 'That which was first is true.' In our religion Christ's faith was first truly taught by Christ himself, by his apostles, and by many good men who from the beginning succeeded next unto them. And as for this controversy of the Sacrament, I am persuaded, that those old writers who wrote before the controversy and the usurping of the see of Rome, all agree in this truth, if they are well understood.'

"I am glad to hear," said Master Secretary, "that you so well esteem the doctors of the church."

"Now, as for universality, it may have two meanings. One to understand that to be universal, which, from the beginning in all ages, has been allowed; another, to understand universality for the multitude of our age, or of any other particular age."

"No, no," saith Master Secretary, "these three always agree, and where there is one, there are all the rest." And here he and I changed many words: and finally, to be short, in this matter we did not agree.

"There was none," quoth Master Fecknam, "before Berengarius, Wickliffe, and Huss, and now, in our days, Carolstadt, and Ecolampadius. And Carolstadt saith, Christ pointed to his own body and not to the Sacrament, and said, 'This is my body.' And Melancthon writes to one Micronius (Myconius said I) these or like words: 'I can find no well grounded reason to cause me to dissent from the belief of our forefathers.'"

Thus when he had spoken at length, with many other words, "Sir," said I, "it is certain that others before these have written of this matter. Not by the way only, as almost all the old writers, but even designedly, and their books treat of it alone, as Bertram."

"Bertram," said the Secretary: "what man was he?[*] who was he? how do you know?" with other questions.

"Sir," quoth I, "I have read his books: he proposes the same which is now in controversy, and answers so directly, that no man may doubt but that he affirms, that the substance of bread remains still in the Sacrament; and he wrote unto Charlemagne."

"Marry," quoth he, "mark, for there is a mistake. He wrote to Henry, and not Charles; for no author makes any such mention of Bertramus."

"Yes," quoth I, "Trithemius, in his Catalogue of illustrious writers, speaks of him. Trithemius was but of late time; but he speaks," quoth I, "of them that were of antiquity." Here, after much talk of Bertram,

"What authors have you," quoth Master Secretary, "that make the Sacrament a figure?"

"Sir," quoth I, "you know, I think, that Tertullian in plain words speaks thus: 'This is my body, that is to say, a figure of my body.' And Gelasius saith plainly, that 'The substance of bread remains.' And Origen saith likewise, 'That which is sanctified, as touching the matter or substance, passeth away into the draught.'" This

[*] See the note prefixed to the Treatise on the Lord's Supper.

when I had englished, Master Secretary said to me, "You know very well, as well as any man." And here, if I would, I might have been set in a fool's paradise by his commendation of my learning, and that I was 'a man of much reading.' But this I would not take at his hand. He set me not up so high, but I brought myself as low again: and here was much ado.

"As for Melancthon," quoth I, "whom Master Fecknam spake of, I marvel that you allege him, for we are nearer an agreement here in England, than the opinion of Melancthon is to you. For, in this point, we all agree, that there is in the Sacrament but one material substance· and Melancthon, as I think, saith there are two.

"You say truth," quoth Master Secretary: "Melancthon's opinion is so. But I pray you, you have heard that the Sacrament was in old time so reverenced, that many were forbidden to be present at the ministration thereof, Catechumens," quoth he, " and many others."

"Truth, sir," quoth I, "there were some called Hearers, some Penitents, some Catechumens, and some ' Energumeni,' which were commanded to depart."

"Now," quoth he, "how can you then make but a figure or a sign of the Sacrament, as that book does, which is set forth in my lord of Canterbury's name. I think you can tell who made it, did not you make it?" And here was much murmuring of the rest, as though they would have given me the glory of the writing of that book, which yet was said by some there to contain the most heinous heresy that ever was.

"Master Secretary," quoth I, "that book was made of a great learned man, who is able to do the like again : as for me, I ensure you, be not deceived in me, I was never able to do or to write any such thing: he passes me no less, than the learned master his young scholar."

Now, here every man would have his saying, which I pass over, as not much material to tell. "But, sir," quoth I, " methinks it is not charitably done, to bear the people in hand that any man does so lightly esteem the Sacrament, as to make of it only a figure. For that 'only' makes it a bare figure without any more profit, which that book often denies, as appears most plainly to the reader."

"Yes," quoth he, " that they do."

"No, sir," quoth I, of a truth: " and as for me, I

ensure you I make no less of the Sacrament than thus—I say whosoever receives the Sacrament, he receives therewith either life or death.'

"No," quoth Master Secretary, "scripture saith not so."

"Sir," quoth I, "although not in the same sound of words, yet it does in the same sense, and St. Augustine saith, in the sound of words also: for St. Paul saith: 'The bread which we break, is it not the partaking or fellowship of the body of Christ?' And St. Augustine says: 'Eat life, drink life.'"

Then said Master Pope, "What can you make of it when you say, there is not the real body of Christ? Which I do believe: and I pray God I may never believe otherwise. How can it bring, as you say, either life or death, when Christ's body is not there?"

"Sir," quoth I, "when you hear God's word truly preached, if you believe it and abide in it, you shall and do receive life withal: and if you do not believe it, it brings unto you death: and yet Christ's body is still in heaven, and not carnal in every preacher's mouth."

"I pray you tell me," quoth he, "how can you answer to this: 'which shall be given for you:' Was the figure of Christ's body given for us?"

"No, sir," quoth I, "but the very body itself, whereof the Sacrament is a sacramental figure.

"How say you then," quoth he, "to the words 'Which shall be given for you?'"

"Forsooth," quoth I, "Tertullian's exposition makes it plain, for he saith, 'The body is a figure of the body.' Now add this to, 'Which shall be given for you,' and it agrees exceedingly well."

"In faith," quoth he, "I would give forty pounds that you were of a good opinion. For I assure you, I have heard you, and had an affection to you."

"I thank you, Master Pope, for your heart and mind, and you know," quoth I, "I were a very fool if I would, in this matter, dissent from you, if, in my conscience, the truth did not inforce me so to do. For I know, as you may perceive, it is somewhat out of my way, if I esteemed worldly gain."

"What say you," quoth he, "to Cyprian? Does he not say plainly, 'The bread which the Lord delivered, being changed, not according to the form, but according to the nature thereof, by the omnipotent word, is made flesh.'"

"True, sir, so he says, and I answer even the same which once I preached at Paul's Cross in a sermon, for which I have been as unjustly and as untruly reported as any poor man has been. For there I, speaking of the Sacrament, and inveighing against them that esteemed it no better than a piece of bread, told even the same thing of Penitents, Hearers, Catechumens, and Energumeni, that I spake of before, and I bade them depart as unworthy to hear the mystery:" and then I said to those that are saints: " Cyprian, the martyr, shall tell you how it is that Christ calls it, saying, ' Bread is the body, meat, drink, flesh, because that unto this material substance is given the property of the thing whereof it beareth the name.' " And this place I then explained as the time would then suffer, that the material substance of bread doth remain. Master Fecknam, who, as is reported to me, belied me openly as to the matter at Paul's cross, heard all this my talk (looking as red as scarlet in his face) and answered me not one word.

"You know well," quoth Master Secretary, " that Origen and Tertullian were not catholics, but erred."

" Sir," quoth I, " there is none of all the doctors that are holden in all points, but they are thought to have erred in some things. But yet I never heard that it was either laid to Origen's charge or to Tertullian's, that ever they were thought to have erred in this matter of the Sacrament."

"What," quoth Master Chomley, late chief justice, " doth not Christ say plainly, that it is his very flesh, and his very blood, and we must needs eat him, or we can have no life?" " Sir," quoth I, " if you will hear how St. Augustine expounds that place, you shall perceive that you are wrong." And when I began to tell St. Augustine's mind in his book Of Christian Doctrine: " Yea, yea," quoth Master Secretary, " that is true, St. Augustine takes it figuratively indeed."

" Forty years ago," quoth Master Fecknam, " all were of one opinion in this matter."

" Forty years ago," quoth I, " all held that the bishop of Rome was supreme head of the universal church.

" What then?" Master Fecknam began to say, but Master Secretary said, " That was but a positive law."

" A positive law?" quoth I. " No, sir, he would not have it so: for it is in his decrees, that he challenged it by Christ's own word. For his decree saith: 'The church of Rome was advanced above all other churches in the world, not by any synodical constitutions, nor yet any councils, but by the lively voice of the Lord, according as the Lord said to Peter: Thou art Peter,' &c. And in another place he declareth 'Thou art Cephas, that is to say, the head.'"

"Tush, it was not counted an article," quoth Master Secretary, "of our faith."

"Yes," said I, "if you call that an article of faith which is to be believed under pain of damnation. For he saith: 'We do absolutely determine, declare, and pronounce, that every creature is subject to the obedience of the bishop of Rome upon necessity of salvation.'"

And when we spake of laws and decrees, Master Roger Chomley thought himself much wronged, that he could not be suffered to speak, the rest were so ready to interrupt him: and then he up and told a long tale what laws were of kings of England made against the bishop of Rome, and was vehement to tell how they of the clergy alway did fly to him. And here, because he seemed to speak of many things beside our purpose, whereof we spake before, he was answered of his own fellows, and I let them talk.

Finally, we departed in peace, and Master Secretary promised in the end, that of their talk there should come to me no harm. And after I had made my moan for lack of my books, he said they were all once given to him: and as I know, said he, who hath them now, write me the names of such as you would have, and I will speak for you the best I can.

CERTAIN

GODLY, LEARNED, AND COMFORTABLE
CONFERENCES,

BETWEEN

THE TWO REVEREND FATHERS AND HOLY MARTYRS,

DR. NICHOLAS RIDLEY,

LATE BISHOP OF LONDON,

AND

MASTER HUGH LATIMER,

SOMETIME BISHOP OF WORCESTER,

DURING THE TIME OF THEIR IMPRISONMENT.*

"*At the name of Jesus let every knee bow.*" Phil. ii.

Ridley. "A BISHOP ought to be unreproveable, as the steward of God, cleaving fast to the true word of doctrine," &c. (Titus, i.) All worldly respects put apart, of shame, death, loss of goods, and worldly commodities, let me have, I pray you, your advice in these matters following. That is, your assent and confirmation in these things, what you judge that God doth allow, and your best counsel and advertisement where you think otherwise, and your reasons for both the same. For the wise man saith, "One brother which is helped of another, is like a well-defended city." (Prov. xviii.)

* "Till the Kentish insurrection, under Wyat, had furnished the tower with crowds of prisoners, the bishops appear to have had separate rooms, with the opportunity of meeting sometimes, when they were indulged to take the benefit of the air in the garden of the tower; but at those interviews they were guarded. Ridley was desirous of a serious conference with his fellow-prisoners to sift his own opinions, and correct, or strengthen them from the experience of those veterans. He knew his life was at stake, and he verily believed the truth of Christ was so also: he would not willingly

The causes that move me to abstain from the mass, are these:

J. It is done in a strange tongue, which the people do not understand, contrary to the doctrine of the apostle. (1 Cor. xiv.)

Latimer. Where is no understanding, there is neither edifying, nor comfort; for besides that they speak to the air, the mind receives no profit; they are as aliens one to another. The parishioners will say, their priests are mad, whereas all things might be done so that they may edify. Let every man know, that the things which I write, saith St. Paul, are the commandments of the Lord. Such absurdities are to be eschewed.*

Ridley. II. There is also wanting, the showing of the Lord's death, contrary to the mind of the apostle, "As often as ye shall eat this bread, and drink of this cup, ye shall show the Lord's death till he come." (1 Cor. xi.) What showing can be there, where no man heareth, that is to say, understands what is said? No man, I mean of the common people, for whose profit the prayer of the church ought especially to serve.

Latimer. Christ saith, "Woe be unto you, that take away the key of knowledge." (Luke, xi.) The papists study by all means to make the people ignorant, lest their ignorant Sir Johns† should be had in less estimation or despised, which is quite contrary to St. Paul's practice, who wished that all men might be full, filled with all knowledge, and to be perfect in Christ Jesus. (Col. i.) The institution of Christ, if it were rehearsed in the vulgar tongue, would be not only a consecration, but also a fruitful preaching, for the edification of the hearers. Whereas, in the popish mass it is neither understood nor heard, whilst the common people are utterly ignorant what their priests do, or what they go about, whether they bless or curse.

---

rush on death through tortures, for a mistaken question, or a point of little importance; nor weakly betray the cause of truth either over-reached by their sophistry, or terrified by their cruelties. He therefore desired the sincere advice of these true friends either to point out his error, or confirm his resolution. For which purpose he wrote to them, setting down his own reasons, and leaving a blank under each, which he wished those venerable fathers to fill up with their observations or corrections. Latimer's answers are preserved." (*Gloucester Ridley's Life of Bishop Ridley*, 444.) Cranmer, Ridley Latimer, and Bradford, were confined together part of the time they were in the tower, probably after these conferences had passed in writing.

* Rejected, avoided.   † Romish priests.

The apostles understood Christ, when he celebrated his supper; therefore these papists swerve from Christ in their mass.

Ridley. III. There is no communion, but it is made a private table, whereas, indeed it ought to be a communion, for St. Paul saith, "The bread, which we break, is the partaking of the body of Christ." (1 Cor. x.) And Christ brake, distributed, and said, "Take and eat." But they make it a private table: it is open. For where they are many priests, who will communicate, they do it not at one table or altar, but every one of them have their altars, masses, and tables.

Latimer. To make that private, which Christ made common, and willed to be communicated, may seem to be the workmanship of antichrist himself. The canons of the apostles excommunicate those who being present at common prayer, &c. do not also receive the holy communion. And unto the same agrees the decree of Anacletus: "When the consecration is done, saith he, let all such communicate as intend not to be excommunicated." Tertullian saith, "That which is first, is true; that which is latter, is counterfeited." But the papists say, "We do it privately, because we do it for others." But where have you your commission to mass and sacrifice for others?

Ridley. IV. The Lord's commandment of communicating the cup unto the lay people, is not observed according to the word of the Lord: "Drink ye all of this."

Latimer. Paul saith, "As often as ye shall eat of this bread, and drink of this cup, ye shall show the Lord's death." (1 Cor. xi.) So that, not the partaking of the one only, but of both, is a showing of the Lord's death; because in his death the blood was divided from the body, it is necessary that the same division be represented in the Supper; otherwise the Supper is not a showing of the Lord's death.

"Let a man examine himself," &c. But this word, homo,' is of both genders: therefore, it is as well commanded to the woman to drink of the cup, as the man, &c. But the king's argument, once against me, was this — "' When ye come together to eat,' Paul saith not to drink."—I answered, it was not needful, seeing that a little before he had made mention of both in these words: "And so let him eat of that bread, and drink of that cup." That is to say, as well the woman as the man. Under the name of bread, which betokens all sustenance of the body, drink is also understood in the scriptures. Otherwise they would say, that Christ did not drink after his resurrection with his disciples, except Peter had said, we did eat and drink with him after he rose from death. (Acts, x.)

Ridley. V. They servilely serve the holy sign, as St. Augustine speaks, instead of the thing signified, whilst the sacramental bread, by a solemn or common error, is adored and worshipped for the flesh of the Son of God.

Latimer. If you deny unto them their corporeal presence and transubstantiation, their fantastical adoration will, by and by,* vanish away. Therefore, be strong in denying such a presence, and then you have won the field.

Furthermore, in the first Supper, celebrated by Christ himself, there is no mention made of adoration of the elements. He said, "Eat ye, and drink ye," not worship ye. Therefore, against adoration may be spoken that saying of Christ concerning divorce, "From the beginning it was not so." But the devil secretly, and by little and little, infects all Christ's ordinances; and as for the private mass, with all the sinews thereof, what manner of thing it is, may be easily perceived by the ready acceptation of the people, whose hearts are prone to evil, even from their youth. (Gen. viii.)

Ridley. VI. They pluck away the honour from the only sacrifice of Christ, whilst this sacramental and mass-sacrifice is believed to be propitiatory, and such a one as cleanseth the souls, both of the quick and the dead. Contrary to what is written to the Hebrews, "With one offering hath he made perfect for ever them that are sanctified." And again, "Where remission of these things (that is, where Jesus) is, there is no more offering for sin."

Latimer. By his own person he hath purged our sins. (Heb. xi.) The words, 'by his own person,' have an emphasis, or vehemence, which drives away all sacrificing priests from such office of sacrificing; seeing that which He hath done by himself, He hath not left to be perfected by others; so that the putting off our sins may more truly be thought past and done, than a thing to come and to be done. "If any man sin." (1 John, ii.) He saith not, let him have a priest at home to sacrifice for him, but "we have an Advocate," the virtue of whose one oblation endureth for ever St. Paul saith, "They that serve the altar, are partakers with the altar;" even so the Lord hath ordained, that they

* At once, soon.

which preach the gospel should live of the gospel. (1 Cor.ix.) Why doth he not rather say, they that sacrifice in the mass?

Ridley. VII. There are manifold abuses and superstitions in the mass, and about the mass. Salt is conjured, that it may be a conjured salt for the salvation of the believers, to be a salvation and health, both of the mind and of the body, unto everlasting life, to all those who receive it. Water is conjured, that it may be made a conjured water, to chase away all the power of the enemy, to chase away devils, &c. Bread also has a second blessing, that it may be health of mind and body to all them that receive it. If we think that such strength is to be given to salt, water, and bread; or, if we judge that these things are able to receive any such virtue or efficacy, what leave we to Christ, our Saviour? But, if we think not so, why then do we pray on this sort? Forasmuch as all prayer ought to be done of faith.

Latimer. As touching the abuses of the mass, I refer you to a little book, the title whereof is Mistress Missa,* where she was justly condemned and banished under pain of burning. But the devil has brought her in again, to bring us to burning.

Ridley. VIII. The priest turns himself from the altar, and speaketh unto the people in an unknown tongue, saying, "Dominus vobiscum, orate pro me, fratres et sorores," &c.; that is, The Lord be with you, and pray for me, brothers and sisters: and turning from the people, he saith in Latin, "Let us pray, and the peace of the Lord be always with you." Also, the people, or at least he which supplies the place of the people, is compelled three times to say, "Amen," when he has not heard a word of what the priest hath prayed or spoken, except these few words, "Per omnia secula seculorum."† Whereas, to the answering of "Amen," St. Paul wills the answerer, not only to hear, but also to understand, the things that were spoken. (1 Cor. xiv.)

Latimer. Yea, and, "Ite, missa est,"‡ must be sung to them with a great rolling up and down of notes, so bidding them go home fasting, when he§ hath eaten and drunken up all himself alone. A fellow, once rebuked for going away before mass was ended, answered, that it was not good manners to tarry till he were bidden to go. After

* By Dr. Turner. † For ever and ever.
‡ Go, it is dismissed. § The priest.

that he was blamed for not taking holy bread, he answered, that he was bidden to go away before.

Ridley. IX. The priest, when he lifteth up the Sacrament, murmurs to himself these words: "Hæc quotiescunque feceritis, in mei memoriam facietis;" that is, "As often as you do these things, ye shall do it in remembrance of me." He seems by his words to speak unto the people, but he suffers not his voice to be heard of the people.

Latimer. I cannot tell to whom the mass-man speaks, as he is a-lifting, seeing that neither Christ bade him lift, neither are the people allowed to do those things: and as for that form of words, it is of their own framing. But the papists do all things well, be they ever so much deceitful workers, taking upon them the vizor* and title of the church, as it were sheep's clothing, as though they were the ministers of righteousness: whereas, indeed, they are the devil's ministers, whose end shall be according to their deeds. (2 Cor. ii.) They roll out their Latin language by heart, but in so doing they make the poor people of Christ altogether ignorant; and so much as in them lies, they keep them back from that which St. Paul calls the best knowledge, (1 Cor. ii.) which is, to know rightly the things which are given unto us of Christ. But this is the matter, so long as the priests speak Latin, they are thought by the people to be marvellously well learned.

Ridley. X. More yet of the canon†—"Upon the which vouchsafe to look with thy merciful and cheerful countenance." What means this prayer for the Sacrament itself, if it be as they say, the body of Christ, if it be God and man? How should the Father not look with a cheerful countenance upon his own well-beloved Son? Why do not we rather pray for ourselves, that we, for his sake, may be looked upon of the Father with a cheerful countenance?

Latimer. To this let them answer, that so pray—except, peradventure, this prayer was used long before it was esteemed to be the body of Christ really and corporeally. And then this prayer makes well to destroy the popish opinion, and shows that it is not the opinion of the church, nor so ancient as they babble. There are other prayers of the mass, which, peradventure, are of like effect; but I have forgotten all massing matters, and the mass itself I

---

* Mask, appearance.   † The canon or service of the mass.

utterly detest and abhor: and so I confessed openly before our Diotrephes* and others.

Ridley. XI. The canon says: "Command these to be carried by the hands of thy holy angel unto thy high altar," &c. If we understand the body or blood of Christ to be meant, wherefore do we so soon desire the departure of them, before they have been received? And wherefore brought we them hither by making of them, to let him go so soon?

Write again, I beseech you, fathers and brethren, most dearly beloved in Christ; spare not my paper, for I look ere it be long that our common enemy will first assault me, and I wish, from the bottom of my heart, to be helped not only by your prayers, but also by your wholesome counsels.†

Latimer. As Peter, when he said, Let us make here three tabernacles, spake, and wist not what; so, peradventure, our massmen cannot tell what they say, speaking so manifestly, against themselves. So that the old proverb may very well be spoken of them, 'Liars have need to have good memories.'

Against the Sacrifice of the Mass yet more, by H. Latimer.

JOHN BAPTIST saith, "A man can receive nothing, except it be given him from heaven." And St. Paul saith, "No man taketh honour to himself, but he that is called of God, as was Aaron," &c. But to offer Christ, is a great and weighty matter, therefore ought no man to take it upon him without a manifest calling and commission. But where have our sacrificers so great an office committed unto them? Let them show their commission, and then sacrifice. Peradventure they will say, 'do this,' is all one with saying, 'offer this.' Then I ask, what was there done? What was demonstrated by this pronoun, 'this?' Or, what did they see done, to whom these words,

---

* Bishop Gardiner and the council.

† This paragraph shows that the conference was carried on in writing. Gloucester Ridley (p. 451) says, "Much paper being left for his further thoughts, Latimer wrote a considerable deal against the sacrifice of the mass. proving that there is no mention of it in scripture."

'Do this,' were spoken? If the whole action of Christ, it all that Christ did, be meant by these words, and 'this,' and 'do,' is nothing else but to offer; then the whole action of Christ is, to be offered of the priests, neither can they, but in so doing, satisfy the commandment. And so it should appear, that neither was there any sacrament instituted for the lay people, seeing that no such sacrifice has been done at any time, or is to be done, of the lay people; neither does it avail much to eat or drink it, but only to offer it. Now the text has not, that any part of Christ's action was to offer, forasmuch as the text does not declare that Christ himself then offered. And so the action of offering is not contained in the pronoun 'this.'

Go through every word. First, 'to take,' is not to offer; 'to break,' is not to offer; 'to give to the disciples,' is not to offer, and so on. Worcester* said once to me that to offer was contained in 'Benedicere,' which is not true; for 'Benedicere' is to give thanks. But Christ had often given thanks to God before, without any such offering. And if, in giving thanks, Christ offered his body, seeing that after he had given thanks, he said, 'This is my body;' then in speaking those words, he did not change the bread into his body, forasmuch as he had offered before those words were spoken.

St. Paul hath these words to the Hebrews, speaking of Christ: 'that he might be a merciful and a faithful high-priest in things concerning God, for to purge the people's sins. So that it may appear, that the purging of our sins rather depends thereon, that Christ was the high-priest offering, than that he was offered; except that he was of himself willingly offered. Then it is not necessary he should be offered by others; I will not say a marvellous presumptuous act, that the same should be attempted of any, without a manifest vocation; for it is no small matter to make an oblation. And yet I speak nothing,† that it tends partly to the derogation of Christ's cross; besides also that the offerer ought to be of more excellency than the thing offered.

The minister of the gospel hath rather to do for Christ to the people, than for the people with God, except it be in praying and giving of thanks; and so hath the people as well to do with God for the minister. The office o reconciliation standeth in preaching, not in offering

* Bishop Heath.   † I might further say.

"We are messengers in the room of Christ," saith St. Paul; he doth not say, 'We offer unto God for the people. If Christ offered in his Supper, for whom, I pray you? For all. Then his latter oblation made on the cross, cannot be thought to be done for all men, for it was not done for them for whom the oblation was made in the Supper; except, peradventure, he offered twice for the self-same: and that would argue the imperfectness of the sacrifice. "Feed ye, as much as in you lieth, the flock of Christ:" (1 Pet. 5.) nay, sacrifice rather for the flock of Christ, if the matter be as it is pretended; and it is a marvel that Peter did forget so high an office, seeing in these days sacrificing is so much esteemed, and preaching almost nothing at all. Who art thou, if thou ceasest to feed?* A good catholic. But who art thou, if thou ceasest to sacrifice and say mass? At the least, a heretic! From whence come these perverse judgments, except, peradventure, they think that in sacrificing they feed, and then what need is there of a learned pastor? Seeing no man is so foolish, but he can soon learn to sacrifice and say mass.

Paul wrote two epistles to Timothy, and one to Titus, two clergymen. He made therein a long sermon *ad clerum*,† but not one word of this mass sacrifice, which could not have been done, if there had been such a one, and so highly to be esteemed. I have read over of late the New Testament three or four times deliberately, yet can I find there neither the popish consecration, nor yet their transubstantiation, nor their oblation, nor their adoration, which are the very sinews and marrow-bones of the mass.

Christ could not be offered, but propitiatorily; yet now, 'Do this,' is as much as to say, 'Sacrifice and offer my body under a piece of bread,' and it is available, but we cannot tell for how much. Ah! thieves, have ye robbed the realm of lands and goods with your sacrifice; and now you cannot tell how much your sacrifice is available! As who say, it is so much available, that the value cannot be expressed, nor too dear bought with both lands and goods. "The eye hath not seen, and the ear hath not heard," &c. This is a fine-spun thread, a cunning piece of work, worthily qualified and blanched, be ye sure. But the worldlings will not see, they will not have that religion that hath the cross annexed to it.

All popish things, for the most part, are man's inventions,

* Preach to the people. † To the clergy.

whereas they ought to have the holy scripture for the only rule of faith. When Paul made allegations for himself before Felix, the high deputy, he did not extend his faith beyond the written word of God; "Believing all things (saith he) which are written in the law and the prophets;" making no mention of the rabbins. "Moreover, they have Moses and the prophets," saith Abraham in the parable, not their persons, but their writings. Also, "Faith cometh by hearing, and hearing by the word of God." (Rom. x.) And again, "Blessed are they which hear the word." (Luke xi.) "The things, which have not their authority from the scriptures, may as easily be despised as allowed," saith St. Jerome.

Therefore, whether it is of Christ, or of his church, or of any other manner of thing, which belongs to our faith and life, I will not say.* "If we," saith St. Augustine, "who are not worthy to be compared to him that said not only 'if we,' but also forthwith added that "if an angel from heaven shall teach any thing, besides that ye have received (in the scriptures of the law and gospel,) accursed be he." (Gal. i.) Our Diotrephes with his papists are under this curse. But how are the scriptures, say they, to be understood? St. Augustine answers, giving this rule, "The circumstances of the scriptures, saith he, enlighten the scriptures, and so one scripture expounds another, to a man that is studious, well willing, and often calling upon God in continual prayer, who giveth his Holy Spirit to them that desire it of him."

So that the scripture is not of any private interpretation at any time. For such a one, though he were a layman, fearing God, is much more fit to understand holy scripture than any arrogant and proud priest, yea, than the bishop himself, be he ever so great and glistering in all his pontificals. But what is to be said of the Fathers? How are they to be esteemed? St. Augustine answers, giving this rule also, that we should not, therefore, think it true, because they say so, though they ever so much excel in holiness or learning; unless they are able to prove their saying by the canonical scriptures, or by a good probable reason; meaning that to be a probable reason, as I think, which orderly follows upon a right collection and gathering out of the scriptures.

Let the papists go with their long faith, be you

* Give an opinion myself.

contented with the short faith of the saints, which is revealed unto us in the written word of God. Adieu to all popish fantasies. Amen. For one man, having the scripture and good reason for him, is more to be esteemed himself alone, than a thousand such as they, either gathered together, or succeeding one another. The Fathers have both herbs and weeds, and papists commonly gather the weeds and leave the herbs. And the Fathers speak many times more vehemently in sound of words, than they meant indeed, or than they would have done, if they had foreseen what sophistical wranglers would have succeeded them. Now, the papists are given to brawl about words, to maintain their own inventions, and rather follow the sound of words, than attain unto the meaning of the Fathers, so that it is dangerous to trust them in citing the Fathers.

In all ages the devil has stirred up some light heads to esteem the Sacraments but lightly, as to the empty and base signs; whom the Fathers have resisted so fiercely, that in their fervour they seem in sound of words to run too far the other way, and to give too much to the Sacraments, when they, in truth, did think more measurably. And, therefore, they are to be read warily, with sound judgment. But our papists, if they seem to have but a little sounding to their purpose, they will outface, brave, and brag all men—it must needs be, as they will have it. Therefore, there is no remedy, namely, when they have the master bowl in their hand and rule the roast; but patience. Better it is, to suffer what cruelty they will put unto us, than to incur God's high indignation.

Wherefore, good my lord, be of good cheer in the Lord, with due consideration of what he requires of you, and what he promises you. Our common enemy shall do no more than God will permit him. "God is faithful, who will not suffer us to be tempted above our strength." (1 Cor. x.) Be at a point, what you will stand unto, stick unto that, and let them both say and do what they list. They can but kill the body, which otherwise is of itself mortal. Neither yet shall they do that when they list, but when God will suffer them, when the hour appointed is come. To use many words with them, shall be but in vain, now they have a bloody and deadly law prepared for them. But it is very requisite that you give a reasonable account of your faith, if they will quietly hear you, (1 Pet. ii.) else you know, in a wicked place of judgment a man may keep silence after the example of Christ. Let them not deceive you with their sophistical sophisms and fallacies; you know that many false things have more appearance of truth, than things that are most true. Therefore, Paul gives a watch-word, saying, " Let no man deceive you with likeliness of speech." (Col. ii.) Neither is it requisite, that with the contentious you should follow strife of words, which tend to no edification, but to the subversion of the hearers, and the vain bragging and ostentation of the adversaries.

Fear of death most powerfully persuades a great number. Be well aware of that argument, for that persuaded Shaxton,* as many men thought, after he had once made a good profession, only before the judgment-seat. The flesh is weak, but the willingness of the spirit shall refresh the weakness of the flesh. The number of the criers under the altar, must needs be fulfilled. If we are segregated† thereunto, happy are we. That is the greatest promotion which God giveth in this world, to be such Philippians, " to whom it is given not only to believe, but also to suffer," &c. (Phil. i.)

But who is able to do these things? Surely, all our ability, all our sufficiency, is of God. He requires and he promises. Let us declare our obedience to his will, when it shall be requisite, in the time of trouble, yea, in the midst of the fire. When that number is fulfilled, which I doubt not shall be shortly, then have at the papists, when they shall say, " Peace, all things are safe;" when Christ shall come to keep his great parliament, to the redress of all things, that are amiss. But he shall not come, as the papists feign, hiding himself, and to play bo-peep, as it were, under a piece of bread, but he shall come gloriously, to the terror and fear of all papists, but to the great consolation and comfort of all, that will here suffer for him. " Comfort yourselves one another with these words." (1 Thess. iv.)

Lo! sir, I have blotted your paper vainly, and played the fool egregiously. But so I thought better, than not to do your request at this time. Pardon me, and pray for me: pray for me, I say, pray for me, I say. For I am sometimes so fearful, that I would creep into a mouse-hole; sometimes God visits me again with his comfort. So he cometh and goeth, to teach me to feel and to know

* Shaxton, once bishop of Salisbury, recanted.
* Set apart.

mine infirmity, to the intent I should give thanks to Him that is worthy, lest I should rob him of his duty, as many do, and almost all the world.

Fare you well,
HUGH LATIMER.

What credence is to be given to papists, may appear by their racking, writhing, wringing, and monstrously injuring of God's holy scripture, as appears in the pope's laws. But I dwell here now in a school of obliviousness.* Farewell, once again. And be you steadfast and immoveable in the Lord. Paul loved Timothy marvellously well, notwithstanding, he saith unto him, "Be thou partaker of the afflictions of the gospel." And again, "Harden thyself to suffer afflictions. Be faithful unto death, and I will give thee a crown of life, saith the Lord." (2 Tim. i. iv. Rev. ii.)

* A place where I forgot all that I have learned.

A

SECOND CONFERENCE*

BETWEEN

RIDLEY AND LATIMER

IN PRISON.

Nicholas Ridley to Master Latimer.

In writing again, you have done me unspeakable pleasure, and I pray, that the Lord may requite it you in that day. For I have received great comfort at your words, but yet I am not so filled withal, but that I thirst much more now, than before, to drink more of that cup of yours, wherein you mingle unto me the profitable with the pleasant. I pray you, good father, let me have one draught more to comfort my stomach. For, surely, except the Lord assist me with his gracious aid, in the time of his service I know I shall play but the part of a white-livered knight.† But truly my trust is in Him, that in mine infirmity he shall prove himself strong, and that he can make the coward to fight like a man in his cause. Sir, now I look daily

---

* "The judgment and advice of Latimer was so pleasing to Ridley, that he desired another conference, in which he mentions the artifices and threatenings of Gardiner and Bonner, under the borrowed names of Diotrephes and Antonius, with his manner of replying to them. Both of those bishops harboured an implacable resentment against him, as he had sat commissioner at the deprivation of both of them. Yet such was Ridley's character, that they thought their cause wanted his countenance and assent to recommend it and make it universally victorious. They therefore had their emissaries to tamper with him, and if possible inveigle him to the mass, as if his bare presence at it would reconcile the people to it. This is the point they labour, and he resolves against, in this second Conference with Latimer: which shows that he had been attacked on this point, and determined not to be persuaded or tempted to comply in that respect, and that being disappointed they gave way to their original resentment, and threatened him with the severity of the laws against those who would not act in compliance with them."—*G. Ridley's Life of Bishop Ridley,* p. 455.

This conference is recommended to the reader's attentive perusal, as affording a valuable and authentic summary of part of the grounds upon which the confessors in the reign of Mary were contented to be led to the stake.—*Wordsworth's Ecclesiastical Biography,* vol. iii. p. 319.

† Cowardly soldier.

when Diotrephes with his warriors shall assault me, therefore I pray you, good father, for that you are an old soldier, and an expert warrior, and, God knoweth, I am but a young soldier, and as yet but of small experience in these feats, help me, I pray you, to buckle on my harness. And now I would have you to think that these darts are cast at my head by some one of Diotrephes' or Antonius' soldiers.

The I. Objection of Antonius.*

All men marvel greatly, why you, after the liberty which you have granted unto you, more than the rest, do not go to mass, which is a thing, as you know, now much esteemed of all men, yea, of the queen herself.

The Answer.

Ridley. Because "no man, that layeth hand on the plough, and looketh back, is fit for the kingdom of God." And also for the self-same cause, why St. Paul would not suffer Titus to be circumcised: which is, that the truth of the gospel might remain with us uncorrupted. And again, "If I build again the things which I destroyed, I make myself a trespasser." There is also another cause, lest I should seem by outward fact to allow the thing, which, I am persuaded, is contrary to sound doctrine, and so should be a stumbling-block unto the weak. But, "Woe be unto him, by whom offence cometh! it were better for him, that a mill-stone were hanged about his neck, and he cast into the midst of the sea."

Latimer. Except the Lord help me, you say. Truth it is. For "Without me, saith he, you can do nothing:" much less suffer death of our adversaries, through the bloody law, now prepared against us. But it follows, "If ye abide in me and my words abide in you, ask what you will, and it shall be done for you." What can be more comfortable? Sir, you make answer yourself so well that I cannot better it. Sir, I begin now to smell what you mean by travailing thus with me. You use me, as Bilney did once, when he converted me; pretending as though he would be taught of me, he sought ways and means to teach me, and so do you. I thank you, therefore, most heartily. For indeed you minister armour unto me, whereas I was unarmed before and unprovided, saving that I give myself to prayer for my refuge.

* By Antonius he means some popish persecutor, alluding to the story of Victor, lib. iii. de persec. Africæ.—*Fox.*

Objection II.

Antonius. What is it then, that offends you so greatly in the mass, that you will not vouchsafe once either to hear it or see it? And from whence comes this new religion upon you? Have not you used in times past to say mass yourself?

Ridley. I confess unto you my fault and ignorance. But know you, that for these matters I have done open penance* long ago, both at Paul's Cross, and also openly in the pulpit at Cambridge, and, I trust, God has forgiven me this mine offence, for I did it in ignorance. But, if you are desirous to know, and will vouchsafe to hear what things do offend me in the mass, I will rehearse unto you those things, which are most clear, and seem to repugn most manifestly against God's word. And they are these.

The strange tongue—the want of the showing of the Lord's death—the breaking of the Lord's commandment of having a communion—the Sacrament is not communicated to all, under both kinds, according to the word of the Lord—the sign is servilely worshipped, instead of the thing signified—Christ's passion is injured, forasmuch as this mass sacrifice is affirmed to remain for the purging of sins. To be short, the manifold superstitions and trifling fondness,† which are in the mass and about the same.

Latimer. Better a few things well pondered, than to trouble the memory with too much. You shall prevail more with praying, than with studying, though a mixture be best. For so one shall alleviate the tediousness of the other. I intend not to contend much with them in words, after a reasonable account of my faith given; for it shall be but in vain. When they have no more to say, they will say as their fathers said, " We have a law, and by our law he ought to die."—" Be ye stedfast and unmoveable," saith St. Paul. And again, " Stand fast." And how oft is this repeated, " If ye abide, if ye abide," &c. But we shall be called obstinate, sturdy, ignorant, heady, and what not? So that a man hath need of much patience, having to do with such men.

Objection III

Antonius. But you know how great a crime it is, to

* Openly declared my sorrow † Folly.

separate yourself from communion or fellowship of the church, or to make a schism or division. You have been reported to have hated the sect of the Anabaptists, and always to have impugned the same. Moreover, this was the pernicious error of Novatus, and of the heretics called Cathari, that they would not communicate with the church.

Ridley. I know that the unity of the church is to be retained by all means, and the same is necessary to salvation. But I do not take the mass, as it is at this day, for the communion of the church, but for a popish device, whereby both the commandment and institution of our Saviour Christ, for the oft frequenting of the remembrance of his death, is eluded, and the people of God are miserably deluded. The sect of the Anabaptists, and the heresy of the Novatians, ought of right to be condemned: forasmuch as, without any just or necessary cause, they wickedly separated themselves from the communion of the congregation.* For they did not allege that the Sacraments were unduly ministered, but turning away their eyes from themselves, wherewith, according to St. Paul's rule, they ought to examine themselves, and casting their eyes upon others, either ministers or communicants with them, they always reproved some thing, for which they abstained from the communion, as from an unholy thing.

Latimer. I remember, that Calvin beginneth to refute the Interim† after this sort, with this saying of Hilary: "The name of peace is beautiful, and the opinion of unity is fair, but who doubteth that to be the true and only peace of the church, which is Christ's?" I would you had that little book, there should you see how much is to be given to unity. St. Paul, when he requires unity, he joineth straight withal, "according to Jesus Christ," but no further. Diotrephes‡ now of late did ever harp upon Unity, Unity, "Yea Sir," (quoth I), "but in verity, not in popery. Better is a diversity, than a unity in popery." I had nothing again but scornful jeers, with commandment to the tower.

---

* Ridley here refers to the German fanatics, who had recently engaged in open rebellion at Munster and elsewhere.
† The Interim was a decree of the emperor Charles V. in 1548, settling the points in dispute between the protestants and the papists in a manner favourable to the latter.
‡ Bishop Gardiner.

Objection IV.

Antonius. But admit there are in the mass that which peradventure might be amended, or at least made better: yea, seeing you will have it so, admit there be a fault, if you do not consent thereto, why do you trouble yourself in vain? Do not you know, both by Cyprian and Augustine that communion of Sacraments doth not defile a man, but consent of deeds?

Ridley. If it were any one trifling ceremony, or if it were some one thing of itself indifferent, although I would wish nothing should be done in the church, which doth not edify the same, yet for the continuance of the common quietness, I could be content to bear it. But forasmuch as things done in the mass tend openly to overthrow Christ's institution, I judge that by no means either in word or deed, I ought to consent unto it. As for that which is objected out of the Fathers, I acknowledge it to be well spoken, if it be well understood. But it is meant of those who suppose they are defiled, if any one secret vice be either in the ministers or in them that communicate with them, and is not meant of those who abhor superstition and wicked traditions of men, and will not suffer the same to be thrust upon themselves or upon the church instead of God's word and the truth of the gospel.

Latimer. The very marrow-bones of the mass are altogether detestable, and therefore by no means to be borne withal, so that of necessity the mending of it is to abolish it for ever. For, if you take away oblation and adoration, which do hang upon consecration and transubstantiation, the most papist of them all will not set a button by the mass, as it is a thing which they esteem not, but for the gain that followeth thereon. For, if the English Communion, which of late was used, were as gainful to them as the mass has been heretofore, they would strive no more for their mass. From thence groweth the grief.

Objection V.

Antonius. Consider in what dangers you cast yourself if you forsake the church. And you cannot but forsake it, if you refuse to go to mass. For the mass is the Sacrament of unity. Out of the ark there is no salvation. The church is the ark, and Peter's ship. You know this saying well enough ; " He shall not have God to be his Father, who acknowledgeth not the church to be his mother." Moreover, " Without the church, saith St. Augustine, be the life ever so well spent, it shall not inherit the kingdom of heaven."

Ridley. The holy catholic, or universal church, which is the communion of saints, the house of God, the city of God, the spouse of Christ, the body of Christ, the pillar and stay of the truth ; this church I believe, according to the Creed. This church I reverence and honour in the Lord. But the rule of this church is the word of God, according to which rule, we go forward unto life. And as many as walk according to this rule, I say with St. Paul, " Peace be upon them and upon Israel, which pertaineth unto God."

The guide of this church is the Holy Ghost. The marks, whereby this church is known unto me in this dark world, and in the midst of this crooked and froward generation, are these—the sincere preaching of God's holy word—the due administration of the Sacraments—charity —and faithful observing of ecclesiastical discipline according to the word of God. And that church or congregation, which is garnished with these marks, is in very deed that heavenly Jerusalem, which consists of those which are born from above. This is the mother of us all. And, by God's grace, I will live and die the child of this church. Out of this, I grant, there is no salvation, and, I suppose, the residue of the places objected, are rightly to be understood of this church only.

" In times past," saith Chrysostom, " there were many ways to know the church of Christ, that is to say, by good life, by miracles, by chastity, by doctrine, by ministering the Sacraments. But from the time that heresies took hold of the churches, it is only known by the Scriptures which is the true church. They have all things in outward show, which the true church hath in truth. They have temples like unto ours," &c. And in the end he concludes, " Wherefore only by the Scriptures do we know which is the true church."

To that which they say, " The mass is the Sacrament of unity ;" I answer, The bread which we break, according to the institution of the Lord, is the Sacrament of the unity of Christ's mystical body. " For we, being many, are one bread and one body, forasmuch as we all are par-

Second Conference with Latimer 85

takers of one bread." But in the mass the Lord's institution is not observed: " For we are not all partakers of one bread, but one devoureth all," &c. So that, as it is used, it may seem a Sacrament of singularity, and of a certain special privilege for one sect of people, whereby they may be discerned from the rest; rather than a Sacrament of unity, wherein our knitting together in one is represented.

Latimer. Yea, what fellowship hath Christ with antichrist? Therefore it is not lawful to bear the yoke with papists. " Come forth from among them, and separate yourselves from them, saith the Lord." It is one thing to be the church indeed, another thing to counterfeit that church. Would to God, it were well known what is the forsaking of the church. In the king's days that is dead, who was the church of England? The king and his fautors,* or the massmongers in corners? If the king and the fautors of his proceedings, why are not we now the church, who abide in the same proceedings? If clancular† massmongers might be of the church, and yet oppose the king's proceedings, why may not we as well be of the church, who oppose the queen's proceedings?

Not all that are covered with the title of the church, are the church indeed. " Separate thyself from them that are such," saith St. Paul. From whom? The text hath before, " If any man follow other doctrine," &c.— " He is puffed up and knoweth nothing," &c. Weigh the whole text, that you may perceive what is the fruit of contentious disputations. But wherefore are such men said to know nothing, when they know so many things? You know the old verses

> Hoc est nescire, sine Christo plurima scire ;
> Si Christum bene scis, satis est, si cætera nescis.

That is, "This is to be ignorant—to know many things without Christ. If thou knowest Christ well, thou knowest enough, though thou know no more." Therefore would St. Paul know nothing but Jesus Christ crucified, &c. As many as are papists and massmongers, they may well be said to know nothing, for they know not Christ: forasmuch as in their massing they take much away from the benefit and merit of Christ.

---

* Those who aided him. Latimer refers to Edward VI., and the promoters of the Reformation.
† Secret.

Objection VI.

Antonius. That church which you have described unto me is invisible, but Christ's church is visible and known. For else why would Christ have said, " Tell it unto the church?" For he had commanded in vain to go unto the church, if a man cannot tell which it is.

Ridley. The church which I have described is visible; it has members, which may be seen, and also I have before declared by what marks and tokens it may be known. But if either our eyes are so dazzled, that we cannot see it, or satan has brought such darkness into the world, that it is hard to discern the true church: that is not the fault of the church, but either of our blindness, or of satan's darkness. But yet, in this most deep darkness, there is one most clear candle, which, of itself alone, is able to put away all darkness. " Thy word is a candle unto my feet, and a light unto my steps." (Psalm cxix.)

Objection VII.

Antonius. The church of Christ is a catholic or universal church, dispersed throughout the whole world. This church is the great house of God. In this church are good men and evil mingled together, goats and sheep, corn and chaff. It is the net, which gathers all kinds of fishes. This church cannot err, because Christ hath promised it his Spirit, which shall lead it unto all truth, and that the gates of hell shall not prevail against it; but that he will be with it unto the end of the world. Whatsoever it shall loose or bind upon earth, shall be ratified in heaven, &c. This church is the pillar and stay of the truth: this is it, for which,[*] St. Augustine saith, he believes the gospel. But this universal church allows the mass, because the greater part of the same allows it. Therefore, &c.

Ridley. I grant that the name of the church is taken after three divers manners in the scripture. Sometimes, for the whole multitude of those who profess the name of Christ, of which they are also named christians. But, as St. Paul saith of the Jews, " Not every one is a Jew, that is a Jew outwardly, &c. Neither all that are of Israel are counted the seed." Even so, not every one who is a christian outwardly, is a christian indeed. For " If any man have not the Spirit of Christ, the same is

[*] By whose authority

none of his." Therefore that church, which is his body, and of which Christ is the head, consists only of living stones and true christians, not only outwardly in name and title, but inwardly in heart and in truth.

Secondly. But forasmuch as this church, as touching the outward fellowship, is contained within that great house,* and has with the same, the outward society of the sacraments, and ministry of the word, many things are spoken of that universal church, which St. Augustine calls the mingled church, which cannot truly be understood, but only of that purer part of the church. So that the rule of Tyconius concerning the mingled church, may here well take place;† when there is attributed unto the whole church that which cannot agree unto the same, but for one part thereof; that is, either for the multitude of good men, which is the very true church indeed; or for the multitude of evil men, which is the malignant church and synagogue of satan. And therein is also the third view of the church, of which, although there is less mention in the scriptures in that signification; yet in the world, even in the most famous assemblies of Christendom, this church hath borne the greatest swing.‡ This distinction presupposed of the three sorts of churches, it is an easy matter, by a figure called synecdoche, to give to the mingled and universal church that which cannot truly be understood but only of the one part thereof.

But if any man will stiffly affirm, that universality so pertains unto the church, that whatsoever Christ hath promised to the church, it must needs be understood of that, I would gladly know of the same man where that universal church was, in the time of the patriarchs and prophets, of Noah, Abraham, and Moses at such times as the people would have stoned him;—of Elijah, of Jeremiah;—in the times of Christ, and the dispersion of the apostles,—or in the time of Arius, when Constantius was emperor, and Felix, bishop of Rome, succeeded Liberius?§

It is worthy to be noted, that Lyra writeth upon Matthew, " The church doth not stand in men, by reason of

* Family. † Augustin de Doct. Christ. lib. iii. ch. 32
‡ Sway, been most spoken of.
§ The second schism in the church of Rome. Felix succeeded Liberius A.D. 358, who was displaced for holding false doctrines; but Liberius was afterwards restored, upon which great tumults arose, and many were slain even in the churches.

their power or dignity, whether it be ecclesiastical or secular. For many princes and popes and other inferiors have been found to have fallen away from God." Therefore the church consists of those persons in whom is true knowledge and confession of the faith and of the truth. Evil men, as it is said in a gloss* of the Decrees, are in the church in name, and not in deed. And St. Augustine, writing against Cresconius the grammarian, saith, "Whosoever is afraid of being deceived by the darkness of this question, let him ask counsel of the same church of it: which church the scripture points out without any doubtfulness."

All my notes which I have written and gathered out of such authors as I have read in this matter and such like, are come into the hands of those who will not let me have the least of all my written books. Wherein I am forced to complain of them unto God: for they spoil me of all my labours which I have taken in my study these many years. My memory was never good, for help whereof I have used for the most part to gather notes of my reading, and so to place them, that thereby I might have had the use of them, when the time required. But who knoweth whether this is not God's will that I should be thus ordered, and spoiled of the poor learning I had, as methought, in store, to the intent that I, now destitute of that, should, from henceforth, learn only to know, with Paul, Christ and him crucified? The Lord grant me herein to be a good young scholar, and to learn this lesson so well, that neither death nor life, wealth nor woe, &c. make me ever to forget that. Amen. Amen.

Latimer. I have no more to say in this matter; for you yourself have said all that is to be said. That same vehement saying of St. Augustine, " I would not believe the gospel but for the church," was wont to trouble many men: I remember I have read it well qualified of† Philip Melancthon, but my memory is altogether slippery. This it is in effect. The church is not a judge, but a witness. There were in his time those who lightly esteemed the testimony of the church, and the outward ministry of preaching, and rejected the outward word itself, sticking only to their inward revelations. Such rash contempt of the word provoked and drove St. Augustine into that

* Commentary upon. See De penit. dist. i. ca. eccles. lib. i. 53.
† Explained by.

excessive vehemence. In which, after the bare sound of the words, he might seem to such as do not attain unto his meaning, that he preferred the church far before the gospel, and that the church hath a free authority over the same. But that godly man never thought so. It were a saying worthy to be brought forth against those who think the open ministry to be a thing not necessary, if they at all esteemed such testimonies.

I would not stick to affirm, that the more part of the great house, that is to say, of the whole universal church, may easily err. And again, I would not hesitate to affirm, that it is one thing to be gathered together in the name of Christ, and another thing to come together with a mass of the Holy Ghost going before.* For in the first Christ ruleth; in the latter, the devil beareth the swing, and how then can any thing be good that they go about? From this latter shall our six articles come forth again into the light, they themselves being very darkness.

But it is demanded, whether the sounder or better part of the catholic church may be seen of† men or not? St. Paul saith, "The Lord knoweth them that are his." What manner of speaking is this, in commendation of the Lord, if we know as well as he, who are his? Well, thus is the text, "The sure foundation of God standeth still, and hath this seal: the Lord knoweth them that are his. And let every man that nameth the name of Christ depart from iniquity." Now how many are there of the whole catholic church of England which depart from iniquity? How many of the noblemen, how many of the bishops or clergy, how many of the rich men or merchants, how many of the queen's counsellors, yea, how many of the whole realm? In how small room then, I pray you, is the true church within the realm of England? And where is it? And in what state? I had a conceit of mine own, well grounded, as they say, when I began, but now it is fallen by the the way.

* The usual form of opening Romish synods, councils, convocations, &c.; see Strype, *Ecc. Mem.* i. p. 50. It is spoken of by a writer of that day as the "unholy mass of the Holy Ghost, rolled up with descant, prick-song, and organs, whereby men's hearts are ravished wholly from God, and from the cogitations of all such things as they ought to pray for."—*Wordsworth,* vol. iii. p. 333.

† Discerned by.

Objection VIII.

Antonius. General councils represent the universal church, and have this promise of Christ: "Where two or three are gathered together in my name, there am I in the midst of them." If Christ be present with two or three, then much more where there is so great a multitude, &c. But in general councils the mass hath been approved and used. Therefore, &c.

Ridley. Of the universal church, which is mingled of good and bad, thus I think: Whensoever those who are chief in it, who rule and govern the same, and to whom the rest of the whole mystical body of Christ doth obey, are the lively members of Christ, and walk after the guiding and rule of his word, and go before the flock towards everlasting life; then, undoubtedly, councils, gathered together of such guides and pastors of the christian flock, do indeed represent the universal church; and, being so gathered in the name of Christ, they have a promise of the gift and guiding of his Spirit into all truth.

But that any such council hath at any time allowed the mass, such a one as ours was of late, in a strange tongue, and stuffed with so many absurdities, errors, and superstitions; that I utterly deny, and I affirm it to be impossible. For like as there is no agreement between light and darkness, between Christ and Belial; so, surely, superstitions and the sincere religion of Christ; will-worship, and the pure worshipping of God, such as God requires of his, that is, in spirit and truth, can never agree together.

But you will say, where so great a company is gathered together, it is not credible, but there are two or three gathered in the name of Christ. I answer, if there are one hundred good, and two hundred bad, forasmuch as the decrees and ordinances are pronounced according to the greater number of the multitude of voices, what can the lesser number of voices avail? It is a known thing, and a common proverb, "Oftentimes the greater part overcometh the better."

Latimer. As touching general councils, at this present I have no more to say, than you have said. Only I refer you to your own experience, to think of the parliaments and convocations of our country, how and what you have there seen and heard. The greater part in my time brought forth the six articles, for then the king would so have it, being misled by certain persons. Afterwards, the more part repealed the same, our good Josiah willing to have it so. The same articles now again, alas! another greater, but worse part hath restored. O what an uncertainty is this! But after this sort most commonly are man's proceedings. God be merciful unto us! Who shall deliver us from such torments of mind? Therefore death is the best physician, but only unto the faithful, whom she altogether, and at once, delivers from all griefs.—You must think that this is written upon this occasion, because you would needs have your paper blotted.

Objection IX.

Antonius. If the matter should go thus, that, in general councils men should not stand to the greater number of the whole multitude, I mean, of those who ought to give voices, then should no certain rule be left unto the church, by which controversies in weighty matters might be determined. But it is not to be believed, that Christ would leave his church destitute of so necessary a help and safeguard.

Ridley. Christ, who is the most loving spouse of his espoused church, who also gave himself for it, that he might sanctify it unto himself, gave unto it abundantly all things which are necessary to salvation, but yet so, that the church should declare itself obedient unto him in all things, and keep itself within the bounds of his commandments, and not seek any thing, which he teaches not, as necessary unto salvation. Now further, for determination of all controversies in Christ's religion, Christ himself hath left unto the church not only Moses and the prophets, whom he willeth his church in all doubts to go unto and ask counsel at; but also the Gospels and the rest of the New Testament. In the which, whatsoever is heard in Moses and the prophets, whatsoever is necessary to be known unto salvation, is revealed and opened.

So that now we have no need to say, Who shall climb up into heaven, or who shall go down into the depth, to tell what is needful to be done? Christ hath done both, and has commended unto us the word of faith, which also is abundantly declared unto us in his written word; so that, hereafter, if we walk earnestly in his way, to the searching out of his truth, it is not to be doubted but that through the certain benefit of Christ's Spirit, which he has promised unto his, we may find it, and obtain everlasting life. Should men ask counsel of the dead for the living, saith Isaiah? "Let them go rather to the law and to the testimony," &c. Christ sends them that are desirous to know the truth, unto the scriptures, saying, "Search the scriptures." I remember a like thing well spoken by Jerome, "Ignorance of the scriptures is the mother and cause of all errors." And in another place, as I remember in the same author, "The knowledge of the scriptures is the food of everlasting life."

But now, methinks, I enter into a very broad sea, in that I begin to show either out of the scriptures themselves, or out of the ancient writers, how much the holy scripture is of force to teach the truth of our religion. But this it is that I am now about, that Christ would have the church, his spouse, in all doubts to ask counsel at the word of his Father, written, and faithfully left and commended unto it in both Testaments, the Old and the New. Neither do we read that Christ in any place has laid so great a burden upon the members of his spouse, as to command them to go to the universal church. "Whatsoever things are written, saith Paul, are written for our learning:" and, it is true that "Christ gave unto his church some apostles, some prophets, and some evangelists, some shepherds and teachers, to the edifying of the saints, till we all come to the unity of faith," &c. But, that all men should meet together, out of all parts of the world, to define the articles of our faith, I neither find it commanded of Christ, nor written in the word of God.

Latimer. There is a diversity betwixt things pertaining to God or faith, and politic or civil matters. For, in the first, we must stand only to the scriptures, which are able to make us all perfect and instructed unto salvation, if they are well understood. And they offer themselves to be well understood only to those who have good will, and give themselves to study and prayer. Neither are there any men less apt to understand them than the prudent and wise men of the world. But in the other, that is, in civil or politic matters, oftentimes the magistrates tolerate a lesser evil to avoid a greater; as they who have this saying oft in their mouths, "Better an inconvenience than a mischief." And "It is the property of a wise man, saith one, to dissemble many things, and he that cannot dissemble cannot rule.' In which saying they betray themselves, that they do not earnestly weigh what is just, what is not.

Wherefore, forasmuch as men's laws, if in this respect only, that they are devised by men, are not able to bring any thing to perfection, but are enforced of necessity to suffer many things out of square, and are compelled sometimes to wink at the worst things; seeing, they know not otherwise how to maintain the common peace and quiet; they ordain that the more part shall take place. You know what these kind of speeches mean, " I speak after the manner of men."—" Ye walk after the manner of men."—" All men are liars."—And that of St. Augustine, " If ye live after man's reason, ye do not live after the will of God."

Objection X.

Antonius. If you say the councils have sometimes erred, or may err, how then should we believe the catholic church? For the councils are assembled by the authority of the catholic church.

Ridley. From " may be," to " be indeed," is no good argument; but from " being," to " may be," no man doubts but it is a most sure argument. But now it is too manifest that councils have sometimes erred. How many councils were there in the east part of the world, which condemned the Nicene council? And all those who would not forsake the same, they called by a slanderous name, as they thought, ' Homoousians.' Were not Athanasius, Chrysostom, Cyril, and Eustachius, men very well learned, and of godly life, banished and condemned as noted heretics, and that by wicked councils? How many things are there in the canons and constitutions of the councils, which the papists themselves do much dislike? But here, peradventure, one man will say unto me, " We will grant you this in provincial councils, or councils of some one nation, that they may sometimes err, forasmuch as they do not represent the universal church: but it is not to be believed, that the general and full councils have erred at any time."

Here, if I had my books of the councils, or rather such notes as I have gathered out of such books, I could bring something which should serve for this purpose. But now seeing I have them not, I will recite one place only out of St. Augustine, which, in my judgment, may suffice in this matter, instead of many.

"Who knoweth not," saith he, "that the holy scripture is so set before us, that it is not lawful to doubt of it, and that the letters of bishops may be reproved by other wiser men's words, and by councils: and that the councils themselves, which are gathered by provinces and countries, give place to the authority of the general and full councils; and that the former general councils are amended by the latter, when, by some experience of things, either that which was shut up is opened, or that which was hid is known." Thus much from Augustine.

But I will plead with our Antonian upon matter confessed, here with us, when papistry reigned. I pray you, how does that book, which is called "The Bishop's Book," made in the time of king Henry VIII., whereof the bishop of Winchester is thought either to be the first father, or chief gatherer, how does it, I say, sharply reprove the Florentine council, in which was decreed the supremacy of the bishop of Rome,* and that with the consent of the emperor of Constantinople, and of the Grecians? So that, in those days, our learned fathers and bishops of England did not hesitate to affirm, that a general council might err.

But, methinks, I hear another man despising all that I have brought forth, and saying, "These which you have called councils, are not worthy to be called councils, but rather assemblies and conventicles of heretics."—"I pray you, sir, why do you judge them worthy of so slanderous a name?"—"Because," saith he, "they decreed things heretical, contrary to true godliness and sound doctrine, and against the faith of the christian religion." The cause is weighty, for which they ought, of right, so to be called. But if it be so, that all councils ought to be despised, which decree any thing contrary to sound doctrine and the true word, which is according to godliness: forasmuch as the mass, such as we have had here of late, is openly against the word of God, it must then follow of necessity, that all such councils as have approved such masses, ought, of right, to be fled and despised, as conventicles and assemblies of men, that stray from the truth.

Another man alleges unto me the authority of the bishop of Rome, "without which neither can the coun-

* The Florentine council was held A.D. 1439—1442.

cils," saith he, " be lawfully gathered, neither, being
gathered, can they determine any thing concerning religion." But this objection is only grounded upon the
ambitious and shameless maintenance of the Romish
tyranny, and the usurped dominion over the clergy, which
tyranny we Englishmen long ago, by the consent of the
whole realm, have expelled and abjured. And how
rightly we have done it, a little book set forth, De utraque
Potestate, i. e. " Of both the Powers"* clearly shows. I
grant, that the Romish ambition has gone about to chal-
lenge to itself, and to usurp such a privilege from old
time. But the council of Carthage, in the year of our
Lord, 457, openly withstood it, and also the council at
Milevite, in the which St. Augustine was present, prohibited any appellations to be made to bishops beyond
the sea.

Objection XI.

Antonius. St. Augustine saith, " The good men are not
to be forsaken for the evil, but the evil are to be borne
withal for the good." You will not say, I think, that in
our congregations all are evil.

Ridley. I speak nothing of the goodness or evilness of
your congregations, but I fight in Christ's quarrel against
the mass, which utterly takes away and overthrows the
ordinance of Christ. Let that be taken quite away, and
then the partition of the wall that made the strife shall be
broken down. Now to the place of St. Augustine for,
" Bearing with the evil for the good's sake," there ought
to be added other words, which the same writer has expressly in other places. That is, " If those evil men do
cast abroad no seeds of false doctrine, nor lead others to
destruction by their example."

Objection XII.

Antonius. It is perilous to attempt any new thing in
the church, that has not the example of good men. How
much more perilous is it, to commit any act unto which
the example of the prophets, of Christ, and of the apostles
are contrary. But unto this your act, in abstaining from

* The title of this book was " Of the real difference between the
royal and ecclesiastical power." It was written in Latin by Fox,
bishop of Hereford, 1534, and translated by Henry Lord Stafford in
1548.

the church by reason of the mass, the example of the prophets, of Christ, and of the apostles, are entirely contrary. Therefore, &c.

The first part of the argument is evident, and the second part I prove thus. In the times of the prophets, of Christ, and of his apostles, all things were most corrupt, the people were miserably given to superstition, the priests despised the law of God, and, yet notwithstanding, we never read that the prophets made any schisms or divisions; and Christ himself frequented the temple, and taught in the temples* of the Jews. Peter and John went up into the temple at the ninth hour of prayer. Paul, after reading of the law, being desired to say something to the people, did not refuse to do it. Yea further, no man can show, that either the prophets, or Christ, and his apostles refused to pray together with others, to sacrifice or to be partakers of the sacrament of Moses' law.

Ridley. I grant the former part of your argument, and to the second part I say, that although it contains many true things, as of the corrupt state in the times of the prophets, of Christ, and the apostles; and of the temple being frequented of Christ and his apostles; yet, notwithstanding, the second part of your argument is not sufficiently proved; for you ought to have proved, that either the prophets, or Christ, or his apostles, in the temple, communicated with the people, in any kind of worshipping which is forbidden by the law of God, or repugnant to the word of God. But that can no where be showed.

And as for the church, I am not angry with it, and I never refused to go to it, and to pray with the people, to hear the word of God, and to do all other things, whatever may agree with the word of God. St. Augustine, speaking of the ceremonies of the Jews, I suppose in the epistle to Januarius, although he grants that they grievously oppressed that people, both for the number and bondage of the same, yet he calls them burdens of the law, which were delivered unto them in the word of God, not presumptions of men; and which, if they were not contrary to God's word, might after a sort be borne withal. But now, seeing these things are contrary to those which are written in the word of God, whether they ought to be borne of any christian or not, let him judge who is

* Synagogues.

spiritual, who fears God more than man, and loves everlasting life more than this short and transitory life....

Did not the man of God threaten grievous plagues, both unto the priests of Bethel and to the altar which Jeroboam had made there, after his own fantasy? Which plagues king Josiah, the true minister of God, executed at the time appointed.

And where do we read that the prophets or the apostles agreed with the people in their idolatry? When the people went to worship with their hill altars, for what cause, I pray you, did the prophets rebuke the people so much, as for their false worshipping of God, after their own minds, and not after God's word? For what was so great an evil as that was? Wherefore, the false prophets ceased not to malign the true prophets of God, therefore they beat them, they banished them, &c.

How else, I pray you, can you understand what St. Paul alleges, when he says, "What concord hath Christ with Belial? Either what part hath the believer with the infidel? Or how agreeth the temple of God with images? For ye are the temple of the living God, as God himself hath said, I will dwell among them, and walk among them, and I will be their God, and they shall be my people: wherefore, come out from among them, and separate yourselves from them, saith the Lord, and touch no unclean thing, so will I receive you, and will be a Father unto you, and ye shall be my sons and daughters, saith the Lord Almighty."....

The Maccabees put themselves in danger of death, for the defence of the law, yea, and at length died manfully in the defence of the same. " If we praise, saith St. Augustine, the Maccabees, and that with great admiration, because they stoutly stood even unto death, for the laws of the country, how much more ought we to suffer all things for our baptism, for the Sacrament of the body and blood of Christ, &c.?" But the Supper of the Lord, such a one, I mean, as Christ commanded us to celebrate, the mass utterly abolishes and corrupts most shamefully.

Latimer. Who am I, that I should add any thing to this, which you have so well spoken? Nay, I rather thank you, that you have vouchsafed to minister such plentiful armour to me, being otherwise altogether unarmed: saving that he cannot be left destitute of help, who rightly trusts in the help of God. I only learn to die in the reading of the New Testament, and am ever now and then praying unto my God, that he will be a helper unto me in time of need.

Objection XIII.

Antonius. Seeing you are so obstinately set against the mass, that you affirm it is not the true sacrament ordained of Christ, because it is done in a tongue not understood of the people, and for other causes, I cannot tell what : I begin to suspect you, that you think not catholicly of baptism also. Is our baptism, which we use in a tongue unknown to the people, the true baptism of Christ or not? If it is, then the strange tongue does not hurt the mass. If it is not the baptism of Christ, tell me how were you baptized? Or, whether you would that all which were baptized in Latin, should be baptized again in the English tongue?

Ridley. Although I would wish baptism to be given in the vulgar tongue, for the people's sake, who are present, that they may the better understand their own profession, and also be more able to teach their children the same; yet, notwithstanding, there is not the like necessity of the vulgar tongue in baptism, as in the Lord's Supper. Baptism is given to children, who by reason of their age are not able to understand what is spoken unto them, in what tongue soever it be. The Lord's Supper is and ought to be given to them that are waxen.*

Moreover, in baptism, which is accustomed to be given to children in the Latin tongue, all the substantial points, as a man would say, which Christ commanded to be done, are observed. And therefore I judge that baptism to be a perfect and true baptism, and that it is not only not needful, but also not lawful, for any man so christened to be christened again. But yet, notwithstanding, they ought to be taught the catechism of the christian faith, when they shall come to years of discretion; which catechism, whosoever despises, or will not desire to embrace, and willingly learn, in my judgment he plays not the part of a christian man. But in the popish mass are wanting certain substantials, that is to say, things commanded by the word of God to be observed in ministration of the Lord's Supper, of the which there is sufficient declaration made before.

* Grown up.

Latimer. Where you say, "I would wish," surely I would wish that you had spoken more vehemently, and to have said, "It is of necessity, that all things in the congregation should be done in the vulgar tongue, for the edifying and comfort of them that are present." Notwithstanding that the child itself is sufficiently baptized in the Latin tongue.

Objection XIV.

Antonius. Forasmuch as I perceive you are so stiffly, I will not say obstinately, bent, and so wedded to your own opinion, that no gentle exhortations, no wholesome counsels, no other kind of means can call you home to a better mind; there remains that which in like cases was wont to be the only remedy against stiffnecked and stubborn persons; that is, you must be hampered by the laws, and compelled either to obey, whether you will or not, or else to suffer that which a rebel to the laws ought to suffer. Do you not know, that whosoever refuses to obey the laws of the realm, betrays himself to be an enemy to his country? Do you not know, that this is the readiest way to stir up sedition and civil war? It is better that you should bear your own sins, than that, through the example of your breach of the common laws, the common quiet should be disturbed. How can you say you will be the queen's true subject, when you openly profess that you will not keep her laws?

Ridley. O! heavenly Father, the Father of all wisdom, understanding, and true strength, I beseech thee, for thy only Son, our Saviour Christ's sake, look mercifully upon me, wretched creature, and send thine Holy Spirit into my breast; that not only I may understand according to thy wisdom, how this pestilent and deadly dart is to be borne off, and with what answer it is to be beaten back; but, also, when I must join to fight in the field for the glory of thy name, that then, I, being strengthened with the defence of thy right hand, may manfully stand in the confession of thy faith and of thy truth, and continue in the same unto the end of my life, through the same our Lord Jesus Christ. Amen.

Now to the objection. I grant it is reasonable, that he who by words and gentleness cannot be made to yield to what is right and good, should be bridled by the strait correction of the laws. That is to say, he that will not be subject to God's word, must be punished by the laws. It is true that it is commonly said, he that will not obey the gospel must be tamed and taught by rigour of the law. But these things ought to take place against him who refuses to do what is right and just, according to true godliness, not against him that cannot quietly bear superstition and the overthrow of Christ's institution, but hates and detests from his heart such kind of proceedings, and that for the glory of the name of God.

To that which you say, a transgressor of the common laws betrays himself to be an enemy of his country, surely a man ought to look unto the nature of the laws, what manner of laws they are which are broken. For a faithful christian ought not to think alike of all manner of laws; but that saying ought only truly to be understood of such laws as are not contrary to God's word. Otherwise, those who love their country in truth, that is to say, in God, they will always judge, if at any time the laws of God and man are contrary the one to the other, that a man ought rather to obey God than man. And they that think otherwise, and pretend a love to their country, forasmuch as they make their country to fight, as it were, against God, in whom consists the only state of the country, surely, I do think, that such are to be judged most deadly enemies and traitors to their country. For they that fight against God, who is the safety of their country, what else do they, but go about to bring upon their country present ruin and destruction? But they that do so, are worthy to be judged enemies to their country, and are traitors to the realm. Therefore, &c.

But this is the readiest way, you say, to stir up sedition, and to trouble the quiet of the commonwealth; therefore, these things are to be repressed in time by force of laws. Behold, Satan does not cease to practise his old guiles and accustomed subtleties. He ever has this dart in readiness to hurl against his adversaries, to accuse them of sedition, that he may bring them, if he can, in danger of the higher powers; for so has he by his ministers always charged the prophets of God.

Ahab said unto Elias, "Art thou he that troubleth Israel?" The false prophets also complained to their princes against Jeremiah, that his words were seditious, and not to be suffered. Did not the Scribes and Pharisees falsely accuse Christ as a seditious person, and one that spake against Cæsar? Did they not at last cry, "If thou let this man go, thou art not Cæsar's friend?" The orator Tertullus, how did he accuse Paul before Felix, the high-deputy! "We have found this man (saith he) a pestilent fellow, and a stirrer of sedition unto all the Jews in the whole world," &c.

But I pray you, were Christ, Paul, and the prophets, seditious persons, as they were called? God forbid! But they were falsely accused by false men. And wherefore, I pray you, but because they reproved their guiles, superstition and deceits, before the people? And when the others could not bear it, and would gladly have had them taken out of the way, they accused them as seditious persons, and troublers of the commonwealth, that being by this means made hateful to the people and princes, they might the more easily be snatched up, to be tormented and put to death. But how far they were from all sedition, their whole doctrine, life, and conversation well declare.

For that which was objected last of all, that he cannot be a faithful subject to his prince, who professes openly, that he will not observe the laws which the prince hath made, here I would wish that I might have an indifferent judge, and one that feareth God, to whose judgment in this cause I promise and will stand. I answer, therefore, that a man ought to obey his prince, but in the Lord, and never against the Lord. For he that knowingly obeys his prince against God, does not a duty to the prince, but is a deceiver of the prince, and a helper unto him, to work his own destruction. He is also unjust, who gives not to the prince that which is the prince's, and to God that which is God's.

Here comes to my remembrance that notable saying of Valentinian, the emperor, about choosing the bishop of Milan; "Set such a one, " saith he, "in the bishop's seat, to whom if we, as men, do offend at any time, we may submit ourselves." Polycarp, the most constant martyr, when he stood before the chief ruler, and was commanded to blaspheme Christ, and to swear by the fortune of Cæsar, answered with a mild spirit, "We are taught," saith he, " to give honour unto princes, and those powers which be of God, but such honour as is not contrary to God's religion.*

* Euseb. Ecc. Hist. lib. iv c. 4. Niceph. lib. iii. c. 35.

So far you may see, good father, how I have in words, only made as it were, a flourish before the fight, which I shortly look for, and how I have begun to prepare certain kinds of weapons to fight against the adversaries of Christ, and to muse with myself how the darts of the old enemy may be borne off, and after what sort I may smite him again with the sword of the Spirit. I learn, also, hereby, to be in use with armour, and to assay how I can go armed.

In Tyndale, where I was born, not far from the Scottish borders, I have known my countrymen watch night and day in their harness, such as they had, that is, in their jacks* and their spears in their hands, (you call them northern gads,) especially when they had any privy warning of the coming of the Scots. And, so doing, although at every such bickering some of them spent their lives, yet by such means, like pretty† men, they defended their country. And those that so died, I think that they died in a good quarrel, and all the country loved their offspring and progeny the better for their fathers' sakes.

And in the quarrel of Christ our Saviour, in the defence of his own divine ordinances, by which he gives unto us life and immortality, yea, in the quarrel of faith and the christian religion, wherein resteth our everlasting salvation, shall we not watch? Shall we not go always armed, ever looking when our adversary, which, like a roaring lion, seeketh whom he may devour, shall come upon us by reason of our slothfulness? Yea, and woe be unto us, if he can oppress us unawares, which, undoubtedly, he will do, if he find us sleeping.

Let us awake, therefore, I say, and let us not suffer our house to be broken up. Resist the devil, saith St. James, and he will flee from you. Let us, therefore, resist him manfully, and, taking the cross upon our shoulders, let us follow our captain Christ, who by his own blood hath dedicated and hallowed that way, which leadeth unto the Father, that is, to the light which no man can attain, the fountain of everlasting joys.

Let us follow, I say, whither he calleth and allureth us, that after all these afflictions, which last but for a moment, whereby he trieth our faith, as gold by the fire, we may everlastingly reign and triumph with Him in the glory of his Father, and that through the same our Lord Jesus

* Coats of mail, armour. † Brave.

Christ, to whom with the Father and the Holy Ghost be all honour and glory now and for ever. Amen. Amen.

Good father, forasmuch as I have determined with myself to pour forth these my cogitations into your bosom, here, methinks, I see you suddenly lifting up your head towards heaven, after your manner, and then looking upon me with your prophetical countenance, and speaking unto me with these or like words: "Trust not, my son, (I beseech you, vouchsafe me the honour of this name, for in so doing I shall think myself both honoured and loved of you,) trust not, I say, my son, to these word-weapons, for the kingdom of God is not in words, but in power. And remember always the words of the Lord, 'Do not imagine beforehand, what and how you will speak, for it shall be given you even in that same hour, what ye shall speak; for it is not ye that speak, but the Spirit of your Father, which speaketh in you.'"*

I pray you, therefore, father, pray for me, that I may cast my whole care upon him, and trust upon him in all perils. For I know, and am surely persuaded, that whatsoever I can imagine or think aforehand, it is nothing, except he assist me with his Spirit, when the time is. I beseech you, therefore, father, pray for me, that such a complete harness of the Spirit, such boldness of mind, may be given unto me, that I may, out of a true faith, say with David, "I will not trust in my bow, and it is not my sword that shall save me. For he hath no pleasure in the strength of a horse, &c. But the Lord's delight is in them that fear him, and put their trust in his mercy." I beseech you, pray, pray that I may enter this fight, only in the name of God, and that when all is past, I, being not overcome, through his gracious aid, may remain and stand fast in him, till that day of the Lord in which, to them that obtain the victory, shall be given the lively manna to eat, and the triumphant crown for evermore.

Now, father, I pray you, help me to buckle on this armour a little better; for you, being an old soldier, know the deepness of Satan, and you have collared with him ere now, blessed be God that hath ever aided you so

* Such was the case; when these two constant martyrs were brought before their adversaries, bishop Ridley refuted the arguments of the papists with much ability, reasoning with them on their own grounds, but father Latimer adhered simply to scripture and silenced his opponents still more effectually than his companion.

well. I suppose he may well hold you at bay, but, truly, he will not be so willing, I think, to join with you, as with us younglings. Sir, I beseech you, let your servant read this my babbling unto you, and now and then, as it shall seem unto you best, let your pen run on my book; spare not to blot my paper, I give you good leave.

As touching this Antonius, whom I have here made mine adversary, lest peradventure any imagination might carry you amiss, and make you think otherwise than I meant, know that I have alluded to one Antonius, a most cruel bishop of the Arians, and a very violent persecutor of them that were catholic, and of a right judgment. To whom Hunericus, a tyrant of the Vandals, knowing Antonius's fierceness, committed his whole authority, that he should either turn the christians which believed well, unto his false religion, or else punish and torment them at his pleasure.

Which Antonius took in hand to do, and executed the same against two most godly bishops, and most constant in the doctrine which was according to godliness. The name of the one was Eugenius, an aged man, the other was named Habet-Deum. This latter, as it appears by the history of the persecutions of the Vandals,* the tyrant and the false counterfeit bishop desired much to have turned unto their most pestilent heresy. This Habet-Deum was bishop of the city Tamallane, where Antonius had been bishop before. And when Antonius had vexed him, as the story saith, with divers and sundry persecutions, and had found the soldier of Christ always constant in his confession, it is said, that at length, in a great rage, he swore and said to his friends on this wise: "If I make him not of my religion, then am I not Antonius." It is incredible what harms and troubles he put him to, what cruelty he practised against him, and it were too long now to describe the same unto you. But the man of God stood always unmoveable, and in the confession of Christ's faith remained ever unto the end the constant and unfoiled soldier of Christ. I pray to God

---

* Victor, lib. iii. de Persecut. Africæ. The similarity of his own case and that of Latimer to the particulars recorded, respecting these primitive bishops, evidently made a deep impression upon the mind of Ridley, and afforded him support in his trials. Does not this show the advantage of students in divinity becoming acquainted with the history of the Church of Christ?

our heavenly Father, to give me grace, that I may faithfully follow this good bishop Habet-Deum, through our Lord Jesus Christ. Amen.

Latimer. Sir, I have caused my man not only to read your armour unto me, but also to write it out; for it is not only not bare* armour, but also well buckled armour. I see not how it could be better. I thank you even from the bottom of my heart for it, and my prayer you shall not lack, trusting that you do the like for me. For, indeed, THERE IS THE HELP. Many things make confusion in memory. And if I were as well learned as was St. Paul, I would not bestow much amongst them, further than to gall them, and spur-gall them too, when and where occasion were given, and matter come to mind, for the law shall be their sheet anchor, stay, and refuge.

Fare you well in Christ.†

* Armour unfitted for use.

† This conference in writing passed between these venerable fathers, as I apprehend, in January, 1554, when they were in separate apartments, after the mass was publicly restored, which was December 21, and before Wyat's rebellion had so crowded the tower with state prisoners, that the three prelates (and Bradford) were confined together in one apartment, and that rebellion broke out the 26th of January. Thus did this good bishop employ himself in his prison; examining himself, and trying his own spirit carefully, lest ignorance or prejudice should in any degree mislead him; seeking the advice of the elder and more experienced, proposing his reasons, and submitting them to the censure of others, that he might either be better informed and set right, or confirmed in his opinion by their approbation; and yet, not confiding in the mere exercise of reason, but requesting the prayers of good men for God's grace to enlighten his mind in the search of truth, and to strengthen his constancy in the open acknowledgement of it. And while he sought, he gave, assistance; for in laying his reasons before Latimer, and confirming them by the Fathers, he furnished that aged father with arguments and proofs, which the loss of his books, and the failure of his memory, had made him forget, though he held the conclusions firmly. For which Latimer heartily thanks him.—*Gloucester Ridley's Life of Ridley*, p. 485.

Latimer, however, adhered to his resolution, "not to bestow much amongst them," excepting scripture; and from the account of their examinations in Fox, it is evident that their adversaries were the soonest tired of this method of proceeding, although Ridley answered them with much ability, and if they had conducted the disputation fairly, would soon have silenced them.

The early editions of these conferences have some verbal differences from each other, but they are not of material importance. Fox has thrown the two conferences together, and transposed several passages, apparently to concentrate them. They are here given as in the original tracts.

A LAMENTATION

FOR

THE CHANGE OF RELIGION IN ENGLAND;

INCLUDING

A COMPARISON BETWEEN THE DOCTRINE OF THE GOSPEL AND THE ROMISH RELIGION;

WITH

WHOLESOME INSTRUCTIONS TO ALL CHRISTIANS HOW TO BEHAVE THEMSELVES IN TIME OF TROUBLE.

Alas! what misery is thy church brought unto, O Lord, at this day! Of late the word of the Lord was truly preached, was read and heard in every town, in every church, in every village; yea, and in almost every honest man's house.—Alas! now it is exiled, and banished out of the whole realm! Of late, who was not* taken for a lover of God's word, for a reader, for a ready hearer, and for a learner of the same? And now, alas! who dare openly countenance it, but such as are content, in Christ's cause, and for his word's sake, to stand to the danger and loss of all that they have?

Of late there was to be found, of every age, of every degree and kind of people, some that gave their diligence, to learn, as they could, out of God's word the articles of christian faith, the commandments of God, and the Lord's prayer. The babes and the young children were taught these things by their parents, their masters, and weekly by their curates in every church: and the aged folk, who had been brought up in blindness, and in ignorance of those things, which every christian is bound to know, they learned the same, when otherwise they could not, by often hearing their children and servants repeat the same. But now, alas, and alas again! the false prophets of antichrist,

---

* Glad to be. (Ed. 1566.) That edition, printed with three letters of Careless, differs in some verbal respects from the Lamentation as given by Fox. It is entitled, 'A Piteous Lamentation of the miserable Estate of the Church in England, in the time of Queen Mary,' but it does not appear needful to notice these variations in the present edition, which was printed from the copy in Fox's 'Acts and Monuments.'

who are past all shame, openly preach in pulpits unto the people of God, that the catechism is to be accounted heresy: whereby their old blindness is brought home again: for the aged are afraid of the higher powers, and the youth are abashed and ashamed, even of that which they have learned, though it be God's word, and they dare no more meddle with it.

Of late, in every congregation throughout all England, prayer and petition was made unto God, to be delivered from the tyranny of the bishop of Rome, and all his detestable enormities: from all false doctrine and heresy.* Now, alas! satan has persuaded England, by his falsehood and craft, to revoke her old godly prayer, to recant the same, and to provoke the fearful wrath and indignation of God upon her own head.

Of late, by strict laws and ordinances, with the consent of the nobles and commonalty, and full agreement and council of the prelates and clergy, the beast of Babylon was banished hence, by laws, and with other and all means that then could be devised for so godly a purpose. But now, alas! all these laws are trodden under foot: the nobles, the commonalty, the prelates, and clergy are quite changed, and all those others, though they were made in judgment, justice, and truth, and the matter were so good, no more hold than a bond of rushes, or of barley straw; and public perjury no more fears them, than a shadow upon the wall.

Of late it was agreed in England of all hands, according to Paul's doctrine and Christ's commandment, as Paul saith plainly, that nothing ought to be done in the church, in the public congregation, but in that tongue which the congregation could understand. That all might edify thereby, whether it were common prayer, administration of the sacraments, or any other thing belonging to the public ministry of God's holy and wholesome word. But, alas! all is turned upside down, Paul's doctrine is put apart, Christ's commandment is not regarded: for commonly nothing is heard in the church but in a strange tongue, which the people do not understand.

Of late all men and women were taught according to

* The litany used in Edward VIth's reign contained the following petition:—"From the tyranny of the bishop of Rome, and all his abominable enormities, from all false doctrine and heresy, from all hardness of heart," &c.

Christ's doctrine, to pray in that tongue, which they could understand, that they might pray with heart, that which they should speak with their tongue. Now, alas! the unlearned people are brought into that blindness again, to think that they pray, when they speak with their tongues they cannot tell what, and whereof their heart is not mindful at all, for it can understand never a whit thereof.

Of late the Lord's Supper was duly ministered, and taught to be made common to all that were true christians, with thanksgiving, and setting forth of the Lord's death and passion, until his returning again to judge both the quick and the dead. But now, alas! the Lord's table is quite overthrown, and that which ought to be common to all the godly, is made private to a few ungodly, without any kind of thanksgiving, or any setting forth of the Lord's death at all, which the people are able to understand.

Of late all that were endued with the light and grace of understanding of God's holy mysteries, blessed God, who had brought them out of that horrible blindness and ignorance, whereby, in time past, being seduced by satan's subtleties, they believed that the sacrament was not the sacrament, but the thing itself whereof it is a sacrament, that the creature was the Creator; and that a thing which has neither life nor sense, alas! such was the horrible blindness, was the Lord himself; who made the eye to see, and gave all senses and understanding unto man. But now, alas! England is returned again like a dog to its own vomit, and is in a worse case than ever she was before. For it had been better never to have known the truth, than to forsake the truth once received and known: and now, not only that light is turned into darkness, and God's grace is received in vain; but also laws of death are made by the high court of parliament, to maintain by power of the sword, fire, and all kind of violence, that heinous idolatry, wherein adoration is given unto the lifeless and dumb creature, which is only due unto the everliving God: yea, they say, they can and do make of bread both man and God, by their transubstantiation,— O! wicked men, and satan's own brood!

Of late the Lord's cup was distributed at his table, according to his own commandment by his express words in his gospel, as well to the laity as to the clergy, which order Christ's church observed many hundred years after, as all the ancient ecclesiastical writers testify, without contradiction of any of them that can be showed, unto this day. But now, alas! not only the Lord's commandment is broken, and his cup is denied to his servants, to whom he commanded it should be distributed, but, also, there is now set up a new blasphemous kind of sacrifice, to satisfy and pay the price of the sins, both of the dead and of the quick, to the great and intolerable contumely of Christ our Saviour's death and passion, which was and is the one only sufficient, and everlasting available sacrifice, satisfactory for all the elect of God, from Adam the first, to the last that shall be born in the end of the world.

Of late the commandment of God, " Thou shalt not make to thyself any graven image, nor any similitude or likeness of any thing in heaven above, or in earth beneath, or in the water under the earth, thou shalt not bow down to them nor worship them;"—this commandment of God, I say, was graven almost every where in churches,* was learned of every body, both young and old; whereupon images that provoked the simple and ignorant people unto idolatry, as the wise man saith, were taken out of the churches; and it was strictly forbidden that none should any where, either bow down to them, or worship them. But now, alas! God's holy word is blotted and rased out of churches, and stocks and stones are set up in the place thereof. God commandeth his word so to be ordered, that it might be had in continual remembrance at all times, and in every place: and he forbad images and idols to be either made or set in any place where any should bow or worship them. But now, alas! that which God commanded is not passed upon,† and that which he forbids is masterfully‡ maintained by falsehood and craft, and wickedly upholden.

Of late all ministers that were admitted to the public office and ministry of God's holy word, on their admission made a solemn profession before the congregation, that they would teach the people nothing, as doctrine necessary

---

* In the reign of Edward VI. texts of scripture were painted in most of the churches, particularly the second commandment and 1 John. v. 21, " Babes, keep yourselves from images;" for, as yet, many persons desired to see the popish images of saints again worshipped. On the accession of queen Mary those texts were removed.

† Thought of importance.   ‡ Powerfully.

to attain everlasting salvation, but that which is **God's**
own holy word, or which may be grounded thereon without any doubt, whereby many vain, yea, wicked traditions
of man, vanished and melted away of themselves, as it
were, before the fire. But now at one brunt* they are
revived, and are in full hope all to return again, in as
great strength as ever they have been. And how can any
man look for any other thing, but that when you have
received the head, you must also receive the whole body;
or else how can the head abide? The head, under satan,
of all mischief, is antichrist and his brood; and the same
is he which is the Babylonical beast.

The beast is he, whereupon the harlot sitteth. The
harlot is that city, saith John in plain words, which hath
empire over the kings of the earth. She hath a golden
cup of abominations in her hand, whereof she maketh the
kings of the earth to drink, and of the wine of this harlot
all nations have drunk; yea, and kings of the earth have
committed abominations with her; and merchants of the
earth, by her pleasant merchandise, have been made
rich.

Now what city is there in the whole world, that, when
John wrote, ruled over the kings of the earth; or what
city can be read of in any time of the city itself, that challenged the empire over the kings of the earth, but only the
city of Rome, and since then the usurpation of that see has
grown to her full strength? And is it not read, that the
old and ancient writers understood Peter's first epistle
to be written at Rome, which is called by him in the
same epistle, in plain terms, Babylon? By the abomination thereof, I understand all the whole trade of the
Romish religion, carried on under the name and title of
Christ, but which is contrary to the only rule of all true
religion, that is, to God's word. What word of God hath
that devilish drab, for the maintenance of her manifold
abominations, and to set to sale such merchandise wherewith, alas for the madness of man! the wicked harlot hath
bewitched almost the whole world? Did not Peter, the
very true apostle of Christ, of whom this strumpet boast-
eth herself so high, but falsely without all just cause,—
did not he, I say, give all the world warning of her pelf
and trash, of her false doctors and apostles; for this harlot
and beast will be called Dominus Apostolicus,† whoso-

* Violent effort   † The apostolic Lord.

ever say nay? For he speaks thus in his latter epistle: "There were among the people in times past false prophets, as there shall be among you, in time to come, false teachers, which shall privily bring in pestilent sects, even denying the Lord which hath bought them, and redeemed them; procuring to themselves swift damnation; and many shall follow their damnable ways, by whom the way of truth shall be railed upon, and through covetousness, by counterfeit tales or sermons, they shall, saith Peter, make merchandise upon you," &c. And doth not John likewise in his Revelation, after he has reckoned up a great rabblement of this harlot's mystical merchandise, at the last, as though he would knit up all in plain words, without any mist at all, setting out her merchandise, reckon up among the rest, and conclude by saying, "and the souls of men too." Whereupon else, I pray you, rose this true proverb, 'All things for money are set to sale at Rome?' Was not that a worthy commendation of Christ's vicar in earth, that was written by our holy father one of the Alexanders, a bishop of Rome, thus in Latin:—

Vendit Alexander cruces, altaria, Christum,
Vendere jure potest, emerat ille prius.

Thus in English:—

Alexander our holy father, the pope of Rome,
Selleth for money both right and doom:[*]
And all kind of holiness the holy fathers do not stick
To set to sale, ready money for to get.
And eke Christ himself, he dare be bold
To chop and change for silver and gold:
And why should any think this to be sore,
For what doth he sell, but what he bought before?

I grant these verses to be light, and the verse is but rude, but, alas! such conditions are more wicked and abominable than any ability could express. If these had been but the faults of one or a few in number, they had been less pernicious, and might have been taken for personal crimes, not to be imputed unto that see. But now, alas! the matter is more than evident to all that have godly understanding, that these crimes are grounded upon laws, established by custom, and set forth by all kinds of

[*] Justice.

wicked doctrine, falsehood, and craft: and, therefore, now they are not to be esteemed for any man's or for a few men's personal crimes, but they are now by law, custom and doctrine incorporated into that wicked see; and make the body of the beast, whereon the abominable harlot doth sit.

But you would know what is the merchandise which I said she sets forth to sell, for which all her false prophets, with all their jugglings and crafty glosses, cannot bring one jot of God's word. Surely, surely, they are not only all these abominations which are come into the church of England already, whereof I have spoken somewhat before, but also an innumerable rabblement of abominations and wicked abuses, which now must needs follow: such as popish pardons, pilgrimages, Romish purgatory, Romish masses, placebo, dirige, with trentals, and scala cœli,* dispensations, and immunities from all godly discipline, laws, and good order, pluralities, unions, with thousands more.

Now shall come in the flattering friars, and the false pardoners, and play their old pranks and knavery; as they were wont to do. Now you shall have, but of the see of Rome only, and that for money, the canonizing of such saints as have stood stout in the pope's cause, the shrining of relics, and clear absolution from punishment and faults, for any kind of wickedness, if you will pay well for it, for thousands of years! Yea, at every poor bishop's hands and of his suffragan, you shall have the hallowing of churches, chapels, altars, superaltars, chalices, and of all the whole household stuff and adornment, which shall be used in the church according to the Romish guise.;† for all these things must be esteemed of such high price, that they may not be done, but by a consecrated bishop only. Oh Lord, all these things are such as thy apostles never knew. As for conjuring (they call it hallowing, but it is conjuring indeed) of water and salt, of christening of bells and such-like things, what need I to speak? For every priest that can but read, has power, they say, not only to do that, but also such power over

* Various services of the church of Rome. Scala cœli was special indulgences whereby persons resorting to places thus privileged were promised the same benefits as if they ascended the holy stairs at Rome.

† Fashion.--The forms for these and other services and consecrations are to be found in the "Rituale Romanum."

Christ's body, as to make God and man, once at least every day, of a wafer-cake.*

After the rehearsal of the said abominations, and the remembrance of a number more, which, as the Lord knoweth, it vexes me to think upon, and which it were too long to describe: when I consider on the other hand, the eternal word of God, that abideth for ever, and the undefiled law of the Lord, which turneth the soul from all wickedness, and giveth wisdom unto the innocent babes; I mean that milk which is without all guile, as Peter calls it, that good word of God, that word of truth, which must be graven within the heart, and then is able to save men's souls—that wholesome seed, not mortal but immortal, of the eternal and everlasting God, whereby the man is born anew, and made the child of God—that seed of God, whereby the man of God, so being born, cannot sin, as John saith; he meaneth—so long as that seed abides in him—that holy Scripture which hath not been devised by the wit of man, but taught from Heaven by the inspiration of the Holy Ghost, and which is profitable to teach, to reprove, to correct, instruct, and give order in all righteousness, that the man of God may be whole and sound, ready to perform every good work.—When, I say, I consider this holy and wholesome true word, that teaches us truly our bounden duty towards our Lord God in every point, what his blessed will and pleasure is, what his infinite great goodness and mercy is, what he hath done for us, how he hath given his own only, dearly-beloved Son, to death for our salvation, and by him hath sent us the revelation of his blessed will and pleasure. Also what his eternal word wills us both to believe and also to do, and that he for the same purpose inspired the holy apostles with the Holy Ghost, and sent them abroad into all the world, and also made them, and other disciples of Christ, inspired by the same Spirit, to write, and leave behind them the same things that they taught, which, as they proceeded of the Spirit of truth, so by the confession of all that ever were endued with the Spirit of God, were sufficient to the obtaining of eternal salvation.

And, likewise, when I consider that all that man doth profess in his regeneration, when he is received into the holy catholic church of Christ, and is now to be accounted

* A Romish priest may only perform mass once a day, and that is to be fasting.

for one of the lively members of Christ's own body—all
that is grounded upon God's holy word, and standeth in
the profession of that faith, and obedience of those commandments, which are all contained and comprised in
God's holy word. And, furthermore, when I consider whom
our Saviour Christ pronounced in his gospel to be blessed,
and to whom Moses giveth his benedictions in the law;
what ways, the law, the prophets, the psalms, and all holy
Scripture, both new and old, declare to be the ways of
the Lord. Also what is good for man to obtain and abide in
God's favour, which is that faith that justifies before God,
and what is that charity, that doth pass and excel all;
—which are the properties of heavenly wisdom, and which
is that undefiled religion that is allowed of God; which
things Christ himself called the weightier matters of the
law. When I consider what thing is that which only is
available in Christ; and what knowledge it is, that Paul
esteemed so much, that he counted himself only to know.
Also what shall be the manner of that extreme judgment
of the latter day; who shall judge, and by what he shall
judge; and what shall be required at our hands at that
fearful day; how all things must be tried by the fire; and
that such only shall stand for ever, as Christ's word shall
allow, who shall be the Judge of all flesh, to give sentence
upon all flesh, and every living soul, either of eternal
damnation or everlasting salvation; from which sentence
there shall be no place to appeal, no wit which shall serve
to delude, and no power to withstand or revoke.

When I consider all these things, and compare with the
same again and again, all those ways wherein stands the
substance of the Romish religion, whereof I spake before,
it may be evident and easy to perceive, that these TWO
WAYS, these two religions, the one of Christ, the other of
the Romish see, in these latter days, are as far distant the
one from the other, as light and darkness; good and evil;
righteousness and unrighteousness; Christ and Belial.
He that is hard of belief, let him note, and weigh well
with himself the places of the holy Scripture, which are
appointed in the margin whereupon this talk is grounded;*
and by God's grace he may receive some light. And unto
the contemner I have nothing now to say, but to rehearse the saying of the prophet Isaiah, which Paul spake

* These scriptures were written by M. Ridley in the margin, but
were not in the copy which we followed.—*Fox, Acts and Monuments.*

to the Jews in the end of the Acts of the Apostles. After he had expounded unto them the truth of God's word, and declared unto them Christ, out of the law of Moses and the prophets, from morning to night, all the day long, he said unto them that would not believe: "Well spake the Holy Ghost unto our fathers, saying: Go unto this people and tell them: ye shall hear with your ears, and not understand, and seeing, you shall behold, and not see, for the heart of this people is waxed gross and dull, and with their ears they are hard of hearing, and they have shut together their eyes, that they should not see, nor hear with their ears, nor understand with their hearts, that they might return, and I should heal them, saith the Lord God."

Alas! England, alas! that this heavy plague of God should fall upon thee. Alas! my dearly beloved country, what thing is there that now may do thee good? Undoubtedly thy plague is so great, that it is utterly incurable, except by the bottomless mercy, and infinite power of Almighty God. Alas! my dear country, what hast thou done that thou hast thus provoked the wrath of God, and caused him to pour out his vengeance upon thee, for thine own deserts? Canst thou be content to hear thy faults told thee? Alas! thou hast often heard, but wouldest never amend. England, thy faults of all degrees and sorts of men, of magistrates, of the ministers, and of the common people, were never more plainly told, since thou barest that name, than thou didst hear them of late, even before the magistrates, in King Edward's days, but thou heardest them only, and didst not amend at all. For even some of thy greatest magistrates, the king's highness, that innocent, godly-hearted, and peerless young christian prince excepted,* unkindly and ungently, spurned privily against those that went about most busily and most wholesomely to cure their sores; and would not spare to speak evil of them, even unto the prince himself; and yet they outwardly bore a jolly countenance and a fair face towards the same preachers.

I have heard that Cranmer, and another whom I will not name, were both in high displeasure, the one for showing his conscience secretly, but plainly and fully, in the duke of Somerset's cause, and both, but especially Cranmer, for repugning† as they might against the late

* Edward VI. † Opposing.

spoil of the church goods, taken away by commandment of the higher powers, without any law, or order of justice, and without any request of consent from those to whom they belonged. As for Latimer, Lever, Bradford, and Knox, their tongues were so sharp, that they ripped deep into their galled backs, to have cleansed them, no doubt, from that evil matter, which was festered in their hearts, of insatiable covetousness, of filthy carnality and voluptuousness, of intolerable ambition and pride, of ungodly lothsomeness* to hear poor men's causes, and to hear God's word, which those men, those magistrates could never abide. Others there were, very godly men, and well learned, who endeavoured by the wholesome plaisters of God's word, although in a more soft manner of handling the matter; but, alas! all sped alike. Notwithstanding all that could be done of all hands, their disease did not minish, but daily did increase, which no doubt, is no small occasion in that state, of the heavy plague of God, which is poured upon England this day.

As for the other magistrates, as judges of the laws, justices of the peace, sergeants, common lawyers, it may be truly said of them, as of the most part of the clergy, of curates, vicars, parsons, prebendaries, doctors of the law, archdeacons, deans, yea, and I may say, of bishops also, I fear me, for the most part—although I doubt not but God had and ever hath, those whom he in every state knew, and knoweth to be his,—but for the most part, I say, they were never persuaded in their hearts, but only from the teeth forward,† and for the king's sake, in the truth of God's word; and yet these dissembled, and bore a copy of a countenance, as if they had been sound within.

And this dissimulation satan knew well enough, and therefore desired, and has ever gone about, that the high magistrates, by any manner of means, might be deceived in matters of religion, for he being of counsel with the dissimulation in the worldly, knew well enough that he should then bring to pass, and rule all, even after his own will.

Hypocrisy and dissimulation, Saint Jerome well calls a double wickedness, for it loves not the truth, which is one great evil, and also it falsely pretends to deceive the simple. This hypocrisy and dissimulation with God in matters of religion, no doubt, has also wholly provoked the

* Unwillingness. † In outward show.

anger of God. And as for the common people, although there were many good, where they were well and diligently taught, yet God knows, a great number received God's true word and high benefits with unthankful hearts. For it was a great pity, and a lamentable thing, to have seen in many places the people come so unwillingly and so unreligiously to the holy communion, and receive it accordingly; and to the common prayers, and other divine service, which were in all points so godly and wholesomely set forth according to the true vein of God's holy word, in comparison of that blind zeal, and indiscreet devotion, which they had aforetimes to those things, whereof they understood never one whit, nor could be edified by them at all.

And again, as for alms-deeds, which are taught in God's word, whereby we are certain that God is pleased with them, and doth and will require such at our hands, which are a part of true religion, as St. James saith, and such as he saith himself, he setteth more by than by sacrifice—as to provide for the fatherless, infants and orphans, for the lame, aged, and impotent poor needy folk, and to make public provision that the poor that might labour should have wherewith to labour upon, and so be kept from shameful beggary and stealing—in these works, I say how wayward were many, in comparison, I mean, of that great prodigality, whereby in times past they spared not to spend upon flattering friars, false pardons, painting and gilding of stocks and stones to be set up and honoured in churches, plainly against God's word. And yet, because no place is to be defrauded of their just commendations, London, I must confess, for godly works, in Sir Richard Dobs, knight, then lord mayor, his year began marvellous well: the Lord grant the same may so likewise persevere, continue, yea, and increase to the comfort and relief of the needy and helpless, that was so godly begun. Amen.

All these things minister matter of more mourning and bewailing the miserable state that now is; for by this it may be perceived, how England has deserved this just plague of God. And also it is greatly to be feared that those good things, whatsoever they were, that had their beginning in the time when God's word was so freely preached, now, with the exile and banishment of the same, will depart again.

But to return again to the consideration of this miserable

state of Christ's church in England, and to leave further and more exquisite searching of the causes thereof, unto God's secret and unsearchable judgments, let us now see what is best to be done for Christ's little flock. This is one maxim and principle in Christ's law: He that denieth Christ before men, him shall Christ deny before his Father, and all the angels of heaven. And therefore every one that looketh to have everlasting life by Christ our Saviour, let him prepare himself so, that he deny not his master Christ, or else he is but a castaway and a wretch, howsoever he is counted or taken here in the world.

Now then, seeing the doctrine of antichrist is returned again into this realm, and the higher powers, alas! are so deceived and bewitched, that they are persuaded it is true, and that Christ's true doctrines are error and heresy, and the old laws of antichrist are allowed to return with the power of their father again; what can hereafter be looked for, by reason, to the man of God and true christian, abiding in this realm, but extreme violence of death, or else to deny his Master?

I grant that the hearts of princes are in God's hands, and whithersoever he will, he can make them to bow: and also that christian princes in old time used a more gentle kind of punishment, even to them that were heretics indeed, as degradation, and deposition out of their rooms and offices; exile and banishment out of their dominions and countries; and also, as it is read, the true bishops of Christ's church were sometimes intercessors unto princes for the heretics, that they would not kill them, as is read of St. Augustine. But antichrist's kingdom was not so erected at that time, nor accustomed to order them, as now, that would not fall down and worship the beast and his image; for now, even as all the world knows, he does according to the same manner that both John and Daniel have prophesied, that is, by violence of death; and Daniel declared farther, that the kind of death generally should be by sword, fire, and imprisonment. Therefore, if thou, O man of God, dost purpose to abide in this realm, prepare and arm thyself to die; for both by antichrist's accustomed laws, and these prophecies, there is no appearance or likelihood of any other thing, except thou wilt deny thy master Christ, which is loss at the last, both of body and soul, unto everlasting death. Therefore, my good brother or sister in Christ, whatsoever thou art, to thee that canst, and mayest so do, I shall show thee hereafter, that counsel which I think is the best safeguard for thee, both for thy body, and most assuredly for thy soul's health. But first I warn thee to understand me, as speaking to him or her, that are not in captivity, or called already to confess Christ, but are at liberty abroad.

My counsel, I say, therefore is this—flee from the plague, and get thee hence. I consider not only the subtleties of satan, and how he is able to deceive by his false persuasions, if it were possible, even the chosen of God, and also the great frailty, which is oftentimes more in a man, than he knows to be in himself, but which in the time of temptation, will utter itself—I do not only consider these things, I say, but that our master Christ, whose life was and is a perfect rule of the christian man's life, that he himself oftentimes avoided the fury and madness of the Jews, by departing from the country and place.

Paul likewise, when he was sought for in Damascus, and the gates of the city were laid in wait for him, was conveyed away by night, being let down in a basket out of a window over the wall. And Elias, the prophet, fled from the persecution of wicked Jezebel: and Christ our Saviour saith in the gospel, "When they persecute you in one city, flee unto another:" and so did many good, great, learned, and virtuous men of God, who were great and stout champions nevertheless, and stout confessors and maintainers of Christ and his truth, in due time and place. Of such was the great clerk* Athanasius. But this is so plainly lawful by God's word, and the examples of holy men, that I need not stand in it.† Having this for my ground, I say to thee, O man of God, this seems to me to be the most sure way for thy safeguard— to depart and flee far from the plague, and that swiftly also: for truly, before God, I think that the abomination that Daniel prophesied of so long before, is now set up in the holy place. For all antichrist's doctrine, laws, rights, and religion, which are contrary to Christ, and the true serving and worshipping of God, I understand to be that abomination. Therefore, now is the time in England for those words of Christ, "Now then," saith Christ, "let those that be in Judea flee to the mountains." "Then," saith he,—mark this word, '*then*,' for truly I am persuaded, and I trust by the Spirit of God, that this is commanded—

* Divine. † Say further on the subject.

"Then," saith Christ, "they that are in Jewry, let them flee into the mountains, and he that is on the house-top, let him not come down to take away anything out of his house; and he that is abroad in the field, let him not return to take his clothes. Woe be to the women who are with child, and to them that give suck; but pray, that your flight be not in winter, or on the Sabbath-day."

These words of Christ are mystical, and therefore need interpretation.* I understand all those to be in Jewry spiritually, who truly confess one true living God, and the whole truth of his word, according to the doctrine of the gospel of Christ. Such are they whom Christ here biddeth, in the time of the reign of antichrist's abominations, to flee unto the mountains: which signifies places of safeguard, and all such things as are able to defend from the plague. By his bidding him that is in the house-top, not to come down; and him that is in the field, not to return to take with him his clothes—he means that they should speed them to get them away betimes, lest in their tarrying, and trifling about worldly provisions, they should be trapped in the snare before they are aware, and caught by the back, and for gain of small worldly things, endanger and cast themselves into great perils of more weighty matters. And where he saith, "Woe be to those women who are with child, and to them that give suck,"—women great with child, and nigh to their lying down, and to be brought to bed, are not able to travel; nor those women, which are brought to bed, and give their babes suck. By these therefore Christ spiritually understands all such as are in extreme danger, which this word "woe" signifies. All such, I say, as are so hindered by any manner of means, that they are unable to flee from the plague. And where Christ saith, "Pray you that your flight be not in the winter, nor on the Sabbath-day:" in winter, the common course of the year teaches us, that the ways are foul, and therefore it is a hard thing then to take a far journey, for there are many incommodities and dangers of the way in that time of the year: and on the Sabbath-day it was not lawful to journey but a little way. Now Christ therefore, meaning that we should have need, both to speed our journey quickly, which cannot be done in the winter, for the incommodities of the ways, and also to go far, which could not be done on the Sabbath-day; biddeth us

* May be thus accommodated.

therefore pray that our flight be not in the winter, nor on the Sabbath-day: that is, to pray that we may fly in time, and also far enough from the danger of the plague. Now the causes why we should fly, follow in the same place of St. Matthew's gospel, which I now pass over—thou mayest read them there.

And in the eighteenth chapter of the Revelation, the angel is said to have cried mightily with a loud voice: "Fly, my people, out of Babylon, lest you be infected with her faults, and so be made partners of her plagues: for her offences and sins are grown so great, that they swell and are come unto the heavens: certainly the time doth approach, and the Lord's day is at hand." Hear, I beseech you, also holy Paul, that blessed apostle: he plainly forbids us to join or couple ourselves with the unfaithful; "for what fellowship can there be," saith he, "of righteousness with unrighteousness? what company hath light with darkness? or what agreement hath Christ with Belial? or what part hath the faithful with the unfaithful? or how doth the temple of God agree with images or idols? For you are the temple of the living God; as God hath said, I will walk and dwell in them; I will be their God, and they shall be my people; wherefore depart from amongst them, and get you from them, saith the Lord, and touch no unclean thing; and I will receive you; and be to you in the stead of your father, and you shall be unto me as my sons and daughters, saith the almighty Lord."

I do not marvel if this counsel to depart the realm seems different to divers, even of them, I mean, that bear favour towards God. Many, I trust, who are learned, shall think the counsel good. Others there are, peradventure who will rather think it a thing that may, indeed, by God's word be lawfully done, rather than to be counselled to be done; for, peradventure, they will say, we should counsel a man always to do that which is best of all, and most perfect; but to spend a man's life boldly in Christ's cause, is best of all, and most perfect, and to flee may seem to smell of cowardice. In many things, that which is best for one at some times, is not best for all at all times; and it is not most perfect nor proper for a child to covet to run before he can go. I will not here make a discourse in this matter, what might here be objected, and what might be answered again: I leave that to the wise and eloquent men of the world.

This is my mind, which I would thou shouldest know, O man of God, as I would wish; and I pray to almighty God, that every true christian, either brother or sister, after they are called, and brought into the wrestling-place, to strive in Christ's cause for the best game, (that is, to confess the truth of the gospel, and of the christian faith, in hope of everlasting life,) should not shrink, nor relent one inch, nor give back, whatever shall befall, but stand to their tackle, and stick by it even unto death, as they desire that Christ shall stick by them at the latter day. So, likewise, I dare not wish nor counsel any, either brother or sister, of their own swing,* to start up into the stage, or to cast themselves either before, or further in danger than time and need shall require. For, undoubtedly, when God sees his time, and it is his pleasure that his glory shall be set forth, and his church edified by thy death and confession, means will be found by his fatherly universal providence, that thou, without thine own presumptuous provocation, shalt be lawfully called to do thy feat, and to play thy part. The miserable end that one Quintus came unto, may be a warning, and a fearful example, for all men to beware of presumption and rashness in such things for evermore, as Eusebius writes in his Ecclesiastical History.

But there are a third sort of men, who also desire to be counted favourers of God's word, and are, I fear, far more in number, and worse to be persuaded to that which is the godly mean.—I speak of such as will, peradventure, say or think, that my former counsel, which was to flee the infection of the antichristian doctrine, by departing out of the realm, is more than needeth, and that ways and means may be found, both to abide, and also to be clear out of danger of the aforesaid plague. If that could be found truly agreeable to God's word, both to abide, and also to be clear out of danger of the aforesaid plague, I would be as glad to hear it, God is my witness, as those who think otherwise. Yes, peradventure, some will say, it may be thus. Thou mayest keep thyself, thy faith, and thy religion close to thyself, and inwardly and privately worship God in spirit and truth, and outwardly see that

* Their own fancy.

thou art no open meddler, nor talker, nor transgressor of common order;—so mayest thou be suffered in the commonwealth, and yet use thy religion without offence of thy conscience.

In some other countries, peradventure, this might be used; and in England what shall be, God knows; but it was never so yet, as far as I have ever known or heard. And how can it be, but either thou must transgress the common order, and the Romish laws and customs, which have been used in England, in times past of popery, and now, it is certain, they return again. I say, thou must either break these rites, laws, and customs, and so bewray thyself, or else, if thou art indeed a man of God, thou shalt offend thy conscience; for, in observing them, thou shalt be compelled to break God's laws, which is the rule of conscience to the man of God. For how canst thou resort every holy day to the church, and bear a face to worship the creature for the Creator, as thou must do, and, peradventure, confess it also with thy mouth, and sprinkle thyself with thy conjured water?

Thou must be contributor, also, to the charges of all their popery, as of books of antichrist's service, of lights, of the rood-loft, of the sepulchre, for setting up and painting of images, nay, indeed, of idols; and thou must bear a face to worship them also, or else thou must be had by the back.* Thou must serve their turn, to give the holy loaves, as they call it, which is nothing but a very mockery of the Lord's holy table. Thou must be a contributor to the charges of all the disguised apparel, that the popish sacrificing priest, like unto Aaron, must play his part in. Yea, when the pardoner goes about, or the flattering friar begs for the maintenance of superstition, except thou do as thy neighbours do, look not to live long in rest. If any of thy household die, if thou wilt not pay money for ringing and singing, for requiems, masses, diriges, and commendations, and such like trumpery of the antichristian religion, thinkest thou that thou shalt be reckoned for a catholic man, or for amicus Cæsaris?† A hundred things more may be reckoned, and many of more weight, and of more evident superstition and idolatry, than some of these which I have now rehearsed, which God knows are bad enough: but these are enough to declare, and to set before thine eye what I intend; that is, if thou abide and

* Taken to prison.　　† Cæsar's friend. John xix. 12.

wilt dwell in England, thou must either do these, and many others more, contrary to God's word, which forbids not only that which is evil, but also saith, "Abstain from all things that have any appearance of evil:" or else, if thou wilt not do them, how thou canst live in England at rest, safe from the stake, truly I cannot tell.

But, peradventure, as a man is always ready to find and invent some colour to cloak his conscience, to do what his heart desires, thou wilt say, Though at any time I shall be forced to do any of these things and such like, yet I will have no confidence in them; but outwardly with my body. I will keep my heart unto God, and will not do that of mine own mind willingly, nor except to avoid another inconvenience. I trust, therefore, God will hold me excused, for he shall have my heart—what can I do more?

O, my friend, beware, for God's sake, and know that the subtleties of satan are deep. He that is not able to perceive them by God's word, is heavily laden; pray, therefore, with David; "Lord, let me not have a mind to invent excuses for to cloak my sin." Examine, my dear friend, these your wily ways by the word of God, and if they agree, you may use them: if not, know, that though they may seem ever so fine and goodly, yet, indeed, they are of satan's brood. God's word is certain, that forbids to worship the creature for the Creator, for that is heinous idolatry, and against the first commandment of God. And it is also against the second commandment of the first table to bow down, or to worship any images of God, or of any other thing; and God's word requires not only the belief of the heart, but also the confession of the mouth. And to bear part of the charges to maintain ungodly things, what is that, but, in thy so doing, a consent to the thing done? Now, consenters and doers, God's word accounts both to be guilty. And by St. Paul's doctrine, which was inspired him by the Spirit of God, it is not lawful to do ill that thereof good may come.

Thy heart, thou sayest, God shall have, and yet thou wilt suffer thy body to do the thing that God doth abhor. Beware, O man; take heed what thou sayest. Man may be deceived, but no man can deceive God, for he is called, and he is truly, the Searcher of the heart. Now, to give God thy heart, is to give him thy whole heart, to love him, to dread him, and to trust in him above all other things. "He that hath my commandments, (saith Christ,) and

observeth and keepeth them, it is he that loveth me."
And to dread God above all other, is rather willingly to
incur the danger and peril of all fearful things, than
willingly to do that which is contrary to his blessed will
and commandment. And to trust in him above all things,
is to trust assuredly to his promise of reward, and his tuition, and his goodness and mercy, and to prefer that above
all things in the world, seem they never so strong, so wise,
or so good. Now how canst thou say truly, that God
hath thy heart after this manner (which is to have thy
heart indeed) when thy deeds declare far another thing?
Thy body, O man, is God's, and all the parts thereof, even
as thy soul is.—He made them both, and Christ with his
blood redeemed them both, and is Lord of both, for he
bought them both dearly; and darest thou suffer any part
of either of them to do service to satan? Surely, in so
doing, thou committest sacrilege and dost rob God; thou
defilest the lively temple of the living God, if thou sufferest thy body to do satan's service. Do you not know,
saith St. Paul, that your body is a lively temple of God?
And may a man then take and use any part thereof but in
the service of God? No, surely, it is not lawful for the
man of God so to do, either with hand, tongue, foot, or
any part of the whole body.

Doth not Paul command the Romans, that which pertains to every christian soul. "As you have in times past,"
saith he, "given your members to do service unto uncleanness and wickedness, from one wickedness to another: so
now give your members to do service unto righteousness.
that you may be sanctified." And I pray you, good brother, what do you think is to bear the mark of the beast
in the forehead, and in the hand, that St. John speaks of?
I know we ought to speak warily of God's mysteries,
which he showed by the Spirit of prophesying to his servant John. Yet to read them with reverence, and to pray
for the same, so much as God knoweth is necessary for
our time to know, I think is necessary and good. Wherefore, I will tell thee what I suppose is to bear the beast's
mark, and I commit the judgment of mine interpretation,
as in all other things, to the spiritual man. I suppose he
bears the beast of Babylon's mark in his forehead, who
is not ashamed of the beast's ways, but will profess them
openly, to set forth his master the beast Abaddon. And,

likewise, he bears his mark in his hand, that will and does practise the works of the beast with his power and hand.

And, likewise, I will tell thee who I think is to be signed in the forehead for the servant of God, whereof John also speaks, reckoning up many thousands of every tribe so to have been signed. I suppose he is signed in the forehead as the servant of God, whom God has appointed of his infinite goodness, and has given him grace and strength stoutly to confess him and his truth before the world. And to have grace and strength to confess Christ, and the doctrine of the cross, and to lament and mourn for the abominations of antichrist, I suppose is to be signed with Tau,* whereof Ezekiel the prophet speaks. Thus I suppose these prophecies are to be understood spiritually; and to look for corporeal marks, to be seen in men's foreheads, or in their hands, is nothing else but to look that there should come some brute beast out of Babylon, or some elephant, leopard, lion, or camel, or some such other monstrous beast with ten horns, that should do all the wonderful things spoken of in John; and yet John speaks of a beast; but I understand him to be so called, not that he shall be any such brute beast, but that he is, and shall be, the child of perdition, who for his cruelty and beastly manners is well called a beast.

The carnal Jews knew that there was a promise made, that Elias should come before Christ the Messiah, the anointed of God, to prepare his ways: they knew also, that there was a promise of Messiah, that he should come and be a king, and reign in the house of David for evermore; but they understood all so grossly and carnally, that they neither knew Elias nor Messiah, when they came. For they looked for Elias to come down from heaven in his own person, and for Messiah to come and reign in worldly pomp, power, riches, and glory; when the prophecies of both were to have been understood spiritually. Of Elias that he should not come in person, but in spirit; that is, one who should be endued with the spirit, and gifts, and grace of Elias, which was, indeed, John Baptist, as Christ himself declared to his apostles. And of Messiah's reign, all the prophets were to be understood as speaking of the reign of his spiritual kingdom over the house of Jacob and the true Israelites for evermore. And

* The letter T, or a cross. Rev. xiii. xiv. xx.—See Dr. A. Clarke's Commentary on Ezek. ix.

so by their gross and carnal understanding, they mistook both Elias and the true Messiah, and, when they came knew neither of them.

So, likewise, I fear me, nay, it is certain, that the world, which is destitute of the light of the Spirit of God (for the world is not able to receive him, saith St. John), neither doth nor shall know the beast, nor his marks, though he rage cruelly and live ever so beastlike, and though his marked men are in number like the sand of the sea. The Lord, therefore, vouchsafe to open the eyes of the blind with the light of grace, that they may see, and perceive, and understand the words of God, after the mind of his Spirit. Amen.

Here remain two objections, which may seem weighty, and which may, peradventure, move many not to follow the former counsel. The first reason is, a man will say; "O, sir, it is no small matter you speak of, to depart from a man's own native country into a strange realm. Many men have such great hindrances, that it is impossible that they can, or may do so. Some have lands and possessions, which they cannot carry with them: some have father, mother, wife, children, and kinsfolk, from whom to depart is a hard thing, and almost the same as to suffer death. And to go to a strange country that thou knowest not, neither the manner of the people, or how thou mayest away* either with the people or with the country! Or what a hard thing it is to live among a strange people, whose tongue thou dost not understand," &c.

I grant that you may heap a number of worldly incommodities, which are very likely to ensue upon the departure out of a man's own native country—I mean out of the whole realm into a strange land: but what of all these, and a thousand more of the like sort? I will set unto them one saying of our Saviour Christ, which unto the faithful child of God, and the true christian, is able to countervail all these, yea, and to weigh them down. Christ our Saviour saith in Luke: "If any man come to me, and do not hate his father and mother, (he means, and will not in my cause forsake his father and mother,) his wife, children, and brethren, yea, and his life too, he cannot be my disciple; and whosoever doth not bear his cross and come after me, he cannot be my disciple." And in the same place he declares by two parables, one of a

* Bear, or live satisfactorily with.

builder, and the other of a king that is a warrior, that
every man who will not in Christ's cause forsake all that
ever he hath, cannot be his disciple. Look at the place
who will: the matter is so plainly set forth, that no
glosses, nor cloaking of conscience to the man of God,
can serve to the contrary. Many places there are for the
same purpose, for the embracing of Christ's cross, when
Christ and his cause lay it upon our back: but this is so
plain, that I need here rehearse no more.

This latter reason and objection, whereof I spake before,
is of more force, and includes a necessity which, according
to the common saying, 'hath no law,' and therefore it
is more hard to shape a good answer for it. This may be
objected of some: 'Alas! sir, I grant all these things do
grieve me; and because I understand that they do not
agree with God's word, which is the rule of my conscience
I loath either to look on them, or to hear them. But, sir,
alas! I am an impotent man, an aged man, a sick man, a
lame man, or I have so many small infants and a lame
wife, who all live by my labour, and by my provision: if
I leave them they will starve, and I am not able to carry
them with me, such is my state. Alas! sir, what shall I
do?'—And these causes may happen to some men of God,
whereby either it shall be utterly impossible for them to
depart the country, or else, in departing, they shall be
enforced to forsake such in extreme necessity, the care of
whom both God and nature have committed unto them.

Alas! what counsel is here to be given? O lamentable
state! O sorrowful heart! that neither can depart, and
without extreme danger and peril, is not able to tarry still!
And these are they whom our Saviour Christ saw before
should be, and called them in his prophecy of the latter
time, women with child, or travailing women, and women
that give their small babes suck. Christ lamenting, and
not cursing, the state of such as are not able to fly the
infection of the pestiferous plague of antichrist's abominations,
saith: "Woe be to the women with child and travailing
women, and women that give suck in those days."
For these, alas! my heart mourneth the more, the less I
am able to give any comfortable counsel, but this, that
as they look for everlasting life, they should always abide
still in the confession of his truth, whatsoever shall befall;
and to put their trust for the rest now wholly in God,
who is able to save them against all appearance; and

Lamentation for the change of religion.

commonly in extremities, when all worldly comfort fails, and the danger is at the highest, he is wont, after his accustomed mercy, to be most ready to put his helping hand then unto his people.

God suffered Daniel to be cast into the den of lions, and the three children into the hot burning furnace, and yet he saved them all. Paul was plucked out of the mouth of the lion, as he saith of himself, and in Asia he was brought into such trouble, that he looked for nothing but for present death, and yet He that raised the dead to life again, brought him out of all his troubles, and taught him, and all others that are in troubles for Christ's cause, not to trust to themselves, but in almighty God.

Of God's gracious aid in extreme perils towards them that put their trust in him, all scripture is full, both old and new. What danger were the patriarchs often brought into; as Abraham, Isaac, and Jacob, but above all others Joseph—and how mercifully were they delivered again! In what perils was Moses when he was fain to fly for his life! And when was he sent again to deliver the Israelites from their servile bondage? Not before they were brought into extreme misery. And when did the Lord mightily deliver his people from Pharaoh's sword? Not before they were brought into such straits, that they were so compassed on every side, the main sea on one side, and the main host on the other, that they could look for nothing else, (yea, what did they else, indeed, look for?) but either to have been drowned in the sea, or else to have fallen on the edge of Pharaoh's sword. The judges who wrought most wonderful things in the delivery of the people, were ever given when the people were brought to the most misery before, as Othniel, Ehud, Shamgar, Gideon, Jephtha, Samson. And so was Saul endued with strength and boldness from above, against the Ammonites, Philistines, and Amalekites, for the defence of the people of God. David, likewise, ever felt God's help most sensibly in his extreme persecutions.

What shall I speak of the Prophets of God, whom God suffered so often to be brought into extreme perils, and so mightily delivered them again: as Elias, Jeremiah, Daniel, Micah, and Jonas, and many others, of whom it were too long to rehearse and set out at large?

And did the Lord use his servants otherwise in the new law after Christ's incarnation? Read the Acts of the

Apostles, and you shall see no. Were not the apostles cast into prison, and brought out by the mighty hand of God? Did not the angel deliver Peter out of the strong prison, and bring him out by the iron gates of the city, and set him free? And when, I pray you? Even the very night before Herod appointed to have brought him to judgment for to have slain him, as he had a little before killed James, the brother of John. Paul and Silas, after they had been sore scourged, and were put into the inner prison, and there were laid fast in the stocks; I pray you, what appearance was there that the magistrates should be glad to come the next day themselves to them, to desire them to be content, and to depart in peace? Who provided for Paul, that he should be safely conducted out of all danger, and brought to Felix, the emperor's deputy, when the high-priests, the pharisees, and rulers of the Jews had conspired to require judgment of death against him, he being fast in prison, and also more than forty men had sworn each one to another, that they would never eat nor drink until they had slain Paul? A thing so wonderful, that no reason could have invented, or man could have looked for it—God provided Paul's own sister's son, a young man that disappointed that conspiracy and all their former conjuration.* How the thing came to pass, you may read in the twenty-third of the Acts; I will not be tedious here with the rehearsal thereof.

Now, to descend from the apostles to the martyrs that followed next in Christ's church, and in them likewise to declare how gracious our good God ever hath been, to work wonderfully with those who have been in extreme perils in his cause, it were matter enough to write a long book. I will here name but one man and one woman, that is Athanasius, the great clerk and godly man, stoutly standing in Christ's cause against the Arians; and that holy woman, Blandina, standing so constantly in all extreme pains, in the simple confession of Christ. If you will have examples of more, look and you shall have both these and a hundred more in the Ecclesiastical History of Eusebius, and in the Tripartite History.

But notwithstanding all these examples, both of holy scripture, and of other histories, I fear the weak man of God, incumbered with the frailty and infirmity of the flesh, will now and then have thoughts and qualms, as they call

* Binding themselves by a mutual oath.

them, run over his heart, and will think thus. 'All these things which are rehearsed out of the scripture, I believe to be true, and of the rest truly I do think well, and can believe them also to be true; but all these we must needs grant were special miracles of God, which now in our days we see are ceased; and to require them at God's hands, were it not to tempt God?'

Well, beloved brother, I grant that such were great wonderful works of God, and we have not seen many such miracles in our time, either because our sight is not clear (for truly God worketh his part with his people in all times), or else because we have not the like faith as they had for whose cause God wrought such things, or because, after he had sufficiently set forth the truth of his doctrine by such miracles, the time of so many miracles to be done was expired. Which of these is the most special cause, or whether there are any others, God knoweth: I leave that to God. But know thou this, my well-beloved in God, that God's hand is as strong as ever it was; he may do what his gracious pleasure is, and he is as good and gracious as ever he was. Man changes as a garment doth, but God, our heavenly Father, is the same now that he was, and shall be for evermore.

The world without doubt, this I do believe, and therefore I say it, draws towards an end; and in all ages God hath had his own manner, according to his secret and unsearchable wisdom, to use his elect. Sometimes to deliver them, and to keep them safe; and sometimes to suffer them to drink of Christ's cup, that is, to feel the smart, and to feel the whip. And though the flesh smarteth at the one, and feeleth ease in the other, is glad of the one, and sore vexed in the other; yet the Lord is the same towards them in both, and loves them no less when he suffers them to be beaten, yea, and to be put to bodily death, than when he works wonders for their marvellous delivery. Nay, rather he does more for them, when he stands by them in anguish of the torments, and strengthens them in their faith, to suffer in the confession of the truth and his faith the bitter pangs of death; than when he opens the prison-doors and lets them loose: for here he does but respite them to another time, and leaves them in danger to fall into like peril again; and there he makes them perfect, to be without danger, pain, or peril, after that for evermore. But this his love towards them,

howsoever the world doth judge fit, is one, both when he
delivers, and when he suffers them to be put to death. He
loved Peter and Paul as well when, after they had, according
to his blessed will, pleasure, and providence,
finished their courses, and done their services appointed
them by him here in preaching of the gospel, the one was
beheaded, and the other was hanged or crucified by the
cruel tyrant Nero, as Ecclesiastical History saith; he
loved them as well at that time as when he sent the angel
to bring Peter out of prison, and for Paul's delivery he
made all the doors of the prison to fly wide open, and the
foundation of the same to tremble and shake like an earthquake.

Thinkest thou, O man of God, that Christ our Saviour
had less affection to the first martyr Stephen, because he
suffered his enemies, even at the first conflict, to stone him
to death? No surely: nor for James, John's brother, who
was one of the three that Paul calleth primates or principals
amongst the apostles of Christ. He loved him never
a whit the worse than he did the others, although he suffered
Herod the tyrant's sword to cut off his head. Nay,
does not Daniel say, when speaking of the cruelty of
antichrist's time: "And the learned—he means the truly
learned in God's law—shall teach many, and shall fall
upon the sword, and in the flame—that is, shall be burnt
in the flaming fire—and in captivity,"—that is, shall be in
prison, and be spoiled and robbed of their goods for a
long season. And in the same place of Daniel, it follows:
"And of the learned there are, which shall fall or be overthrown,
that they may be known, tried, chosen, and made
white,"—he means to be burnished and scoured anew,
picked and chosen, and made fresh and lusty. If that
then was foreseen that it should be done to the godly
learned, and for such gracious causes, let every one to
whom any such thing happens by the will of God, be glad
in God and rejoice, for it is to God's glory and to his own
everlasting wealth. Wherefore, well is he that ever he was
born, for whom God has provided thus graciously, having
grace of God, and strength of the Holy Ghost, to stand
stedfastly in the height of the storm. Happy is he that
ever he was born, whom God, his heavenly Father, has
vouchsafed to appoint to glorify him, and to edify his
church by the effusion of his blood.

To die in Christ's cause is a high honour, to which no

man certainly shall or can aspire, except those to whom God vouchsafes that dignity: for no man is allowed to presume to take unto himself any office of honour, but he who is thereunto called of God. Therefore John saith well, speaking of those who have obtained the victory by the word of his testimony, that they loved not their lives, even unto death.

And our Saviour Christ saith: " He that shall lose his life for my cause, shall find it." And this manner of speech pertains not to one kind of christians,* as the worldly doth wickedly dream, but to all that truly pertain unto Christ. For when Christ had called unto him the multitude together with his disciples, he said unto them (mark, that he said not this to the disciples and apostles only, but he said it to all), "Whosoever will follow me, let him forsake or deny himself, and take up his cross and follow me: for whosoever will save his life, shall lose it"—he means whosoever will, to save his life, both forsake or leave him and his truth,—" and whosoever shall lose his life for my cause and the gospel's sake, shall save it: for what shall it profit a man if he shall win the whole world, and lose his own soul, his own life? or what shall a man give to recompense that loss of his own life, and of his own soul? Whosoever shall be ashamed of me and my words,—that is, to confess me and my gospel, before this adulterous and sinful generation, of him shall the Son of man be ashamed, when he cometh in the glory of his Father with the holy angels."

Know thou, O man of God, that all things are ordained for thy behoof, and for the furtherance of thee towards thy salvation. " All things," saith St. Paul, " work with the good to goodness," even the enemies of God; and such kind of punishments whereby they go about to destroy them, shall be forced by God's power, might, and fatherly providence, to do them service.

It is not as the wicked think, that poverty, adversity, sickness, tribulation, yea, the painful death of the godly, are tokens that God does not love them; but quite the contrary, as all the whole course of scripture evidently declares; for then he would never have suffered his most dearly beloved, the patriarchs, to have had such troubles, his prophets, his apostles, his martyrs, and chief champions and maintainers of his truth and gospel, to have

* Not to those alone who lived in the days of the apostles.

been murdered and slain so cruelly by the wicked · " of the which some were racked (as the apostle saith), and would not be delivered, that they might receive a better resurrection. Some were tried by mockings and scourgings, yea, moreover, by bonds and imprisonments: they were stoned; they were hewn and cut asunder; they were tempted; they were slain by the sword; they wandered up and down in sheeps' skins and goats' skins, being forsaken, afflicted, and tormented; such men as the world were not worthy to have, wandering in the wilderness, in mountains, in dens and caves of the earth. All these were approved by the testimony of faith, and received not the promise, because God provided better for us, that without us they should not be consummated.' They tarry for us undoubtedly, longing for the day; but they are commanded to have patience; " yet," saith the Lord, " a little while," until the number of their fellow-servants be fulfilled, and of their brethren which are yet to be slain, as they were.

Now, O thou man of God, for our Lord's sake, let us not, for the love of this life, tarry too long, and be an occasion of delay of that glorious consummation, in hope and expectation whereof they departed in the Lord, and which also the living, endued with God's Spirit, ought so earnestly to desire and to groan for, with all the creatures of God. Let us all with John, the servant of God, cry in our hearts unto our Saviour Christ: " Come, Lord Jesus, come." For when Christ, who is our life, shall be made manifest and appear in glory, then shall the children of God appear what they are, even like unto Christ; for this our weak body shall be transfigured, and made like unto Christ's glorious body, by the power whereby he is able to subdue all things unto himself: then that which now is corruptible, shall be made incorruptible: that which now is vile, shall then be made glorious; that which now is weak, then shall rise mighty and strong; that is, the gross and carnal shall be made fine and spiritual, for then we shall see and have the unspeakable joy and fruition of the glorious majesty of our Lord, even as he is.

Who or what then shall hinder us to jeopardy—to jeopardy? yea, to spend, this life, which we have here, in Christ's cause, in our Lord God's cause? O, therefore, thou man of God, thou who art laden, and burdened like unto a woman with child, so that thou canst not fly this plague, yet if thou desire earnestly after such things as I have spoken of, stand fast, whatsoever shall befall, in thy Master's cause; and take this thy hindrance from flying, for a calling of God, to fight in thy master Christ's cause. Of this be thou certain, they can do nothing unto thee, which thy Father is not aware of, or has not foreseen before; they can do no more than it shall please him to suffer them to do for the furtherance of his glory, the edifying of his church, and thine own salvation. Let them do what they shall do, seeing that to thee, O man of God, all things shall be forced to serve, and to work with thee unto the best before God. O be not afraid, and remember the end.

All this which I have spoken for the comfort of the lamentable case of the man whom Christ likened to women with child, I mean to be spoken likewise to the captive and prisoner in God's cause: for such I count to be, as it were, already summoned and pressed to fight under the banner of the cross of Christ, and, as it were, soldiers allowed and taken up for the Lord's wars, to do their Lord and Master good and honourable service, and to stick to him, as men of trusty service in his cause, even unto death; and to think that to lose their life in his cause, is to win it in eternal glory for evermore.

Therefore, now to conclude, and to make an end of this treatise, I say unto all that love God our heavenly Father, that love Christ Jesus our Redeemer and Saviour; that love to follow the ways of the Holy Ghost who is our Comforter and Sanctifier of all; unto all that love Christ's spouse and body, the true catholic church of Christ, yea, that love life and their own soul's health—I say unto all these, Hearken, my dear brethren and sisters, all you that are of God, of all sorts, ages, dignities, or degrees; hearken to the word of our Saviour Jesus Christ, spoken to his apostles, and meant to all his, in Saint Matthew's gospel: " Fear not them which kill the body, for they cannot kill the soul; but fear him more who may destroy, and cast both body and soul into hell-fire. Are not two sparrows sold for a farthing? and one of them shall not fall or light upon the ground without your Father; all the hairs of your head being numbered. Fear them not, you are much more worth than the little sparrows."—" Every one that confesseth me before men, him shall I likewise confess before my Father which is in heaven. But whosoever shall deny me before men, I shall deny him likewise before my Father which is in heaven."

The Lord grant us therefore, of his heavenly grace and strength, that here we may so confess him in this world, amongst this adulterous and sinful generation, that he may confess us again at the latter day before his Father which is in heaven, to his glory and our everlasting comfort, joy, and salvation.

To our heavenly Father, to our Saviour and Redeemer Jesus Christ, and to the Holy Ghost, be all glory and honour now and for ever. Amen.

[The Lamentation is here reprinted from the Acts and Monuments: the only other early edition has the date 1566 prefixed: it was printed by William Powell, and has many verbal variations from the edition of Fox.]

A TREATISE OR LETTER OF BISHOP RIDLEY

WHICH HE WROTE AS HIS

LAST FAREWELL

TO ALL HIS TRUE AND FAITHFUL FRIENDS IN GOD, A LITTLE BEFORE HE SUFFERED;

WITH A SHARP ADMONITION TO THE PAPISTS, THE ENEMIES OF TRUTH.*

AT the name of Jesus let every knee bow, both of things in heaven, and things in earth, and things under the earth; and let every tongue confess, that Jesus Christ is the Lord, unto the glory of God the Father. Amen.

As a man, minding to take a far journey, and to depart from his familiar friends, commonly and naturally has a desire to bid his friends farewell before his departure: so likewise I, now looking daily when I should be called to depart hence from you, O! all ye, my dearly beloved brethren and sisters in our Saviour Christ, that dwell here in this world; and having a like mind towards you all, and also, blessed be God for this, such time and leisure, (whereof right heartily I thank his heavenly goodness:) I bid you all, my dear brethren and sisters in Christ, that dwell upon the earth, after such manner as I can, farewell.

Farewell, my dear brother George Shipside: whom I have ever found faithful, trusty, and loving in all states and conditions, and now in the time of my cross, above all others, to me most friendly and stedfast; and also, which pleases me best, above all other things, ever hearty in God's cause.

* After Ridley was condemned, he remained in prison a fortnight before he was burned. Gloucester Ridley says, "Having now in immediate prospect his crown of martyrdom, he was desirous that his life might continue useful to the last, by discharging the affection and duties which the several relations in which he stood might require, so far as his wishes, his prayers, and his advice might effect; and therefore wrote his Farewell to them, not to be published till after his death, that it might have all the weight of the last words of a dying friend."

Farewell, my dear sister Alice, his wife. I am glad to hear of you, that you take Christ's cross, which now is laid (blessed be God) both on your back and mine, in good part. Thank God, who has given you a godly and loving husband. See that you honour him, and obey him according to God's law. Honour your mother-in-law, his mother, and love all those that pertain unto him, being ready to do them good, as it shall lie in your power. As for your children, I doubt not of your husband, but that He, who hath given him a heart to love and fear God, and in God them that pertain unto him, will also make him friendly and beneficial unto thy children, even as if they had been his own.

Farewell, my well-beloved brother, John Ridley, of the Waltown, and you, my gentle and loving sister Elizabeth: whom, besides the natural league of amity, your tender love, which you were said ever to bear towards me above the rest of your brethren, binds me to love. My mind was to have acknowledged this your loving affection, and to have acquitted it with deeds, and not with words alone. Your daughter Elizabeth I bid farewell, whom I love for the meek and gentle spirit that God has given her, which is a precious thing in the sight of God.

Farewell, my beloved sister of Unthanke, with all your children, my nephews and nieces. Since the departure of my brother Hugh, my mind was to have been unto them in the stead of their father: but the Lord God must and will be their Father, if they will love him, and fear him, and live according to his law.

Farewell, my well-beloved and worshipful cousins, Master Nicholas Ridley of Wyllimountswick and your wife; and I thank you for all your kindness showed both to me, and also to all your own kinsfolk and mine. Good cousin, as God has set you in our stock and kindred, not for any respect of your person, but of his abundant grace and goodness, to be, as it were, the leader, to order and conduct the rest, and has also endued you with his manifold gifts of grace, both heavenly and worldly, above others; so I pray you, good cousin (as my trust and hope is in you), continue and increase in the maintenance of truth, honesty, righteousness, and all true godliness; and, to the uttermost of your power, withstand falsehood, untruth, unrighteousness, and all ungodliness, which is forbidden and condemned by the word and laws of God.

Farewell, my young cousin Ralph Whitfield. Your time was very short with me: my mind was to have done you good, and yet you suffered in that little time a loss; but I trust it shall be recompensed as it shall please almighty God.

Farewell, all my kindred and countrymen, farewell in Christ altogether. The Lord, who is the searcher of secrets, knoweth that according to my heart's desire, my hope was of late, that I should have come among you, and have brought with me abundance of Christ's blessed gospel, according to the duty of that office and ministry whereunto I was chosen, named, and appointed among you, by the mouth of our late peerless prince King Edward, and also openly declared in his court by his privy council.

I warn you all, my well-beloved kinsfolk and countrymen, that you be not amazed or astonished at the kind* of my departure or dissolution; for I assure you I think it the greatest honour that ever I was called unto in all my life. And therefore I thank my Lord God heartily for it, that it hath pleased him to call me of his great mercy unto this high honour, to suffer death willingly for his sake and in his cause: unto which honour he called the holy prophets, and his dearly beloved apostles, and his blessed chosen martyrs. For you know that I no more doubt, but that the causes wherefore I am put to death, are God's causes and the causes of the truth, than I doubt that the gospel which John wrote is the gospel of Christ, or that Paul's epistles are the very word of God.

And to have a heart willing to abide and stand in God's cause and in Christ's quarrel even unto death, I ensure thee, O man, it is an inestimable and an honourable gift of God, given only to the true elect and dearly beloved children of God, and inheritors of the kingdom of heaven! For the holy apostle and martyr in Christ's cause, St. Peter, saith, "If ye suffer rebuke in the name of Christ, (that is, in Christ's cause and for his truth's sake,) then ye are happy and blessed: for the glory of the Spirit of God resteth upon you." If for rebuke suffered in Christ's name, a man is pronounced blessed and happy, by the mouth of that holy apostle; how much more happy and blessed is he, that hath the grace to suffer death also. Wherefore, all you that are my true lovers and friends,

* Manner.

rejoice, and rejoice with me again, and render with me hearty thanks to God, our heavenly Father, that for his Son's sake, my Saviour and Redeemer Christ, he hath vouchsafed to call me, being else, without his gracious goodness, in myself but a sinful and vile wretch—to call me, I say, unto this high dignity of his true prophets, of his faithful apostles, and of his holy elect and chosen martyrs, that is, to die and to spend this temporal life in the defence and maintenance of his eternal and everlasting truth.

You who are my countrymen dwelling upon the borders, where alas! the true man often suffers much wrong at the thieves' hand—you know that if a man who went out with his neighbour to help him to rescue his goods again is slain by a thief, as often happens there,* you know that the more cruelly he was slain, and the more stedfastly he stuck by his neighbour in the fight against the face of the thief, the more favour and friendship shall all his posterity have for the slain man's sake, from all them that are true, as long as the memory of this fact and his posterity shall endure. Even so, you that are my kinsfolk and countrymen, know that howsoever the blind, ignorant, and wicked world hereafter shall rail upon my death, which they cannot do worse than their fathers did of the death of Christ our Saviour, of his holy prophets, apostles, and martyrs; know ye, I say, that both before God, and all them that are godly, and that truly know and follow the laws of God, ye have, and shall have, by God's grace, cause ever to rejoice, and to thank God highly, and to think good of it, and in God to rejoice of me, your flesh and blood, whom God of his gracious goodness hath vouchsafed to associate unto the blessed company of his holy martyrs in heaven. And I doubt not in the infinite goodness of my Lord God, nor in the faithful fellowship of his elect and chosen people, but at both their hands in my cause, you shall rather find the more favour and grace. For the Lord saith, that he will be both to them and theirs that love him the more loving again for a thousand generations. The Lord is so full of mercy to them, I say, and theirs, who love him indeed.

---

* Ridley here alludes to the disorders which prevailed in the districts upon the borders between England and Scotland, the effects of which were daily witnessed by his relations and friends in Northumberland.

And Christ saith again, that "no man can show more love, than to give his life for his friend."

Now also, know ye, all my true lovers in God—my kinsfolk and countrymen, that the cause, wherefore I am put to death, is after the same sort and condition, but it more nearly touches God's cause, and in more weighty matters. For, to speak generally, both are in God's cause, both in the maintenance of right, both for the commonwealth, and both for the weal also of the Christian brother: although there is in these two no small difference, both concerning the enemies, the goods stolen, and the manner of the fight.

For you all know, that when the poor true* man is robbed by the thief of his own truly-gotten goods, whereupon he and his household should live, he is greatly wronged; and the thief, in stealing and robbing with violence the poor man's goods, offends God, transgresses his laws, and is injurious both to the poor man and to the commonwealth. So, I say, you all know, that even here, in the cause of my death, it is with the church of England; I mean the congregation of the true chosen children of God in this realm of England, which I acknowledge not only to be my neighbours, but rather the congregation of my spiritual brethren and sisters in Christ; yea, members of one body, wherein by God's grace I am, and have been grafted in Christ.

This church of England had of late, of the infinite goodness and abundant grace of almighty God, great substance, great riches of heavenly treasure, great plenty of God's true and sincere word, the true and wholesome administration of Christ's holy sacraments, the whole profession of Christ's religion, truly and plainly set forth in baptism, the plain declaration and understanding of the same, taught in the holy catechism, to be learned of all true Christians.

This church had also a true and sincere form and manner of the Lord's Supper, wherein, according to Jesus Christ's own ordinance and holy institution, Christ's commandments were executed and done. For upon the bread and wine set upon the Lord's table, thanks were given; the commemoration of the Lord's death was had; the bread was broken in the remembrance of Christ's body torn upon

* Honest.

the cross; and the cup was distributed in the remembrance of Christ's blood shed; and both were communicated unto all that were present, and would receive them, and they were exhorted by the minister so to do.

All was done openly in the vulgar tongue, so that every thing might be both easily heard and plainly understood by all the people, to God's high glory, and the edification of the whole church.

This church had of late the whole divine service, all common and public prayers ordained to be said and heard in the common congregation, not only framed and fashioned to the true vein of holy scripture, but also all things were set forth, according to the commandment of the Lord and St. Paul's doctrine, for the people's edification, in their vulgar tongue.

It had also holy and wholesome homilies in commendation of the principal virtues which are commended in scripture, and likewise other homilies against the most pernicious and capital vices, which alas! reign in this realm of England.

This church had, in matters of controversy, articles so penned and framed after the holy scripture, and grounded upon the true understanding of God's word, that, in short time, if they had been universally received, they should have been able to have set in Christ's church much concord and unity in Christ's true religion, and have expelled many false errors and heresies, wherewith this church, alas! was almost overgrown.

But alas! of late, into this spiritual possession of the heavenly treasure of these godly riches, thieves are entered in, who have robbed and spoiled all this heavenly treasure away. I may well complain of these thieves, and cry out upon them with the prophet, saying: (Psalm 79) " O Lord God, the gentiles, heathen nations, are come into thy heritage, they have defiled the holy temple, and made Jerusalem an heap of stones :" that is, they have broken and beat down to the ground thy holy city. This heathenish generation, these thieves of Samaria, these Sabæans and Chaldeans, these robbers, have rushed out of their dens, and have robbed the church of England of all the aforesaid holy treasure of God. They have carried it away, and overthrown it, and in the stead of God's holy word, the true and right administration of Christ's holy sacraments, as of baptism and others, they mixed their ministry with men's foolish fantasies, and many wicked and ungodly traditions.

In the stead of the Lord's holy table, they give the people, with much solemn disguising, a thing which they call their mass; but indeed and in truth it is a very mask ing and mockery of the true Supper of the Lord. Or rather I may call it a crafty juggling, whereby these false thieves and jugglers have bewitched the minds of the simple people, so that they have brought them from the true worship of God, unto pernicious idolatry, and make them believe that to be Christ our Lord and Saviour, which indeed is neither God nor man, nor has any life in itself, but in substance is the creature of bread and wine, and, in use of* the Lord's table, is the sacrament of Christ's body and blood. And for this holy use, for which the Lord hath ordained them in his table, to represent unto us his blessed body torn upon the cross for us, and his blood there shed, it pleased him to call them his body and blood, which understanding† Christ declares to be his true meaning, when he saith: "Do this in remembrance of me." And again St. Paul likewise sets out the same more plainly, speaking of the same sacrament, after the words of the consecration, saying: "As often as ye shall eat of this bread, and drink of this cup, ye shall set forth (he meaneth with the same) the Lord's death until his coming again." And here again these thieves also have robbed the people of the Lord's cup, contrary to the plain words of Christ written in his gospel.

Now for the common public prayers, which were in the vulgar tongue, these thieves have brought in again a strange tongue, whereof the people understand not one word. Wherein what do they else, but rob the people of their divine service, wherein they ought to pray together with the minister? And to pray in a strange tongue, what is it but as St. Paul calls it, barbarousness, childishness, unprofitable folly, yea, and plain madness?

For the godly articles of unity in religion, and for the wholesome homilies, what do these thieves place instead, but the pope's laws and decrees, lying legends, feigned fables and miracles, to delude and abuse the simplicity of

---

* When used at.
† Sense in which Christ's words are to be understood

the rude people? Thus this robbery and theft is not only committed, nay, sacrilege and wicked spoil of heavenly things is made, but also, instead of the same, is brought in and placed the abominable desolation of the tyrants Antiochus, of proud Sennacherib, of the shameless-faced king, and of the Babylonical beast. Unto this robbery, this theft and sacrilege, I cannot consent, nor, God willing, ever will, so long as breath is in my body, because it is blasphemy against God, high treason unto Christ, our heavenly King, Lord, Master, and our only Saviour and Redeemer: for it is plainly contrary to God's word and to Christ's gospel. It is the subversion of all true godliness, and against the everlasting salvation of mine own soul, and of all my brethren and sisters, whom Christ my Saviour hath so dearly bought with no less price, than with the effusion and shedding forth of his most precious blood. Therefore, all ye, my true lovers in God, my kinsfolk and countrymen, for this cause, I say, know ye, that I am put to death, which by God's grace I shall willingly take, with hearty thanks to God therefore, in certain hope, without any doubting, to receive at God's hand again, of his free mercy and grace, everlasting life.

Although the cause of the true man, slain by the thief while helping his neighbour to recover his goods again, and the cause, wherefore I am to be put to death, in a general sense are the same, as I said before, yet there is no small difference. These thieves, against whom I do stand, are much worse than the robbers and thieves of the borders. The goods which they steal are much more precious; and their kinds of fight are far different. These thieves are worse, I say; for they are more cruel, more wicked, more false, more deceitful, and crafty; for those will but kill the body, but these will not stick to kill both body and soul. Those for the general theft and robbery are called, and indeed are, thieves and robbers, but these for their spiritual kind of robbery are called sacrilegious, as you would say, church robbers. They are more wicked, for those go about only to spoil men of worldly things, worldly riches, gold and silver, and worldly substance— these go about in the ways of the devil, their ghostly* father, to steal from the universal church, and particularly from every man, all heavenly treasure, true faith, true charity, and hope of salvation in the blood of our Saviour

* Spiritual.

Jesus Christ: yea, to spoil us of our Saviour Christ, of his gospel, of his heavenly Spirit, and of the heavenly heritage of the kingdom of heaven, so dearly purchased unto us by the death of our Master and Saviour Christ.

These are the goods and godly substance, whereupon the christian must live before God, and without which he cannot live; these goods, I say, these thieves, these church robbers go about to spoil us of. The which goods, to the man of God, excel and far pass all worldly treasure: so that to withstand even unto death, such thieves as go about to spoil both us and the whole church of such goods, is most high and honourable service done unto God.

These church robbers also are much more false, crafty, and deceitful, than the thieves upon the borders: for they have not the craft so to commend their theft, that they dare avouch it, and therefore, acknowledging themselves to be evil, they steal commonly in the night; they dare not appear at judgments and sessions, where justice is executed; and when they are taken and brought thither, they never hang any man, but they ofttimes are hanged for their faults. But these church robbers can so cloak and colour their spiritual robbery, that they can make the people believe falsehood to be truth, and truth falsehood; good to be evil, and evil good; light to be darkness, and darkness light; superstition to be true religion, and idolatry to be the true worship of God; and that which is in substance the creature of bread and wine, to be none other substance but only the substance of Christ, the living Lord, both God and man! And with this their falsehood and craft, they can so juggle and bewitch the understanding of the simple, that they dare avouch it openly in court and in town, and fear neither hanging, nor beheading, as the poor thieves of the borders do; but stout and strong like Nimrod, they dare condemn whosoever will go about to betray* their falsehood, to be burned in flaming fire, quick and alive.

The kind of fight against these church robbers is also of another sort and kind, than that which is against the thieves of the borders. For there the true men go forth against them with spear and lance, with bow and bill, and all such kind of bodily weapons as the true men have; but here, as the enemies are of another nature, so the watchmen of Christ's flock, the warriors that fight in the

* Expose, make known.

Lord's war, must be armed and fight with another kind of
weapons and armour. For here the enemies of God, the
soldiers of antichrist; although the battle is set forth
against the church by mortal men, being flesh and blood,
and nevertheless members of their father the devil; yet,
since their grand master is the power of darkness, their
members are spiritual wickedness, wicked spirits, spirits of
errors, of heresies, of all deceit and ungodliness; spirits
of idolatry, superstition, and hypocrisy, which are called by
St. Paul principalities and powers, lords of the world,
rulers of the darkness of this world, and spiritual subtleties concerning heavenly things. Therefore our weapons
must be fit and meet to fight against such: not carnal nor
bodily weapons, as spear and lance, but spiritual and heavenly. We must fight against such with the armour of
God, not intending to kill their bodies, but their errors,
their false craft and heresies, their idolatry, superstition,
and hypocrisy, and save, as much as lieth in us, both their
bodies and souls.

And therefore, as St. Paul teaches us, we fight not
against flesh and blood; that is, we fight not with bodily
weapons to kill the man, but with the weapons of God,
to put to flight his wicked errors and vice, and to save
both body and soul. Our weapons therefore are faith,
hope, charity, righteousness, truth, patience, prayer unto
God; and our sword, wherewith we smite our enemies,
and beat and batter and bear down all falsehood, is the
word of God. With these weapons, under the banner of
the cross of Christ, we fight, ever having our eye upon
our grand master, duke,* and captain, Christ; and we
reckon ourselves to triumph, and to win the crown of everlasting bliss, when, enduring in this battle without any
shrinking or yielding to the enemies, after the example of
our grand captain Christ, our master, after the example
of his holy prophets, apostles, and martyrs; when, I say,
we are slain in our mortal bodies by our enemies, and are
most cruelly and without mercy murdered down like sheep.
And the more cruel, the more painful, the more vile and
spiteful is the kind of death, whereunto we are put, the
more glorious in God, the more blessed and happy we
reckon, without all doubt, our martyrdom to be.

And thus much, dear lovers and friends in God, my
countrymen and kinsfolk, I have spoken for your comfort,

* Leader (dux).

lest by my death, of whose life you looked, peradventure, sometimes to have had honesty, pleasures, and commodities, you might be abashed or think any evil: whereas you have rather cause to rejoice, if you love me indeed, because it has pleased God to call me to a greater honour and dignity than ever I enjoyed either in Rochester or in the see of London, or ever should have had in the see of Durham, whereunto I was last of all elected and named. Yea, I count it greater honour before God to die in his cause (whereof I nothing doubt), than any earthly or temporal promotion or honour, that can be given to a man in this world.

And who is he that knows the cause to be God's, to be Christ's quarrel, and of his gospel—to be the common weal of all his elect and chosen children of God, of all the inheritors of the kingdom of heaven: who is he, I say, that knows this assuredly by God's word, and the testimony of his own conscience, as I, through the infinite goodness of God, not of myself, but by his grace, acknowledge myself to do—who is he, I say, that knows this, and both loves and fears God, indeed and in truth; and loves and believes his master Christ, and his blessed gospel, loves his brotherhood, the chosen children of God, and also striveth and longeth for everlasting life—who is he, I say again, that would not or cannot find in his heart to be content to die in this cause?

The Lord forbid that there should be any who should forsake this grace of God! I trust in my Lord God, the God of mercies, and the Father of all comfort, through Jesus Christ our Lord, that he, who hath put this mind, will, and affection, by his Holy Spirit, in my heart, to stand against the face of the enemy in his cause, and to choose rather the loss of all my worldly substance, yea, and of my life also, than to deny his known truth—I trust that he will comfort me, aid me, and strengthen me evermore, even unto the end; and enable me to yield up my spirit and soul into his holy hands, whereof I most heartily beseech his most holy sacred Majesty, of his infinite goodness and mercy, through Jesus Christ our Lord. Amen.

Now I have taken my leave of my countrymen and kinsfolk, and as the Lord lends me life and gives me leisure, I will bid my other good friends in God, of other places, also, farewell. And whom first or before others but the university of Cambridge, where I have dwelt longer, found more faithful and hearty friends, received more benefits, the benefits of my natural parents only excepted, than ever I did even in mine own native country wherein I was born.

Farewell, therefore, Cambridge, my loving mother and tender nurse. If I should not acknowledge thy manifold benefits, yea, if I should not for thy benefits, at the least, love thee again, truly I were to be counted ungrateful and unkind. What benefits hast thou, that thou usest to give and bestow upon thy best beloved children, that thou thoughtest too good for me? Thou didst bestow on me all thy school degrees: of thy common offices, the chaplainship of the university, the office of proctorship, and of a common reader: and of thy private advantages and emoluments in colleges, what was it that thou madest me not partner in? First, to be scholar, then fellow; and, after my departure from thee, thou calledst me again to a mastership of a right worshipful college. I thank thee, my loving mother, for all this thy kindness, and I pray God, that his laws and the sincere gospel of Christ may ever be truly taught and faithfully learned in thee.

Farewell, Pembroke Hall, of late mine own college, my cure, and my charge: what case thou art in now, God knoweth; I know not well. Thou wast ever named since I knew thee, which is now thirty years ago, as studious, well learned, and a great setter forth of Christ's gospel and of God's true word. So I found thee, and, blessed be God, so I left thee indeed: woe is me for thee, mine own dear college, if ever thou suffer thyself by any means to be brought from that way. In thy orchards* (the walls, butts, and trees, if they could speak, would bear me witness) I learned, without books,† almost all Paul's epistles, yea, and, I ween, all the canonical epistles, save only the Apocalypse. Of which study, although in time a great part departed from me, yet the sweet savour thereof I trust I shall carry with me into heaven; for the profit thereof I think I have felt all my lifetime ever after. And, I know, that lately there were that did the like; whether they abide there now or not, I cannot tell. The Lord grant that this zeal and love toward that part of

---

* There is a walk in the garden of Pembroke college still distinguished by the name of Ridley's Walk.
† "v heart.

God's word, which is a key and true commentary to all the holy scriptures, may ever abide in that college so long as the world shall endure.

From Cambridge I was called into Kent by the archbishop of Canterbury, Thomas Cranmer, that most reverend father and man of God, and by him sent to be vicar of Herne, in East Kent: wherefore, farewell, Herne, thou worshipful and wealthy parish, the first cure whereunto I was called to minister God's word. Thou hast heard from my mouth ofttimes the word of God preached, not after the popish methods, but after Christ's gospel. Oh, that the fruit had answered to the seed! And yet I must acknowledge that I am thy debtor for the doctrine of the Lord's Supper, which at that time, I acknowledge, God had not revealed unto me; but I bless God for all that godly virtue and zeal of God's word, which the Lord then, by preaching of his word, did kindle manifestly, both in the heart, and in the life, and in the works, of that godly woman there, my lady Fiennes. The Lord grant that his word took like effect there in many other more.

Farewell, thou cathedral church of Canterbury, the metropolitan see, whereof once I was a member. To speak things pleasant unto thee I dare not, for danger of conscience and displeasure of my Lord God; and to say what lieth in my heart were now too much, and I fear were able to do thee now but little good. Nevertheless, for the friendship I have found in some there, and for charity sake, I wish thee to be washed clean from all worldliness and ungodliness, that thou mayest be found of God according to thy name, Christ's church, in deed and in truth.

Farewell, Rochester, some time my cathedral see, in whom, to say the truth, I found much gentleness and obedience; and I trust thou wilt not say the contrary, but that I used it to God's glory and thine own profit in God—oh, that thou hadst and mightest have continued and gone forward in the way of God's law, wherein I left thee! Then thy charge and burden should not have been so terrible and dangerous, as I suppose, verily, it is like to be, alas! on the latter day.

To Westminster, other advertisement in God I have not now to say, than I have said before to the cathedral church of Canterbury: and so God give thee of his grace, that thou mayest learn in deed and in truth to please him according to his own laws, and thus fare you well.

Oh! London, London, to whom now may I speak in thee, or whom shall I bid farewell? Shall I speak to the prebendaries of St. Paul's? Alas! all that loved God's word and were true setters forth thereof, are now, as I hear say, some burnt and slain, some exiled and banished, and some held in hard prison, and appointed daily to be put to most cruel death for Christ's gospel's sake. As for the rest of them, I know they could never brook me well, nor could I ever delight in them.

Shall I speak to the see wherein of late I was placed almost, but not fully, the space of three years? But what may I say to it, being, as I hear say I am, deposed and expelled by judgment, as an unjust usurper of that place. Oh! judgment, judgment! can this be just judgment, to condemn the chief minister of God's word, the pastor and bishop of the diocese, and never bring him into judgment, that he might have heard what crimes were laid to his charge, nor ever suffer him to have any place or time to answer for himself? Thinkest thou, that hereafter, when true justice shall have place, this judgment can ever be allowed, either of God or of man! Well, as for the cause and whole matter of my deposition and the spoil of my goods which thou possessest, I refer it unto God, who is a just judge; and I beseech God, if it be his pleasure, that my personal wrong be not laid to thy charge in the latter day: this only can I pray for.

O! thou now wicked and bloody see; why dost thou set up again many altars of idolatry, which by the word of God were justly taken away? Why hast thou overthrown the Lord's table? Why dost thou daily delude the people, masking in thy masses instead of the Lord's Holy Supper, which Chrysostom, yea, the Lord himself, saith, ought to be common as well to the people as to the priest? How darest thou deny to the people of Christ, contrary to his express commandment in the gospel, his holy cup?

Why babblest thou to the people the common prayer in a strange tongue, wherein St. Paul commands, in the Lord's name, that no man shall speak before the congregation, except it should be afterwards declared in their common tongue, that all might be edified? Nay, hearken, thou harlot of Babylon, thou wicked limb of antichrist.

thou bloody wolf—why slayest thou down and makest havoc of the prophets of God? Why murderest thou so cruelly Christ's poor silly* sheep, which will not hear thy voice, because thou art a stranger, and will follow none other but their own pastor Christ's voice?

Thinkest thou to escape, or that the Lord will not require the blood of his saints at thy hands? Thy god, which is the work of thy hands, and whom thou sayest thou hast power to make—*that* thy deaf and dumb god,† I say, will not, indeed, and cannot, make thee escape the revenging hand of the high and almighty God, although thou art not ashamed to call him thy Maker. But be thou assured, that the living Lord, our Saviour and Redeemer, who sitteth on the right hand of his Father in glory; he seeth all thy wicked ways, and thy cruelty done to his dear members, and he will not forget his holy ones, and his hands thou shalt never escape. Instead of my farewell to thee, now I say—Fye upon thee, fye upon thee, filthy drab, and all thy false prophets!

Yet, O thou London, I may not leave thee thus. Although thy episcopal see, being now joined in league with the seat of satan, hath thus now handled me and the saints of God, yet I do not doubt, but in that great city there are many secret mourners, who daily mourn for that mischief, who never did, and never will, consent to that wickedness, but do detest and abhor it as the ways of satan. But these secret mourners I will here pass by, and bid them farewell with their fellows hereafter, when the place and occasion shall more conveniently require.

Among the worshipful of the city, and especially those who were in the office of the mayoralty, yea, and other citizens also, whom to name now it will not be necessary, in the time of my ministry, which was from the latter parts of Sir Rowland Hill's year unto Sir George Barnes's year, and a great part thereof, I acknowledge that I found no small humanity and gentleness, as methought. But to say the truth, I do esteem above all other for true christian kindness, that which is showed in God's cause, and done for his sake. Wherefore, O Dobbes, Dobbes, alderman and knight, thou in thy year didst win my heart for evermore, for that honourable act, that most blessed work of God, of the erection and setting up of Christ's holy

---

* Weak, simple.   † The consecrated wafer or host.

hospitals and truly religious houses, which by thee and through thee were begun.*

For thou, like a man of God, when the matter was moved for the relief of Christ's poor silly members, to be holpen from extreme misery, hunger, and famine; thy heart, I say, was moved with pity, and, as Christ's high honourable officer in that cause, thou calledst together thy brethren, the aldermen of the city, before whom thou breakedst the matter for the poor. Thou didst plead their cause; yea, and not only in thine own person thou didst set forth Christ's cause, but, to further the matter, thou broughtest me into the council-chamber of the city before the aldermen alone, whom thou hadst assembled there together, to hear me speak what I could say as an advocate, by office and duty, in the poor man's cause. The Lord wrought with thee, and gave thee the consent of thy brethren, whereby the matter was brought to the common-council, and so to the whole body of the city, by whom, with a uniform consent, it was committed to be drawn, ordered, and devised, by a certain number of the most wise and politic citizens, endued, also, with godliness and with ready hearts to set forward such a noble act, that could be chosen in all the whole city. And they, like true and faithful ministers, both to their city and their master Christ, so ordered, devised, and brought forth the matter, that thousands of poor members of Christ, who else for extreme hunger and misery should have famished and perished, shall be relieved, holpen, and brought up, and shall have cause to bless the aldermen of that time, the common-council, and the whole body of the city, but especially thee, O! Dobbes, and those chosen men by whom this honourable work of God was begun and wrought; and that as long, throughout all ages, as that godly work shall endure, which I pray almighty God may be ever unto the world's end. Amen.

And thou, Sir George Barnes, (the truth is to be confessed to God's glory, and to the good example of others,) thou wast in thy year not only a furtherer and continuer of that which was well begun by thy predecessor; but

---

* Dobbes was lord-mayor of London in 1552, the last year of the reign of king Edward VI. He was active in promoting the foundation of the hospitals of Bethlehem, St. Bartholomew, Bridewell, and Christ, which were established by royal charter a few weeks before the death of the king.

also didst labour so to have perfected thy work, that it should have been complete, and a perfect spectacle of true charity and godliness unto all Christendom. Thine endeavour was to have set up a house of occupation, both that all kinds of poor persons, being able to work, should not have lacked whereupon they might have been profitably occupied, to their own relief, and to the profit and commodity of the commonwealth of the city: and, also, to have retired thither the poor babes brought up in the hospitals, when they had come to a certain age and strength: and, also, all those who in the hospitals had been cured of their diseases. And to bring this to pass thou obtainedst, not without great diligence and labour, both of thee and thy brethren, from that godly king, Edward, that christian and peerless prince's hand, his princely place* of Bridewell. And other things to the performance of the same, and under what condition, is not unknown. That this, thine endeavour, hath not had full success, the fault is not in thee, but in the condition and state of the time, which the Lord of his infinite mercy vouchsafe to amend, when it shall be his gracious will and pleasure.

Farewell now, all ye citizens that are of God, of what state and condition soever ye be: undoubtedly, in London you have heard God's word truly preached. My heart's desire and daily prayer shall be for you, as for whom, for my time I know I am accountable to my Lord God, is that ye never swerve, either for loss of life or worldly goods, from God's holy word, and yield unto antichrist; whereupon must needs follow the extreme displeasure of God, and the loss, both of your bodies and souls, in perpetual damnation, for evermore.

Now that I have gone through the places where I have dwelt any space in the time of my pilgrimage here upon earth; remembering that for the space of king Edward's reign, which was the time of mine office in the sees of London and Rochester, I was a member of the higher house of parliament; therefore, seeing my God hath given me leisure and the remembrance thereof, I will bid my lords of the temporality farewell. They shall have no just cause, by God's grace, to take what I intend to say in ill part. As for the spiritual prelacy that now is, I have nothing to say to them, except I should repeat again a

* Palace.

great part of what I have said already to the see of London.

To you, therefore, my lords of the temporality, will I speak; and this would I have you first to understand, that when I wrote this, I looked daily when I should be called to the change of* this life, and thought that this, my writing, should not come to your knowledge, before the time of the dissolution of my body and soul should be expired. And therefore, know ye, that I had before mine eyes only the fear of God, and christian charity toward you, which moved me to write. For of you hereafter I look not in this world either for pleasure or displeasure. If my talk shall do you ever so much pleasure or profit, you cannot promote me, nor, if I displease you, can you hurt me, or harm me, for I shall be out of your reach. Now, therefore, if you fear God, and can be content to hear the talk of him that seeketh nothing at your hands, but to serve God and to do you good, hearken what I say.

I say unto you, as St. Paul saith to the Galatians, I wonder, my lords, what hath bewitched you, that you are so suddenly fallen from Christ unto antichrist; from Christ's gospel unto men's traditions; from the Lord, that bought you, unto the bishops now of Rome. I warn you of your peril—be not deceived, except you will be found willingly consenters unto your own death. For if you think thus, "We are laymen; this is a matter of religion: we follow as we are taught and led; if our teachers and governors teach us and lead us amiss, the fault is in them, they shall bear the blame." My lords, this is true, I grant you, that both the false teacher and the corrupt governor shall be punished for the death of their subject, whom they have falsely taught and corruptly led; yea, and his blood shall be required at their hands; but yet, nevertheless, that subject shall die the death himself also; that is, he shall also be damned for his own sin; for "if the blind lead the blind," Christ saith, not the leader only, but he saith, "both shall fall into the ditch."

Shall the synagogue and the senate of the Jews, (think ye,) which forsook Christ, and consented to his death, be excused, because Annas and Caiaphas, with the scribes and pharisees, and their clergy, taught them amiss? Yea, and also Pilate, their governor, and the emperor's lieutenant, who by his tyranny put him to death without

* Depart from.

cause. Forsooth, no my lords, no; for notwithstanding that corrupt doctrine, or Pilate washing of his hands, neither shall excuse the synagogue, nor the seigniory, or Pilate; but at the Lord's hand, for the effusion of that innocent blood, on the latter day all shall taste of the deadly whip. You understand what I mean; therefore I will pass over this, and return to tell you how you are fallen from Christ to his adversary the bishop of Rome.

And lest, my lords, ye may peradventure think thus openly to call the bishop of Rome Christ's adversary; or, to speak it in plain terms, to call him antichrist; is done in mine anguish; and that I do but rage, and as a desperate man do not care what I say, or upon whom I rail —therefore, that your lordships may perceive my mind, and thereby understand that I speak the words of truth and sobriety, as St. Paul said unto Festus, be it known unto your lordships, that as concerning the bishop of Rome, I neither hate the person, nor the place; for I assure your lordships, (and the living Lord before whom I speak beareth me witness,) I think many a good holy man, many martyrs and saints, have sat and taught Christ's gospel truly in that place; which, therefore, justly may be called apostolici; that is, true disciples of the apostles, and also that church and congregation of christians, the apostolic church, yea, and that for some hundred years after the same was first erected and builded upon Christ by the true apostolical doctrine, taught by the mouths of the apostles themselves.

If you would know how long that was, and how many hundred of years, I will not be too bold, to be curious in pointing the precise number of years. But thus I say, so long and so many hundred years as that see truly taught and preached that gospel and that religion—exercised that power and ordered every thing by those laws and rules, which that see received of the apostles, and, as Tertullian saith, the apostles received of Christ, and Christ of God: so long, I say, that see might well have been called Peter's and Paul's chair and see, or rather Christ's chair, and the bishop thereof apostolicus, or a true disciple and successor of the apostles, and a minister of Christ.

But since that see has degenerated from the profession of truth and true religion, which it received of the apostles at the beginning, and has preached another gospel; has set up another religion, has exercised another power, and

has taken upon it to order and rule the church of Christ
by other laws, canons, and rules, which it never received
of the apostles, nor the apostles, of Christ—which things it
doth at this day, and has continued so doing, alas, alas!
too long a time—since the time, I say, that the state and
condition of that see has thus been changed, in truth it
ought, of duty and of right, to have the names, both of
the see and of the sitter therein changed. For understand,
my lords, it was neither for the privilege of the place nor
the person that the see and bishop thereof were called
apostolic; but for the true profession of Christ's religion,
which was taught and maintained in that see at the first,
and by those godly men. And therefore, as truly and
justly as that see then was called apostolic, for that true
profession of religion, and consanguinity of doctrine with
the religion and doctrine of Christ's apostles: so, as truly
and as justly, for the contrariety of religion and the diversity of doctrine from Christ and his apostles, that see and
the bishop thereof, at this day, both ought to be called, and
are indeed, antichristian.

The see is the seat of satan, and the bishop of the
same, who maintains the abominations thereof, is ANTI-
CHRIST himself indeed. And for the same causes this see,
at this day, is the same, which Saint John calleth in his
Revelation, Babylon, or the harlot of Babylon, and spiritually Sodom and Egypt, the mother of fornications and
of the abominations upon the earth. And with this harlot
all those kings and princes, yea, and all nations of the
earth, which consent to her abominations, and use or
practise the same, do spiritually dwell, and commit most
abominable adultery before God. That is, from the innumerable multitude of them to rehearse some for example
sake, by her dispensations, her pardons and pilgrimages,
her invocation of saints, her worshipping of images, her
false counterfeit religion in her monks and friars, her
traditions, whereby God's laws are defiled. Also, by her
massing and false ministering of God's word and the
sacraments of Christ, quite contrary to Christ's word
and the apostles' doctrine; whereof, in particular, I have
touched in my talk had with the see of London,* and in
other treatises more at large; wherein, if it shall please
God to bring the same to light, it shall appear, I trust, by
God's grace, plainly to the man of God, and to him, whose

* His examinations before bishop Bonner and his clergy.

rule in judgment of religion is God's word—that the religion, the rule and order, the doctrine and faith, which this harlot of Babylon and the beast whereupon she doth sit, maintains at this day with all violence of fire and sword, with spoil and banishment, according to Daniel's prophecy; and with all falsehood, deceit, hypocrisy, and all kinds of ungodliness,—that these things, I say, are as clean contrary to God's word, as darkness is unto light, or light unto darkness; white to black, or black to white; or as Belial unto Christ, or Christ unto antichrist himself.

I know, my lords, and foresaw, when I wrote this, that so many of you as should see this my writing, not being before endued with the Spirit of grace and the light of God's word; that so many, I say, would, at these my words, lord-like stamp, and spurn, and spit thereat. But sober yourselves with patience, and be still, and know that, in my writing of this, my mind was none other, but in God, as the living God bears me witness, both to do you profit and pleasure. And otherwise, as for your displeasure, by the time this shall come to your knowledge, I trust, by God's grace, to be in the hands and protection of the Almighty, my heavenly Father, and the living Lord, who is, as St. John saith, the greatest of all. And then I shall not need, I trow, to fear what any lord, no nor what any king or prince can do unto me.

My lords, if in time past you have been contented to hear me sometimes in matters of religion before the prince in the pulpit, and in the parliament house, and have not seemed to have despised what I have said, when, if you had perceived just occasion, you might then have suspected in my talk, though it had been reasonable, either desire of worldly gain, or fear of displeasure; how much more then have your lordships cause to hearken to my word, and to hear me patiently, seeing that now you cannot justly think of me otherwise, being in this case appointed to die, and looking daily when I shall be called to come before the eternal Judge, but that I only study to serve my Lord God, and to say that which I am persuaded assuredly by God's word shall and doth please him, and profit all them to whom God shall give grace to hear and believe what I say. And I do say even that which I have said heretofore, both of the see of Rome, and of the bishop thereof: I mean according to their present state at this day, wherein, if you will not believe the ministers of God, and the true preachers of his word, verily I denounce unto you, in the words of the Lord, except ye do repent betime, it shall turn to your confusion, and to your smart on the latter day.

Forget not what I say, my lords, for God's sake forget not, but remember it upon your bed. For I tell you, moreover, as I know I must be accountable for this my talk, and for my speaking thus, to the eternal Judge, who will judge nothing amiss; so shall you be accountable for your duty in hearing, and you shall be charged, if you will hearken to God's word, for not obeying the truth.

Alas, my lords, how happens it that this matter is now anew again to be persuaded unto you? Who would have thought of late, but that your lordships had been persuaded indeed sufficiently, or else that you could ever have agreed so uniformly with one consent to the abolishment of the usurpation of the bishop of Rome? If that matter then were but a matter of policy, wherein the prince must be obeyed, how is it now made a matter wherein, as your clergy say now, and so say the pope's laws indeed, standeth the unity of the catholic-church, and a matter necessary for our salvation? Has the time, being so short since the death of the two last kings, Henry the eighth, and Edward his son, altered the nature of the matter? If it have not, but was of the same nature and danger before God then, as it is now; and is now, as it is said by the pope's laws and the instructions set forth in English to the curates of the diocese of York, indeed a matter of necessity to salvation: how then happened it, that you were all, O my lords, so light,[*] and thought so little upon the catholic faith and the unity thereof, without which no man can be saved, that for your princes' pleasures, who were but mortal men, you have forsaken the unity of your catholic faith, that is, forsaken Christ and his holy gospel?

And, furthermore, if it were both then and now so necessary to salvation, how happened it that you all, the whole body of the parliament agreeing with you, did not only abolish and expel the bishop of Rome, but also abjured him in your own persons, and decreed in your acts great oaths to be taken both by the spirituality and tem-

[*] So fickle.

porality, whosoever should enter into any weighty and chargeable office in the commonwealth?

But on the other side, if the law and decree, which makes the supremacy of the see and bishop of Rome over the universal church of Christ, a thing of necessity required unto salvation; if this be an antichristian law, as it is indeed, and such instructions as are given to the diocese of York, are indeed a setting forth of the power of that beast of Babylon, by the craft and falsehood of his false prophets, as of truth, when compared unto God's word, and truly judged by the same, it shall plainly appear that they are: then, my lords, never think but the day shall come, when you shall be charged with this, I mean your undoing of that which once you had well done; and with your perjury and breach of your oath, which oath was done in judgment, justice, and truth, agreeably to God's law.

The harlot of Babylon may well for a time dally with you, and make you so drunken with the wine of her filthy stews and harlotry, as with her dispensations and promises of pardon from punishment and blame, that for drunkenness and blindness you may think yourselves safe! But be you assured, when the living Lord shall try this matter by the fire, and judge it according to his word; when all her abominations shall appear what they are, then you, my lords, I give your lordships warning in time, repent, if you would be happy and love your own souls' health. Repent, I say; or else, without all doubt, you shall never escape the hands of the living Lord, for the guilt of your perjury and the breach of your oath.

As you have banqueted with the Romish harlot in her dispensations, pardons, idolatry, and such like abominations, so shall you drink with her, except you repent in time, of the cup of the Lord's indignation and everlasting wrath, which is prepared for the beast, his false prophets, and all their partakers. For he that is partner with them in their whoredom and abominations, must also be partner with them in their plagues; and in the latter day shall be thrown with them into the lake burning with brimstone and unquenchable fire.

Thus fare ye well, my lords, all. I pray God give you understanding of his blessed will and pleasure, and cause you to believe and embrace the truth. Amen.

ANOTHER FAREWELL

To the prisoners in Christ's gospel's cause, and to all those who, for the same cause, are exiled and banished out from their own country, choosing rather to leave all worldly commodity, than their Master Christ.

FAREWELL, my dearly beloved brethren in Christ, both you, my fellow-prisoners, and you also who are exiled and banished out of your country, because you will forsake all worldly advantages rather than the gospel of Christ.

Farewell, all ye together in Christ, farewell, and be joyful, for you know that the trial of your faith bringeth forth patience, and patience shall make us perfect, whole, and sound on every side: and such, after trial, you know, shall receive the crown of life, according to the promise of the Lord, made to his dearly beloved. Let us, therefore, be patient unto the coming of the Lord. As the husbandman abideth patiently the former and latter rain for the increase of his crop: so let us be patient and pluck up our hearts; for the coming of the Lord approaches apace. Let us, my dear brethren, take example of patience in tribulation from the prophets, who likewise spake God's word truly in his name.

Let Job be to us an example of patience; and the end which the Lord suffered, which is full of mercy and pity. We know, my brethren, by God's word, that our faith is much more precious than any corruptible gold, and yet that is tried by the fire: even so our faith is tried in tribulations, that it may be found, when the Lord shall appear, laudable, glorious, and honourable. For if we for Christ's cause do suffer, it is grateful before God; for thereunto are we called. That is our state and vocation, therewith let us be content. Christ, we know, suffered afflictions for us, leaving us an example, that we should follow his footsteps. For he committed no sin, nor was guile found in his mouth: when he was railed upon and reviled, he railed not again; when he was evil entreated, he did not threaten, but committed the punishment thereof to Him that judgeth aright.

Let us ever have in fresh remembrance those wonderful and comfortable sentences, spoken by the mouth of our Saviour Christ: " Blessed are they which suffer persecution for righteousness' sake, for theirs is the kingdom of heaven. Blessed are ye, when men revile you, persecute you, and speak all evil against you for my sake; rejoice and be glad, for great is your reward in heaven, for so did they persecute the prophets, which were before you." Therefore, let us always bear this in our minds, that if any incommodity happen unto us for righteousness' sake, happy are we, whatever the world thinks of us. Christ, our master, has told us beforehand, that the brother should put the brother to death, and the father the son, and the children should rise against their parents and kill them: and that Christ's true apostles should be hated of all men for his name's sake: but he, that shall abide patiently unto the end, shall be saved.

Let us then in all troubles endure patiently, after the example of our master Christ, and be contented thereat: for he suffered, being our master and Lord; how doth it not then become us to suffer? " For the disciple is not above his master, nor the servant above his lord. It may suffice the disciple to be as his master, and the servant to be as his lord. If they have called the father of the family, the master of the household, Beelzebub, how much more shall they so call them of his household?" " Fear them not, then," saith our Saviour, " for all secrets shall be made plain: there is now nothing secret, but it shall be showed in light." Of Christ's words let us not be ashamed, nor afraid to speak them. For so Christ, our master, commands us, saying, " That which I tell you privily, speak openly abroad: and that which I tell you in your ear, preach it upon the house top." And, " Fear not them which kill the body, for the soul they cannot kill; but fear Him, who can cast both body and soul into hell-fire."

Know ye, that the heavenly Father ever hath a gracious eye and respect towards you, and a fatherly providence for you: so that, without his knowledge and permission, nothing can do you harm. Let us, therefore, cast all our care upon him, and he shall provide that which shall be best for us. For if, of two small sparrows, which both are sold for a farthing, not one of them lighteth on the ground without your Father; and since all the hairs of your head are numbered, fear not then, saith our master Christ, for you are of more worth than many small sparrows.

Let us not hesitate to confess our master Christ, for fear of danger, whatever it shall be, remembering the promise of Christ, saying, "Whosoever shall confess me before men, him will I confess before my Father which is in heaven: but whosoever shall deny me, him will I likewise deny before my Father which is in heaven." Christ came not to give unto us here a carnal amity, and a worldly peace, or to knit his people unto the world in ease and peace: but rather to separate and divide them from the world, and to join them unto himself; in whose cause we must, if we will be his, forsake father and mother, and stick unto him. If we forsake him, or shrink from him, for trouble or death's sake, which he calleth his cross, he will have none of us; we cannot be his.

If for his cause we lose our temporal lives here, we shall find them again and enjoy them for evermore; but if we will not be contented to leave nor lose them here in his cause; then shall we lose them so, that we shall never find them again, but in everlasting death. What though our troubles here are painful for the time, and the sting of death is bitter and unpleasant; yet we know that they shall not last, in comparison of eternity, no, not the twinkling of an eye, and that they, being patiently taken in Christ's cause, shall procure and get us immeasurable heaps of heavenly glory, unto which these temporal pains of death and troubles compared, are not to be esteemed, but to be rejoiced in.

"Wonder not," saith St. Peter, "as though it were any strange matter, that you are tried by the fire (he meaneth of tribulation), which," saith he, "is done to prove you. Nay, rather rejoice in that ye are partners of Christ's afflictions, that in his glorious revelation ye may rejoice with joyful hearts. If ye suffer rebukes in Christ's name, happy are you, for the glory and Spirit of God resteth upon you. Of them God is reviled and dishonoured; but of you he is glorified."

"Let no man be ashamed of that which he suffereth as a christian, and in Christ's cause; for now is the time, that judgment and correction must begin at the house of God: and if it begin first at us, what shall be the end of those, think ye, who believe not the gospel? and if the righteous shall be hardly saved, the wicked and the sinner, where shall they appear? wherefore, they which are afflicted according to the will of God, let them lay down and commit their souls to him by well doing, as to a trusty and faithful Maker."

This, as I said, may not seem strange to us, for we know that all the whole fraternity of Christ's congregation in this world is served with the like, and by the same is made perfect. Also for the fervent love that the apostles had unto their master Christ; and for the great advantages and increase of all godliness, which they felt by their faith to ensue from afflictions in Christ's cause; and thirdly, for the heavenly joys bestowed upon the godly, which shall endure in heaven for evermore: for these causes, I say, the apostles did joy of their afflictions, and rejoiced that they were had and accounted worthy to suffer contumelies and rebukes for Christ's name.

And Paul, as he gloried in the grace and favour of God, whereunto he was brought and stood in by faith; so he rejoiced in his afflictions, for the heavenly and spiritual profit, which he counted to arise from them: yea, he was so far in love with that which the carnal man loaths so much,—that is, with Christ's cross,—that he judged himself to know nothing else but Christ crucified: he will glory, he saith, in nothing else but in Christ's cross; yea, and he blesses all those, as the only true Israelites and elect people of God, with peace and mercy, who walk after that rule and no other.

O! Lord, what a wonderful spirit was that which made Paul, in setting of himself forth against the vanity of satan's pseudapostles,* and in his claim there, that he, in Christ's cause, did excel and pass them all,—what wonderful spirit was that, I say, which made him reckon up all his troubles, his labours, his beatings, his whippings and scourgings, his shipwrecks, his dangers and perils, by water and by land; his famine, hunger, nakedness, and cold, with many more; and the daily care of all the congregations of Christ, among whom every man's pain did pierce his heart, and every man's grief was grievous unto him? O Lord, is this Paul's primacy, whereof he thought it good that he excelled others? Is not this Paul's saying unto Timothy, his own scholar, and does it not pertain to whomsoever will be Christ's true soldier: "Bear thou,"

* False teachers.

saith he, " affliction, like a good soldier of Jesus Christ?" "This is true, if we die with him (he meaneth Christ), we shall live with him; if we suffer with him, we shall reign with him; if we deny him, he shall deny us; if we be faithless, he remaineth faithful; he cannot deny himself."

Paul would have this known to every body; for there is no other way to heaven but Christ and his way: and " all that will live godly in Christ shall (saith St. Paul) suffer persecution." By this way the patriarchs, the prophets, Christ our master, his apostles, his martyrs, and all the godly since the beginning, went to heaven. And, as it hath been of old, that he who was born after the flesh, persecuted him who was born after the Spirit, for so it was in Isaac's time, so, said St. Paul, it was in his time also. And whether it be so now or not, let the spiritual man, the self-same man I mean that is endued with the Spirit of almighty God, let him be judge.

Of the cross of the patriarchs, you may read in their stories, if you read the book of Genesis. Of others, St. Paul, in few words, comprehends much, when speaking generally of the wonderful afflictions, death, and torments, which the men of God, in God's cause, and for the truth's sake, willingly and gladly suffered.

After particularly speaking of many, he saith, " Others were racked and despised, and would not be delivered, that they might obtain a better resurrection. Others again were tried with mockings and scourgings, and moreover, with bonds and imprisonment; they were stoned, hewn asunder, tempted, fell, and were slain upon the edge of the sword; some wandered to and fro in sheeps' pilches,* in goats' pilches, forsaken, oppressed, afflicted: such godly men, as the world was unworthy of, wandering in the wilderness, in mountains, in caves, and in dens; and all these were commended for their faith. And yet they abide for† us the servants of God, and for those, their brethren, who are to be slain, as they were, for the word of God's sake, that none be shut out, but that we may all go together to meet our master, Christ, in the air at his coming, and so to be in bliss with him in body and soul for evermore.

Therefore, seeing we have so much occasion to suffer, and to take afflictions for Christ's name's sake patiently, so many advantages thereby, such weighty causes, so

* Skins' coverings. † Wait for

many good examples, such great necessity, such sure promises of eternal life and heavenly joys from Him that cannot lie; let us throw away whatever might hinder us; all burden of sin, and all kind of carnality; and patiently and constantly let us run for the best game in "this race, that is set before us; ever having our eyes upon Jesus Christ, the leader, captain, and perfecter of our faith, who for the joy that was set before him, endured the cross, not caring for the ignominy and shame thereof, and is set now at the right hand of the throne of God." Consider this, that he suffered such strife of sinners against himself, that ye should not give over, nor faint in your minds. As yet, brethren, we have not withstood unto death, fighting against sin.

Let us never forget, dear brethren, for Christ's sake, that fatherly exhortation of the wise, who speaketh unto us, as unto his children, the godly wisdom of God, saying thus: " My son, despise not the correction of the Lord, nor fall from him, when thou art rebuked of him: for whom the Lord loveth, him he corrects; and scourges every child whom he receives. What child is he, whom the father does not chasten? If ye be free from chastisement, whereof all are partakers, then are ye bastards and no children—Seeing then, when as we have had carnal parents, which chastened us, we reverenced them: shall not we much more be subject unto our spiritual Father, that we might live? And they for a little time have taught us, after their own mind; but this Father teacheth us for our advantage, to give unto us his holiness. All chastisement, for the present time, appeareth not pleasant, but painful: but afterward it rendereth the fruit of righteousness on them which are exercised in it." (Heb. xii.)

Wherefore, let us be of good cheer, good brethren, and let us pluck up our feeble members, that were fallen or began to faint; heart hands, knees, and all the rest; and let us walk upright and straight, that no limping nor halting bring us out of the way. Let us look not upon the things that are present; but with the eyes of our faith let us stedfastly behold the things that are everlasting in heaven; and so choose rather in respect of that which is to come, with the chosen members of Christ to bear Christ's cross, than for this short lifetime, to enjoy all the riches, honours, and pleasure of the broad world.

Why should we christians fear death? Can death

deprive us of Christ, who is all our comfort, our joy, and our life? Nay, forsooth. But on the contrary, death shall deliver us from this mortal body, which loadeth and beareth down the spirit that it cannot so well perceive heavenly things, in which, so long as we dwell, we are absent from God.

Wherefore, understanding our state, since we are christians, that " if our mortal body, which is our earthly house, were destroyed, we have a building, a house not made with hands, but everlasting in heaven ;" therefore we are of good cheer, and know, that when we are in the body, we are absent from God; for we walk by faith and not by clear sight. Nevertheless, we are bold, and had rather be absent from the body and present with God. Wherefore, we strive, whether we are present at home, or absent abroad, that we may always please him. And who, that hath true faith in our Saviour Christ, whereby he knoweth somewhat truly, what Christ our Saviour is; that he is the eternal Son of God, life, light, the wisdom of the Father, all goodness, all righteousness, and whatsoever is good that heart can desire ; yea, infinite plenty of all these, above that which man's heart can either conceive or think, for in him dwelleth the fulness of the Godhead corporeally—and also, that he is given us of the Father, and made of God to be our wisdom, our righteousness, our holiness, and our redemption: who, I say, is he, that believes this indeed, that would not gladly be with his master Christ?

Paul for this knowledge coveted to have been loosed from the body, and to have been with Christ; for he counted it much better for himself, and had rather be loosed than live. Therefore, these words of Christ to the thief on the cross, that asked mercy of him, were full of comfort and solace : " This day thou shalt be with me in paradise."

To die in the defence of Christ's gospel, is our bounden duty to Christ, and also to our neighbour. To Christ, for he died for us, and rose again, that he might be Lord over all. And seeing he died for us, we also, saith St. John, should jeopard,* yea, give our life, for our brethren. And this kind of giving and losing, is getting and winning indeed: for he, that gives or loses his life thus, gets it and wins it for evermore. Blessed are they, therefore, that die

* Endanger, risk.

in the Lord: and, if they die in the Lord's cause, they are most happy of all.

Then let us not fear death, which can do us no harm, otherwise than to make the flesh smart for a moment; for our faith, which is surely fastened and fixed unto the word of God, tells us that anon[*] after death we shall be in peace, in the hands of God, in joy, in solace; and that from death we shall go straight into life. For St. John saith, " he, that liveth and believeth in me shall never die." And in another place, " he shall depart from death unto life." And, therefore, this death of the christian is not to be called death, but rather it is a gate or entrance into everlasting life. Therefore Paul calls it but a dissolution and resolution, and both Peter and Paul call it a putting off this tabernacle or dwelling house: meaning thereby the mortal body, wherein the soul or spirit dwells here in this world for a small time: yea, this death may be called to the christian an end of all miseries. For, so long as we live here, we must pass through many tribulations, before we can enter into the kingdom of heaven. And now, after death has shot his bolt, all the christian man's enemies have done what they can; and after that, they have no more to do.

What could hurt or harm poor Lazarus, who lay at the rich man's gate? Could his former penury and poverty, his miserable beggary and horrible sores and sickness? For so soon as death had stricken him with his dart, so soon came the angels, and carried him straight up into Abraham's bosom. What lost he by death, who from misery and pain is set, by the ministry of angels, in a place both of joy and solace?

Farewell, dear brethren, farewell; and let us comfort our hearts in all troubles and in death, with the word of God: for heaven and earth shall perish, but the word of the Lord endureth for ever.

Farewell, Christ's dearly beloved spouse, here wandering in this world, as in a strange land, far from thine own country, and compassed about on every hand with deadly enemies, which cease not to assault thee, ever seeking thy destruction.

Farewell, farewell, O! ye, the whole and universal congregation of the chosen of God, here living upon earth, the true church militant of Christ, the true mystical body

[*] Directly.

of Christ, the very household and family of God, and the sacred temple of the Holy Ghost. Farewell.

Farewell, O! thou little flock of the high heavenly Pastor Christ, for to thee it hath pleased the heavenly Father to give an everlasting and eternal kingdom. Farewell.

Farewell, thou spiritual house of God, thou holy and royal priesthood, thou chosen generation, thou holy nation, thou won spouse, farewell! farewell!

NICHOLAS RIDLEY.*

* These Farewells appear to have been written between the 1st October, 1555, when he was condemned at Oxford by the bishops of Lincoln, Gloucester, and Bristol, and the 16th of the same month, when he was burned. It was during this interval, that Lord Dacres offered ten thousand pounds to the queen if she would spare Ridley's life. An enormous sum, exceeding one hundred thousand pounds at the present day; but her bigotry prevailed, and the offer was refused.

LETTERS

OF

DR. NICHOLAS RIDLEY,

BISHOP OF LONDON,

Who, after long imprisonment, was cruelly burned
in Oxford, for the constant confession
of God's true Religion,
In the year of our Lord God, 1555, the 16th day of October.

LETTERS.

[Arranged according to the Dates at which they appear to have been written.]

LETTER I.

A Letter of that true pastor and worthy martyr Dr. Ridley; wherein you may see the singular zeal he had to the glory of God and the furtherance of his gospel. written to Sir John Cheke* in King Edward's days.

MASTER CHEKE, I wish you grace and peace. Sir, in God's cause, for God's sake, and in his name, I beseech you for your help and furtherance towards God's word. I did talk with you of late what case I was in concerning my chaplains. I have gotten the good will and grant to be with me, of three preachers, men of good learning, and, as I am persuaded, of excellent virtue, who are able, both with life and learning, to set forth God's word in London, and in the whole diocese of the same, where is most need of all parts in England; for from thence goeth example (as you know) into all the rest of the king's majesty's whole realm. The men's names are these, Master Grindall, whom you know to be a man of virtue and learning. Master Bradford, a man by whom, as I am assuredly informed, God hath and doth work wonders, in setting forth of his word. The third is a preacher, who for detecting and confuting the fanatics and papists in Essex, both by his preaching and by his writing, is enforced now to bear Christ's cross. The two first are scholars in the university. The third is as poor as either of the other twain. Now there is fallen a prebend in Paul's, called

* Sir John Cheke was one of the tutors of Edward VI., when prince of Wales, and afterwards one of the secretaries of state, and a privy counsellor. After the accession of Queen Mary, he obtained leave to retire to the continent, but when popery was fully established, he was seized in the Netherlands by order of king Philip, and being required to turn or burn, he recanted. The papists, by way of triumph, obliged him to be present at the examinations of several of the martyrs. Remorse preyed so heavily on his mind, that he pined away with shame and regret, and died in September, 1557

Cantrelle, by the death of one Layton. This prebend is an honest man's living of £34. and better, in the king's books. I would with all my heart give it unto Master Grindall, and so I should have him continually with me and in my diocese, to preach.

But alas, Sir, I am hindered by the means I fear of such as do not fear God. One Master William Thomas, one of the clerks of the council, hath in times past set the council upon me, to grant that Layton might alienate the said prebend unto him and his heirs for ever. God was mine aid and defender, so that I did not consent unto his ungodly enterprise. Yet I was then handled so before the council, that I granted that whensoever it should fall, I should not give it before I should make the king's majesty acquainted with it, before the collation of it. Now Layton is departed, and the prebend is fallen, and certain of the council, no doubt by this ungodly man's means, have written unto me to stay the collation. And whereas he despairs, that ever I should assent that a preacher's living should be bestowed on him, he has procured letters unto me, subscribed by certain of the counsellor's hands, that now the king's majesty hath determined it shall be appropriated unto the furniture of his highness's stable. Alas, Sir, this is a heavy hearing—when papistry was taught, there was nothing too little for the teachers, when the bishop gave his benefices unto idiots, unlearned and ungodly, because they were kindred, for pleasure, for service, and other worldly respects, all was then well allowed! Now, where a poor living is to be given to an excellent scholar, a man known and tried to have both discretion and also virtue, and such a one as, before God, I do not know a man yet unplaced or unprovided for, more fit to set forth God's word in all England—when a poor living, I say, which is founded for a preacher, is to be given unto such a man, that then an ungodly person shall procure in this sort, letters to stop the same, alas! Master Cheke, this seemeth unto me to be a right heavy hearing. Is this the fruit of the gospel? speak Master Cheke, speak for God's sake in God's cause, unto whomsoever you think you may do any good withal. And if you will not speak, then, I beseech you, let these my letters speak unto Master Gates, to Master Wrothe, to Master Cecill, all of whom I do take for men that fear God.

It was said here constantly, that my lord chamberlain

is departed—Sir, though the day be delayed, yet he has no grant of long life, and therefore I do beseech his good lordship and so many as shall read these letters, if they fear God, to help that neither horse nor yet dog, be suffered to devour the poor livings appointed and founded by godly ordinance, for the ministers of God's word. The causes of conscience which move me to speak and write thus, are not only those which I declared once in the cause of this prebend before the king's majesty's council which now I let pass, but also now that man, Master Grindall, unto whom I would give this prebend, moves me very much, for he is a man known to be both of virtue, honesty, discretion, wisdom, and learning; and besides all this, I have a better opinion of the king's majesty's honourable council, although some of them have subscribed, at this their clerk's crafty and ungodly lure, to such a letter, than to think they will hinder, and not suffer, after request made unto them, the living appointed and founded for a preacher, to be bestowed upon so honest and well learned a man.

Wherefore, I beseech you all, help that with the favour of the council, I may have knowledge of the king's majesty's good pleasure, to give this preacher's living unto Master Grindall. Of late there have been letters directed from the king's majesty, and his honourable council, unto all the bishops, whereby we are charged and commanded, both in our own persons, and also to cause our preachers and ministers, especially to cry out against the insatiable serpent of covetousness, whereby is said to be such a greediness among the people, that each one goeth about to devour the other; and to threaten them with God's grievous plagues, both now presently thrown upon them, and that likewise in the world to come. Sir, what preachers shall I get to open and set forth such matters, and so as the king's majesty and the council do command them to be set forth, if either ungodly men, or unreasonable beasts, be suffered to pull away and devour the good and godly learned preachers' livings. Thus I wish you in God, ever well to fare, and to help Christ's cause as you would have help of him at your most need.*

From Fulham, this present 15th of July, 1551.

Yours in Christ,
NICHOLAS LONDON.

* The request in this letter was complied with.

LETTER II.

A Letter written by bishop Ridley to his well-beloved the preachers within the Diocese of London, setting forth the sins of those times.

AFTER hearty commendations having regard, especially at this time, to the wrath of God, who hath plagued us diversely, and now with extreme punishment of sudden death poured upon us,* for causes best known unto his high and secret judgment; but as it may seem unto man for our wicked living which daily increases; so that not only in our conversations, the fear of God is, alas, far gone from before our eyes, but also the world is grown into that uncharitableness, that one, as it appears plainly, goes about to devour another; moved with insatiable covetousness, and contrary to God's word and will, and to the extreme peril and damnation of Christ's flock, bought so dearly with his precious blood, and to the utter destruction of this whole commonwealth, except God's anger be shortly appeased. Wherein, according to my bounden duty, I shall, God willing, in my own person, be diligent and labour; and I also exhort and require you, first in God's name, and by authority of him committed unto me in that behalf, and also in the king's majesty's name, from whom I have authority and special commandment thus to do—That as you are called to be setters forth of God's word, and to express the same in your lives, so now in your exhortations and sermons, most wholesomely and earnestly, tell unto men their sins, with God's punishments lately poured upon us for the same, now before our eyes; according to that word "Tell unto my people their wickednesses." And especially beat down and destroy, with all

---

* The sweating sickness. It began in London, 9th July, and was most terrible July 12, 1551. People being in the best health, were suddenly taken, and dead in a few hours. This mortality fell chiefly on men of the best age, or between thirty and forty, few women or children, or old men died thereof. Sleeping in the beginning was present death; for if they were suffered to sleep but half a quarter of an hour, they never spake after, nor had any knowledge, but when they woke fell into the pangs of death. Seven honest householders supped together, and before eight o'clock next morning six of them were dead. This sickness followed Englishmen as well in foreign countries as within this realm; wherefore this nation was much afraid of it, and for the time began to repent and remember God, but as the disease relented, the devotion decayed. The first week 800 persons died in London.—*Stowe's Annals.*

your power and ability, that greedy and devouring serpent of covetousness, which now so universally reigns. Call upon God for repentance, and excite to common prayer and amendment of life, with most earnest petitions, that hereby God's hand may be stayed, the world amended, and obedience of subjects and faithfulness of ministers declared accordingly. Thus I bid you heartily well to fare.

From London, July 25, 1551.

Yours in Christ,

NICHOLAS LONDON.

LETTER III.

The manner of Dr. Ridley's handling in the schools at Oxford (in 1554), and of the impudent, spiteful, and cruel dealing of the papists; which he set before his disputation by way of a preface, and is not unfit here to be placed among the letters: translated out of his Latin copy into English.

I NEVER yet in all my life saw or heard any thing done or handled more vainly or tumultuously, than the disputation which was had with me of late in the schools at Oxford. And, surely, I could never have thought that it had been possible to have found any within this realm, being of any knowledge, learning, and ancient degree of school, so brazen-faced and so shameless, as to behave themselves so vainly and so like stage-players, as they did in that disputation.

The Sorbonical clamours,* which, at Paris, when popery most reigned, I in times past have seen, might be worthily thought to have had much modesty, in comparison of this thrasonical† and glorious ostentation. Howbeit, it was not to be wondered at, for those who should there have been moderators, and rulers of others, and who should have given a good example in word, gravity, &c. as St. Paul teaches, (1 Tim. iv.) gave the worst example of all, and did, as it were, blow the trumpet to others to rail, rage, roar, and cry out. By reason whereof, good christian reader, it is manifest that they never sought for

* Scholastic disputations in the university of Paris.
† Vain boasting.

any truth, but only for the glory of the world, and a bragging victory. But besides the innumerable railings, rebukes, and taunts wherewith I was baited on every side, —lest our cause, which, indeed, is God's cause and his church's, should also, by the false examples of our disputations, be evil spoken of and slandered to the world, and so the verity sustain hurt and hinderance thereby; I have thought good to write my answers myself, that whosoever is desirous to know them and the truth withal, may thereby perceive those things which were chiefly objected against me, and also, in effect, what was answered of me to every one of them.

Howbeit, good reader, I confess this to be most true, that it is impossible to set forth either all that was tumultuously spoken, like as by madmen, or objected by so many, who spake oftentimes huddled together, so that one could not well hear another; or all that was answered by me briefly to such and so many different opponents. Moreover, a great part of the time appointed for the disputations, was vainly spent in most contumelious taunts, hissings, clapping of hands, and triumphs more than would be borne even in stage-players, and that in the English tongue, to get the people's favour withal. All which things, when I with godly grief did suffer, and therewithal did openly bewail and witness that the company of learned men, and schools, which were appointed to grave men, and to grave matters, were contaminated and defiled by such foolish and Robin Hood pastimes,* and that those, who were the doers of such things, did but thereby openly show their vanity; I was so far, by my such humble complaint, from doing good, or helping any thing at all, that I was enforced, what with hissing and shouting, and what with authority, to hear such great reproaches and slanders uttered against me, as no grave man without blushing could abide the hearing of the same, spoken by a most vile knave against a most wretched ruffian. At the beginning of the disputation, when I should have confirmed mine answer to the first proposition in few words, and that after the manner of disputations, before I could make an end of my probation, which was not very long, even the doctors themselves cried out, " He speaketh blasphemies! blasphemies! blasphemies!" And when I on my knees most humbly and earnestly besought them

* Alluding to the games on May-day.

that they would vouchsafe to hear me to the end, whereat the prolocutor, somewhat moved, as it seemed, cried out, "Let him read it," there was by and by such a cry and noise of "Blasphemies! blasphemies! blasphemies!" as I, to my remembrance, never heard or read the like, except it be that which is spoken of in the Acts of the Apostles, stirred up of Demetrius the silversmith, and others of his occupation, crying out against Paul, "Great is Diana of the Ephesians, great is Diana of the Ephesians;" and except it were a certain disputation which the Arians had against the orthodox, and such as were of godly judgment, in Africa; where it is said that such as the presidents and rulers of the disputation were, such was also the end of the disputation: all was done in hurly-burly, and the slanders of the Arians were so outrageous that nothing could quietly be heard. So writeth Victor in the second book of his history. And thus the cries and tumults of these men against me now so prevailed, that whether I would or not, I was enforced to leave off the reading of my probations, although they were but short; and of the truth hereof, I have all those that were present, being of any discretion or honesty, to be my witnesses. But hereof will I cease to complain any further.

Know, gentle reader, that Master prolocutor did promise me in the disputations publicly that I should see my answers how they were collected and gathered by the notaries, and that I should have license to add or diminish, to alter or change afterwards, as I should think best would make for me to the answering of the propositions. He promised, moreover, publicly, that I should have both time and place for me to bring in frankly all that I could for the confirmation of mine answers. Now, when he had promised all these things openly in the hearing of other commissioners, and of the whole university of Oxford, yet, good reader, mark this, that in very deed he performed nothing of all that he promised: what faith then shall a man look to find at such judges' hands in the secret mysteries of God, which in their promises, so openly made and so justly due, (I will not speak of the witnesses of the matter,) are found to be so faithless both to God and man?—Well, I will leave it to the judgment of the wise.

And now, for that we can do, let us pray that God would have mercy on his church of England, that yet once, when it shall be his good pleasure, it may clearly see and eagerly embrace, in the face of Jesus Christ, the will of the heavenly Father; and that of his infinite mercy, he would either turn to him the raging and ravening wolves, and most subtle seducers of his people, which are by them altogether spoiled and bewitched, or that of his most righteous judgment he would drive these faithless feeders from his flock, that they may no more be able to trouble and scatter abroad Christ's sheep from their shepherd, and that speedily: Amen, Amen. And let every one that hath the Spirit, (as St. John saith,) say Amen.

Yet further know thou, that when Master prolocutor did put forth three propositions, he commanded us to answer particularly to them all. After our answers, neither he nor his fellows did ever enter into any disputation upon any one of them, saving only of the first; yea, when he had asked us after the disputations upon the first, whether we would subscribe to the whole, in such sort, form, and words, as there are set forth, without further disputation, which we denied to do, by and by he gave sentence against us all, that is, against me, doctor Cranmer, and doctor Latimer, my most dear fathers and brethren in Christ, condemning us as heinous heretics concerning every one of these propositions, and so separated us one from another, sending us severally into sundry and divers houses, to be kept most secretly to the day of our burning; and as before, so he still commanded, that all and every one of our servants should be kept from us; whereto he added, that at his departure thence, pen, ink, and paper should depart from us also. But thanks be to God, that gave me to write this[*] before the use of such things were utterly taken away. Almighty God, who beholdeth the cause of the afflicted, and is wont to loose and look mercifully on the bonds and groanings of the captives, may he vouchsafe now to look upon the causes of his poor church in England, and of his great wisdom and unspeakable mercy, with speed to make an end of our misery. Amen. Amen. Amen.

[*] The report of Ridley's disputation in Oxford, which he penned with his own hands.—*Letters of the Martyrs.*

LETTER IV.

To Doctor Weston, requiring performance of certain promises made by him but never fulfilled, according to the accustomed wily and unfaithful dealing of the papists.

MASTER PROLOCUTOR, you remember, I am sure, how you promised me openly in the schools after my protestation, that I should see how my answers were there taken and written by the notaries, whom you appointed (I admit that no one objected thereto) to write what should be said, and that I should have had license to add unto them, or to have altered them, as upon more deliberation should have seemed best to me. You granted me also, at the delivery of my answer unto your first proposition, a copy of the same. These promises are not performed. If your sudden departure is any part of the cause thereof, yet, I pray you, remember that they may be performed; for performance of promises is to be looked for at a righteous judge's hands.

Now, I send you here mine answers in writing to your second and third propositions, and do desire and require earnestly a copy of the same, and I shall, by God's grace, procure the pains of the writer to be paid for and satisfied accordingly. When I would have confirmed my sayings with authorities or reasons, you said there, openly, that I should have had time and place to say and bring whatsoever I could another time. And the same, your saying, was then and there confirmed by others of the commissioners; yea, and, I dare say, the audience also, thought then that I should have had another day to have brought and said what I could say, for the declaration and confirmation of my assertions. Now, that this was not done, but sentence given so suddenly before the cause was perfectly heard, I cannot but marvel at; and the due reformation of all things which are amiss, I commit unto almighty God, my heavenly Father, who by his dear Son our Saviour Christ (whom he hath made the universal Judge of all flesh) shall truly and righteously judge both you and me.

Master prolocutor, I desire you, and in God's name require you, that you truly bring forth and show all my three answers, written and subscribed with my own hand, unto the higher house of the convocation, and specially unto my lord chancellor, my lords of Durham, Ely, Norwich, Worcester, and Chichester; and also to show and exhibit this my writing unto them, which in these few lines I write here unto you. And that I do make this request unto you by this my writing, know you that I did take witness of them by whom I did send you this writing, and of those who were then present, that is of the bailiffs of Oxford, and of master Irish, alderman, then and there called to be a witness,

By me, N. RIDLEY, 23rd of April, 1554

LETTER V.

Letter from Doctor Ridley to the Archbishop of Canterbury (Cranmer).

I WISH you might have seen these mine answers before I delivered them, that you might have corrected them. But I trust, in the substance of the matter we do agree fully, being both led by one Spirit of truth, and both walking after one rule of God's word. It is reported, that sergeant Morgan, the chief justice of the Common Pleas, is gone mad.* It is said, also, that justice Hales hath recanted, perverted by doctor Moreman. Also, that master Rogers, doctor Crome, and master Bradford, shall be had to Cambridge, and there disputed with as we were here; and that the doctors of Oxford shall go likewise thither, as Cambridge men came hither. When you have read mine answers, send them again to Austen, except you will put any thing to them. I trust, the day of our delivery out of all miseries, and of our entrance into perpetual rest, and unto perpetual joy and felicity, draweth nigh. The Lord strengthen us with his mighty Spirit of grace.

If you have not what to write with, you must make your man your friend. And this bearer deserves to be rewarded, so he may and will do your pleasure. My man is trusty; but it grieves both him and me, that when I send him with any thing to you, your man will not let him come up

---

* The judge who condemned lady Jane Grey. He shortly after went out of his mind, and died raving mad, calling incessantly to have the lady Jane taken away from his sight.

to see you, as he may to Master Latimer, and yours to me.

I have a promise to see how my answers were written in the schools, but as yet I cannot come by it. Pray for me, I pray you, and so shall I for you. The Lord have mercy on his church, and lighten the eyes of the magistrates, that God's extreme plagues light not on this realm of England.

TURN OR BURN.

LETTER VI.

To the brethren remaining in captivity of the flesh, and dispersed abroad in sundry prisons, but knit together in unity of spirit and holy religion in the bowels of the Lord Jesus.

GRACE, peace, and mercy be multiplied among you. What worthy thanks can be rendered unto the Lord for you, my brethren, namely for the great consolation which, through you, we have received in the Lord; that—notwithstanding the rage of satan, who goeth about by all manner of subtle means to beguile the world, and also busily labours to restore and set up his kingdom again, which of late began to decay and fall to ruin—you remain yet still unmoveable, as men surely grounded upon a strong rock!

And now, although satan, by his soldiers and wicked ministers daily, as we hear, draws numbers unto him, so that it is said of him, that he plucketh even the very stars out of heaven; while he driveth into some men the fear of death and loss of all their goods, and showeth and offereth to some others the pleasant baits of the world; namely, riches, wealth, and all kinds of delights and pleasures, fair houses, great revenues, fat benefices, and what not. And all to the intent that they should fall down and worship, not in the Lord, but in the dragon, the old serpent, which is the devil, that great beast and his image; and should be enticed to commit fornication with the harlot of Babylon, together with the kings of the earth, with the lesser beast, and with the false prophets; and to rejoice and be pleasant with her, and to be drunken with the wine of her fornication. (Rev. xvii.)

Yet, blessed be God, the Father of our Lord Jesus Christ, who hath given unto you a manly courage, and hath so strengthened you in the inward man, by the power of his Spirit, that you can contemn, as well all the terrors, as also the vain flattering allurements of the world, esteeming them as vanities, mere trifles, and things of nought. Who hath also wrought, planted, and surely stablished in your hearts so steadfast a faith and love of our Lord Jesus Christ, joined with such constancy, that, by no engines of antichrist, be they ever so terrible or plausible, you will suffer any other Jesus or any other Christ to be forced upon you besides him whom the prophets have spoken of before, the apostles have preached, and the holy martyrs of God have confessed and testified with the effusion of their blood.

In this faith stand fast, my brethren, and suffer not yourselves to be brought under the yoke of bondage and superstition any more. For you know, brethren, how that our Saviour warned his disciples beforehand, that such should come as would point unto the world another Christ, and would set him out with so many false miracles, and with such deceivable and subtle practices, that even the very elect, if it were possible, should be thereby deceived: such strong delusions to come, did our Saviour give warning of before. But continue faithful and constant, and be of good comfort, and remember, that our grand Captain hath overcome the world; for he that is in us, is stronger than he that is in the world, and the Lord promises unto us, that for the elect's sake the days of wickedness shall be shortened.

In the mean season abide and endure with patience, as you have begun—endure, I say, and "reserve yourselves unto better times," as one of the heathen poets said. Cease not to show yourselves valiant soldiers of the Lord, and help to maintain the travailing faith of the gospel. Ye have need of patience, that after ye have done the will of God, ye may receive the promises. "For yet a very little while, and he that shall come will come, and will not tarry," and "the just shall live by faith; but if any withdraw himself, my soul shall have no pleasure in him, saith the Lord. But we are not of them which withdraw ourselves unto damnation, but believe unto the salvation of the soul."

Let us not suffer these words of Christ to fall out of our

hearts by any manner of terrors or threatenings of the world: "Fear not them which kill the body," the rest ye know. For I write not unto you, as to men who are ignorant of the truth, but as those who know the truth, and to this end only, that we, agreeing together in one faith, may take comfort one of another, and be the more confirmed and strengthened thereby. We never had a better or more just cause either to contemn our life, or to shed our blood: we cannot take in hand the defence of a more certain, clear, and manifest truth. For it is not any ceremony for which we contend, but it touches the very substance of our whole religion, yea, even Christ himself.

Shall we, or can we, receive and acknowledge any other Christ, instead of him who alone is the everlasting Son of the everlasting Father, and is the brightness of the glory, and lively image of the substance of the Father, in whom only dwelleth corporeally the fulness of the Godhead, who is the only way, the truth, and the life? Let such wickedness, my brethren, let such horrible wickedness be far from us. "For although there be that are called gods, whether in heaven, or in earth, as there are many gods and many lords, yet unto us there is but one God, who is the Father, of whom are all things, and we in him; and one Lord, Jesus Christ, by whom are all things, and we by him:" but every man hath not knowledge. "This is life eternal," saith St. John, "that they know thee to be the only true God, and Jesus Christ, whom thou hast sent." If any, therefore, would force upon us any other god besides him whom Paul and the apostles have taught, let us not hear him, but let us flee from him, and hold him accursed.

Brethren, ye are not ignorant of the deep and profound subtleties of satan, for he will not cease to rage about you, seeking by all possible means whom he may devour; but play the men, and be of good comfort in the Lord. And although your enemies and the adversaries of the truth set upon you, armed with all worldly force and power that may be; yet be not ye faint-hearted, nor shrink therefore; but trust unto your captain Christ, trust unto the Spirit of truth, and trust unto the truth of your cause, which, as it may by the malice of satan be darkened, so it can never be wholly put out. For we have (high praise be given to God therefore) most plainly, evidently and clearly on our side, all the prophets, all the apostles, and, undoubtedly, all the ancient ecclesiastical writers which have written until of late years past.

Let us be hearty and of good courage, therefore, and throughly comfort ourselves in the Lord. "Be in nowise afraid of your adversaries, for that which is to them an occasion of perdition, is to you a sure token of salvation, and that of God. For unto you it is given, that not only ye should believe on him, but also suffer for his sake." And when you are railed upon for the name of Christ, remember that by the voice of Peter, yea, and of Christ our Saviour also, you are counted with the prophets, with the apostles, and with the holy martyrs of Christ, happy and blessed therefore: "for the glory and Spirit of God resteth upon you. On their part our Saviour Christ is evil spoken of, but on your part he is glorified."

For what else can they do unto you by persecuting you, and working all cruelty and villany against you, but make your crowns more glorious, yea, beautify and multiply the same, and heap upon themselves the horrible plagues and heavy wrath of God? And, therefore, good brethren, though they rage ever so fiercely against us, yet let us not wish evil unto them again, knowing, that whilst for Christ's cause they vex and persecute us, they are like madmen, most outrageous and cruel against themselves, heaping hot burning coals upon their own heads; but rather let us wish well unto them, knowing that we are thereunto called in Jesus Christ, that we should be heirs of the blessing.

Let us pray, therefore, unto God, that he would drive out of their hearts this darkness of error, and make the light of his truth to shine unto them, that they, acknowledging their blindness, may with all humble repentance be converted unto the Lord, and together with us confess him to be the only true God, who is the Father of light, and his only Son Christ Jesus, worshipping him in spirit and verity. Amen.

The Spirit of our Lord Jesus Christ comfort your hearts in the love of God and patience of Christ. Amen.

Your brother in the Lord, whose name this bearer shall signify unto you, ready always by the grace of God to live and die with you.

LETTER VII.

To the brethren which constantly cleave unto Christ in suffering affliction with him and for his sake.

GRACE and peace from God the Father and from our Lord Jesus Christ be multiplied unto you. Amen.

Although, brethren, we have of late heard nothing from you, neither have at this present any news to send you: yet we thought good to write something unto you, whereby you might understand that we have good remembrance of you continually, as we doubt not but you have of us also. When this messenger, coming unto us from you of late, had brought us good tidings of your great constancy, fortitude, and patience in the Lord, we were filled with much joy and gladness; giving thanks to God the Father, through our Lord Jesus Christ, who hath caused his face so to shine upon you, and with the light of spiritual understanding hath so lightened your hearts, that now, being in captivity and bonds for Christ's cause, you have not ceased, as much as in you lieth, by words, but much more by deeds and by your example, to establish and confirm that which, when you were at liberty in the world, you laboured to publish and set abroad by the word and doctrine: that is to say, " holding fast the word of life, you shine as lights in the world in the midst of a wicked and crooked nation;" and that with so much the greater glory of our Lord Jesus Christ, and profit of your brethren, by how much more cruelly satan now rages, and busily labours to darken the light of the gospel.

And as for the darkness that satan now brings upon the church of England, who needs to doubt thereof? Of late time our Saviour Christ, his apostles, prophets, and teachers, spake in the temple to the people of England in the English tongue, so that they might be understood plainly, and without any hardness, by the godly and such as sought for heavenly knowledge in matters, which of necessity of salvation pertained to the obtaining of eternal life. But now those things, which once were written of them for the edifying of the congregation, are read in a strange tongue without interpretation, manifestly against St. Paul's commandment, so that there is no man able to understand them who has not learned that strange and unknown tongue.

Of late days those heavenly mysteries, whereby Christ hath engrafted us into his body, and hath united us one to another,—whereby also, being regenerate and born anew unto God, he hath nourished, increased, and strengthened us,—whereby, moreover, either he hath taught and set forth an order amongst them, which are whole, or else to the sick in soul or body, hath given, as it were, wholesome medicines and remedies: those, I say, were all plainly set forth to the people in their own language, so that what great and exceeding good things every man had received of God ;—what duty every one owed to another by God's ordinance ;—what every one had professed in his vocation, and was bound to observe ; where remedy was to be had for the weak and feeble : he to whom God hath given a desire, and a heart willing to understand those things, might soon perceive and understand. But now all these things are taught and set forth so that the people, redeemed with Christ's blood, and for whose sake they were by Christ himself ordained, can have no manner of understanding thereof at all.

Of late, as we know not how to pray as we ought, our Lord Jesus Christ in his prayer, whereof he would have no man ignorant, and also the Holy Ghost in the psalms, hymns, and spiritual songs, which are set forth in the Bible, did teach and instruct all the people of England in the English tongue, that they might ask such things as are according to the will of the Father, and might join their hearts and lips in prayer together. But now all these things are commanded to be hid and shut up from them in a strange tongue; whereby it must needs follow, that the people neither can tell how to pray, nor what to pray for : and how can they join their hearts and voices together, when they understand no more what the voice signifies, than a brute beast ?

Finally, I here say, that the catechism, which was lately set forth in the English tongue, is now in every pulpit condemned. Oh! devilish malice, and most spitefully injurious to the salvation of mankind purchased by Jesus Christ. Indeed satan could not long suffer that such great light should be spread abroad in the world ; he saw well enough that nothing was able to overthrow his kingdom so much, as if children, being godly instructed in religion, should learn to know Christ while they are yet young; whereby not only children, but the elder sort also and aged folks, that before were not taught to know Christ in their childhood, should now, even with children and babes, be forced to learn to know him. Now, therefore, he roars, now he rages.

But what else do they, brethren, who serve satan, and become his ministers and slaves in maintaining his impiety, but even the same which they did, to whom Christ our Saviour threatens this curse in the gospel: " Woe unto you, which shut up the kingdom of heaven before men, and take away the key of knowledge from them; ye yourselves have not entered in, neither have you suffered them that would enter, to come in."

And from whence shall we say, brethren, that this horrible and mischievous darkness proceeds, which is now brought into the world? From whence, I pray you, but even from the smoke of the great furnace of the bottomless pit, so that the sun and the air are now darkened by the smoke of the pit? Now, even now, out of doubt, brethren, the pit is opened amongst us, and the locusts begin to swarm, and Abaddon now reigneth.

Ye, therefore, my brethren, who pertain unto Christ, and have the seal of God marked in your foreheads, that is, who are sealed with the earnest of his Spirit to be a peculiar people of God, quit yourselves like men, and be strong; " For He that is in us, is stronger than he which is in the world; and you know that all that is born of God overcometh the world; and this is the victory that overcometh the world, even our faith."

Let the world fret, let it rage ever so much, be it ever so cruel and bloody, yet be sure, that no man can take us out of the Father's hands, for he is greater than all; who " hath not spared his own Son, but hath given him to death for us all; and, therefore, how shall he not with him give us all things also? Who shall lay any thing to the charge of God's elect? It is God that justifieth, who then shall condemn? It is Christ that is dead, yea, rather that is risen again, who is also at the right hand of God, and maketh request also for us. Who shall separate us from the love of Christ? Shall tribulation, or anguish, or persecution, or famine, or nakedness, or peril, or sword?" The rest you know, brethren; we are certainly persuaded with St. Paul, by the grace of our

Lord Jesus Christ, that no kind of thing shall be able to separate us from the love of God which is in Christ Jesus our Lord.

Which, that it may come to pass by the grace and mercy of our Lord Jesus Christ, to the comfort both of you and of us all, as we, for our parts, will continually, God willing, pray for you: so, dear brethren in the Lord, with all earnest and hearty request, we beseech you, even in the bowels of our Lord Jesus Christ, that you will not cease to pray for us. Fare you well, dear brethren. The grace of our Lord Jesus Christ be with you all evermore Amen.   Yours in the Lord,
                                                           NICHOLAS RIDLEY.

LETTER VIII.

To Augustine Bernher.

BROTHER AUSTIN, where you desire so earnestly to know my mind of that part of the husband's letter unto his wife, wherein he permits her " to do as she may, when she cannot do what she would," giving this reason, " that she must keep her religion as she may, in this realm, and God shall accept her will, and shall impute the fault to others:" also saying, " What blame is in her, if she use the religion here as she may, though it be not as she would?"—this seemeth to me to be a perilous saying, wherein I fear the man tendereth his wife too much. I wish rather that he had counselled her to depart the realm: for peradventure, she tarrying, to have bidden her openly and boldly, when she should have been commanded to follow ungodliness—to have bidden her, I say, there and then to have confessed the truth, and to have stood in it— he thought, and peradventure knew, was more than she was likely to do. But I suppose, if she had more deeply considered her husband's mind in this writing—that his counsel savoured of a too tender zeal towards her, rather than' contempt of all worldly and carnal affections, which ought to be in Christ's cause; and upon the same had required license to depart the realm; yea, and then had departed indeed, rather than, after certain knowledge had of their ungodly ways, to seem to allow the same by her open acts, and so not to have followed her husband's former counsel.—I think she would thus have offended her husband less than she doth now, in that she hath made his letter (not so warily written, methinks, as I would have wished it had been) if she did so, to come to the knowledge of those who will use it, and construe it to the worst, to the defence and maintenance of ungodly ways.

NICHOLAS RIDLEY.

LETTER IX.

To Master Bradford.

DEARLY beloved, I wish you grace, mercy, and peace. According to your mind I have run over all your papers,* and what I have done, which is but small, therein may appear. . Sir, what shall be best done with these things, now you must consider: for if they come in sight at this time, undoubtedly they must to the fire with their father; and as for any safeguard that your custody can be unto them, I am sure you look not for it: for as you have been partner of the work, so I am sure you look for none other, but to have and receive like wages, and to drink of the same cup.

Blessed be God, who hath given you liberty in the mean season, that you may use your pen to his glory, and to the comfort, as I hear say, of many. I bless God daily in you and all your whole company, to whom I beseech you to commend me heartily. Now I love my countryman in deed and in truth, I mean Dr. Taylor, not now for my earthly country's sake, but for our heavenly Father's sake, whom I heard say, he did so stoutly in time of peril confess. And yet also now for our country's sake and for all our mother's sake—but I mean the kingdom of heaven, and the heavenly Jerusalem—and because of the Spirit which bringeth forth in him, in you, and in your company, such blessed fruits of boldness in the Lord's cause, of patience, and constancy. The Lord, who hath begun this work in you all, perform and perfect this his own deed, until his own day come. Amen.

* This was a treatise of the Communion, with other things, which M. Bradford sent him to peruse, and to give his judgment thereof. *Letters of the Martyrs.*

I perceive you have not been baited as yet, and the cause thereof God knoweth, who will let them do no more to his, than is his blessed will and good pleasure to suffer them to do for his own glory, and to the profit of those who are truly his. For the Father, who guides them that are Christ's to Christ, is more mighty than all they, and no man is able to pull them out of the Father's hands—except, I say, it please our Father, it please our Master Christ, to suffer them, they shall not be able to stir one hair of your head.

My brother P., the bearer hereof, would, that we should say what we think good concerning your mind: that is, not to answer, except you might have somewhat indifferent judges. We are, as you know, separated, and one of us cannot in any thing consult with another, and much strait watching of the bailiffs is about us, that there be no private conference amongst us. And yet, as we hear, the scholars bear us more heavily than the townsmen. A wonderful thing, among so many, never yet scholar offered to any of us, so far as I know, any manner of favour, either for or in Christ's cause.

Now as concerning your demand of our counsel, for my part, I do not mislike that, which I perceive you are minded to do: for I look for none other, but if you answer before the same commissioners that we did, you shall be served and handled as we were, though you were as well learned as either Peter or Paul. And yet further, I think that occasion afterward may be given you, and the consideration of the profit of your auditory may perchance move you to do otherwise. Finally, determinately to say what shall be best, I am not able: but I trust He, whose cause you have in hand, will put you in mind to do that which shall be most for his glory, the profit of his flock, and your own salvation.

This letter must be common to you and master Hooper, in whom and in his prison-fellow good father Crome, I bless God, even from the bottom of my heart: for I doubt not, but they both do to our Master Christ, true, acceptable, and honourable service, and profitable to his flock, the one with his pen, and the other with his fatherly example of patience and constancy, and all manner of true godliness.

But why should I say to you, let this be common among your brethren? Among whom, I dare say, it is with you as it is with us, to whom all things here are common: meat, money, and whatsoever one of us hath that can, or may do, any other good. Although, as I said, the bailiffs and our hosts straitly watch us, that we have no conference or intelligence of any thing abroad, yet God has provided for every one of us in the stead of our servants, faithful fellows, who will be content to hear and see, and to do for us, whatsoever they can. It is God's work surely, blessed be God for his unspeakable goodness! The grace of our Lord Jesus Christ, and the love of God, and the communion of the Holy Ghost, be with you all. Amen, Amen.

As far as London is from Oxford, yet thence we have received of late both meat, money, and shirts, not only from such as are of our acquaintance, but of some whom this bearer can tell, with whom I had never, to my knowledge, any acquaintance. I know for whose sake they do it; to Him, therefore, be all honour, glory, and due thanks; and yet, I pray you, do so much as to show them that we have received their benevolence, and, God be blessed! have plenty of all such things. This I desire you to do, for I know they are of master Hooper and your familiar acquaintance. Master Latimer was crazed;* but I hear now, thanks be to God, that he amendeth again.

Yours in Christ,
NICHOLAS RIDLEY.

LETTER X.

To Master Bradford.

BROTHER BRADFORD, I wish you and your company in Christ, yea, and all the holy brotherhood, that now with you in divers prisons suffer and bear patiently Christ's cross for the maintenance of his gospel; grace, mercy, and peace from God the Father, and from our Lord Jesus Christ.

Sir, considering the state of this chivalry and warfare, wherein, I doubt not, but we are set to fight under Christ's banner and his cross, against our spiritual enemy, the devil and the old serpent, satan; methinks I perceive two things to be his most perilous and most dangerous engines,

* Feeble and unwell.

which he hath to impugn Christ's verity, his gospel, his faith: and the same two also are the most massy posts and most mighty pillars, whereby he maintains and upholds his satanical synagogue.

These two, Sir, they are in my judgment—the one is false doctrine and idolatrous use of the Lord's supper; and the other, the wicked and abominable usurpation of the primacy of the see of Rome. By these two, satan seems to me principally to maintain and uphold his kingdom: by these two, he drives down mightily, alas! I fear me, the third part of the stars in heaven. These two poisonful rotten posts he has so painted over with such a pretence and colour of religion, of unity in Christ's church, of the catholic faith and such like, that the wily serpent is able to deceive, if it were possible, even the elect of God.

Wherefore, John said not without great cause, If any know not satan's subtleties and the dangers thereof, I will wish him no other burden to be laden withal. Sir, because these are his principal and main posts, whereupon stand all his falsehood, craft, and treachery, therefore, according to the poor power that God has given me, I have bent my artillery to shoot at the same. I know it is but little, God knows, that I can do, and my shot I know they value not. Yet will I not, God willing, cease to do the best that I can, to shake those cankered and rotten posts. The Lord grant me good success, to the glory of his name and the furtherance of Christ's gospel. I have now already, I thank God for this present time, spent a good part of my powder in this scribbling, whereof this bearer shall give you knowledge. Good brother Bradford, let the wicked surmise and say what they list, know you for a certainty by God's grace, without all doubt, that in Christ's gospel's cause, against and upon the foresaid God's enemies, I am fully determined to live and die. Farewell, dear brother, and I beseech you, with all the rest of our brethren, to have good remembrance of the condemned heretics, as they call them, of Oxford, in your prayers. The bearer shall certify you of our state. Farewell in the Lord.

From Bocardo.

Yours in Christ,
N. RIDLEY.[*]

---

[*] For the answer to this letter, see Bradford's Letters. Ridley wrote as follows in reply

LETTER XI.
To Master Bradford.

Dearly beloved brother, blessed be God, our heavenly Father, for his manifold and innumerable mercies towards us; and blessed be he that he has spared us thus long together, that each one of us may bless his mercy and clemency in the other, unto this day, above the expectation and hope of any worldly appearance.

Whereas you write of the outrageous rule, that satan, our ghostly enemy, beareth abroad in the world, whereby he stirs up and raises pestilent and heinous heresies, as some to deny the blessed Trinity, some the Divinity of our Saviour Christ, some the Divinity of the Holy Ghost, some the baptism of infants, some original sin, and to be infected with the error of the Pelagians, and to rebaptize those that have been baptized with Christ's baptism already.* Alas! sir, this declares this present time and these days to be wicked indeed. But what else can we look for of satan here and of his ministers, but to do the worst that they can, so far as God shall or will suffer them? And now methinks he is less to be marvelled at in this time, if he bestir himself by all manner of means, that the truth indeed should not take place. For he sees now, blessed be God! that some go about in deed and in truth, not trifling, but, with the loss of all that they are able to lose in this world, goods, lands, name, fame, and life also, to set forth God's word and his truth; and by God's grace shall do, and abide in the same unto the end: now, therefore, it is time to bestir him, I trow.

And as for diversities of errors, what cares he, though one be ever so contrary to another? He reckons all, and so he may, to be his, whosoever prevails, so that truth prevail not. Nevertheless, good brother, I suppose that the universal plague is most dangerous, which at this day is, alas! fostered and masterfully holden up by wit,† worldly policy, multitude of people, power, and all worldly means.

As for others, the devil's galtrops,‡ that he casts in our ways, by some of his busy-headed younkers, I trust they will never be able to do the multitude great harm. For,

---

* The modern reader will observe that the opinions concerning baptism here noticed, do not involve the denial of the doctrines of the Trinity, and others of like importance, referred to in this sentence.—

† Human understanding.

‡ Or, caltrops, instruments made with three spikes, and scattered in front of an army to wound the horses' feet.

blessed be God, these heresies beforetime, when satan by his servants has been about to broach them, have, by God's servants, already, been so sharply and truly confounded, that the multitude was never infected with them, or else, where they have been infected, they are healed again, so that now the peril is not so great.

And where you say, that if your request had been heard, things, you think, had been in better case than they are: know you, that concerning the matter* you mean, I have in Latin drawn out the places of the scriptures, and upon the same have noted what I can for the time. Sir, in those matters I am so fearful, that I dare not speak further, yea, almost none otherwise than the very text does, as it were, lead me by the hand. And where you exhort us to help &c. O Lord, what is else in this world that we now should list to do? I bless my Lord God, I never, as methinks, had more or better leisure to be occupied with my pen in such things as I can do to set forth God's glory, when they may come to light. And I bless my Lord God through Jesus Christ, my heart and my work are therein occupied, not so fully and perfectly as I would, but yet so that I bless God for the same.

Farewell, dear brother; the messenger tarries, and I may not now be longer with you. The Lord, I trust, verily shall bring us thither, where we shall, each one with the other in Christ our Saviour, rejoice, and be glad everlastingly.

Your brother in Christ,
N. RIDLEY.

LETTER XII.

To Master Bradford, prisoner in the King's Bench.

WELL-BELOVED in Christ our Saviour, we all with one heart wish you, with all those that love God in deed and truth, grace and health; and especially to our dearly beloved companions which are in Christ's cause, and the cause both of their brethren, and of their own salvation,

---

* He meaneth here the matter of the election, whereof he afterward wrote a godly and comfortable treatise.—*Letters of the Martyrs.*

Gloucester Ridley says, "In the Martyrs' Letters we are told by Coverdale, that on this occasion Doctor Ridley wrote a treatise of election and predestination, which was in the hands of some person at that time, and he hoped would hereafter come to light; but I never heard that it was published, nor have I been able to meet with it in MS." The great learning and cool judgment of this prelate, and the entire subjection of his imagination to the revealed will of God, make the loss of this treatise much to be lamented.

ready and willing to put their neck under the yoke of
Christ's cross. How joyful it was for us to hear the report of Dr. Taylor, and of his godly confession, &c., I
assure you, it is hard for me to express. Blessed be God,
who was and is the giver of that and all godly strength
and stomach in the time of adversity!

As for the rumours that have, or do go abroad, either
of our relenting or massing,* we trust, that those who
know God and their duty towards their brethren in Christ,
will not be too light of credit to believe them. It is not
the slanderer's evil tongue, but a man's own evil deed, that
can before God defile a man; and, therefore, by God's
grace, you shall never have cause to do otherwise than
you say you do; that is, not to doubt but that we will continue steadfast. The like rumour as you have heard of our
coming to London, has been here spread of the coming of
certain learned men, prisoners, hither from London; but
as yet we know no certainty which of those rumours is, or
shall be, the more true.

Know you, that we have you in our daily remembrance,
and wish you and all the rest of our foresaid companions,
well in Christ. It would do us much comfort if we might
have knowledge of the state of the rest of our most dearly
beloved, which in this troublesome time do stand in
Christ's cause, and in the defence of the truth thereof.
We are in good health, thanks be to God; and yet the
manner of our being treated doth change, as sour ale
doth in summer. It is reported to us by our keepers, that
the university beareth us heavily. A coal chanced to fall
in the night out of the chimney, and burnt a hole in the
floor, and no more harm was done, the bailiffs' servant
sitting by the fire. Another night, there chanced a
drunken fellow to multiply words, and for the same he was
sent to Bocardo.†

Upon these things, as is reported, there is risen a rumour in the town and country about, that we would have
broken the prison with such violence, as, if the bailiffs had
not played the pretty men,‡ we should have made an
escape. We had out of our prison a wall that we might
have walked upon, and our servants had liberty to go

* Recanting or going to mass.
† A filthy prison at Oxford for drunkards, harlots, and the vilest
sort of people.—*Letters of the Martyrs.* Cranmer, Ridley, and
Latimer were then confined in that abominable prison.
‡ Been very active and courageous.

abroad in the town or fields; but now both they and we are restrained from both.

The bishop of Worcester passed through Oxford, but he did not visit us.* The same day our restraint began to be more strict, and the book of the communion was taken from us by the bailiffs, at the mayor's commandment. No man is licensed to come unto us; before they might, that would, see us upon the wall; but that is so grudged at, and so evil reported, that we are now restrained.

Sir, blessed be God, with all our evil reports, grudgings, and restraints, we are joyful in God; and all our care is, and shall be, by God's grace, to please and serve him, of whom we look and hope, after these temporal and momentary miseries, to have eternal joy and perpetual felicity, with Abraham, Isaac, and Jacob, Peter and Paul, and all the blessed company of the angels in heaven, through Jesus Christ our Lord.

As yet, there never was any learned man, or any scholar, or other, that visited us, since we came unto Bocardo, which now in Oxford may be called a college of quondams;† for, as you know, we are no fewer here than three, and I dare say, every one well contented with his portion, which I do reckon to be our heavenly Father's gracious and fatherly good gift.

Thus fare you well. We shall with God's grace one day meet together and be joyful; the day assuredly approaches apace; the Lord grant that it may come shortly; for before that day come, I fear me, the world will wax worse and worse: but then all our enemies shall be overthrown and trodden under foot; righteousness and truth then shall have the victory and bear away the bell; whereof the Lord grant us to be partakers, and all that sincerely love the truth.

We all pray you, as you can, to cause all our commendations to be made to all such as you know visited us and you, when we were in the tower, with their friendly remembrances and benefits. Mistress Wilkinson and Mistress Warcup have not forgotten us, but even since we came into Bocardo have comforted us with their charitable and friendly benevolence: not that else we lack, for God be

---

* Bishop Heath. When he was in trouble in king Edward's reign, Ridley had received him in his house for a year and a half, and had treated him with much kindness.

† Those who had formerly been in authority and respected.

blessed who hitherto hath ever provided sufficiently for us: but it is a great comfort, and an occasion for us to bless God, when we see that he makes them so friendly to tender us, whom some of us were never familiarly acquainted with.

Yours in Christ,

N. RIDLEY.

LETTER XIII.

To bishop Cranmer and bishop Latimer, being separated from him, and prisoners in separate places.

THE cause of my brother's* imprisonment is this, so far as I can perceive There is a young man called Master Grimbold, who was my chaplain, a preacher and a man of much eloquence both in the English and also in the Latin. This man, desiring copies of all things which I had written and done since the beginning of mine imprisonment, my brother, as is said, hath sent copies of all things that I have done. First, a little treatise which Master Latimer and I wrote in the tower, where is, before my sayings N. R., and before Master Latimer's H. L. Also, another draft which I drew out of the evangelists and of St. Paul, that the words of the Lord's Supper are figuratively to be understood, alleging out of the doctors only six; three of the Greek church, which are Origen, Chrysostom, and Theodoret, and three of the Latin church, Tertullian, Augustine, and Gelasius.† He had of my brother also, a copy of my three positions to the three questions here propounded to us at Oxford; then also a copy of my Disputation in the Schools, as I wrote it myself after the Disputation. Also, of the Letter to the brethren in different prisons.

All these things they have gotten from Grimbold, as my brother doth suppose, not that Grimbold hath betrayed him, but as is supposed, one whom my brother trusted to carry his letters unto Grimbold. But it will not sink into my head to think that Grimbold would ever play me such a Judas' part. Although these things are chanced far otherwise than I had thought they should; for my mind was

---

* Master Shipside. Grimbold had obtained some copies of Ridley's writings from him. See note, p. 204.

† This was Ridley's treatise upon the Lord's Supper.

that they should not have come abroad until my body had been laid to rest in peace, yet truly I suppose this is not thus chanced without God's gracious providence which he hath over all his; and I trust that God of his goodness shall turn it to his own glory. For it shall evidently show to the reader of these things which they have, that the cause why I do dissent from the Romish religion is not any study of vain glory or of singularity, but of conscience, of my bounden duty towards God, and towards Christ's church, and the salvation of mine own soul; for which, by God's grace, I will willingly jeopard here to lose life, lands and goods, name and fame, and what else is or can be pleasant unto me in this world.

My brother, as yet, because they neither showed any commission or authority whereby they examined him, nor any thing of his letters, although they said they had them —as yet, I say, my brother hath confessed nothing; but I look for none other but he shall be forced to tell where he had the copies and where they are, and I will be content that he shall say the truth, that he had them all of me, let them come and take them and cast them into the fire; if God know they will promote his glory, they can do no more than he will suffer them.

Because in the book of N. R. and H. L. it is said in the end that H. L. hath caused his servant to write it, I would Austin should have word, if any further search be made, to keep himself out of the way.

God shall reward you both for my brother, you my lord of Canterbury for your meat and daily comfort, and you father L. for your money and comfortable messages. I trust in God that my brother, though he be young, yet will study to learn to bear Christ's cross patiently as a young scholar in Christ's school: God increase his grace in us all. Amen.

LETTER XIV.

To *Augustine Bernher*.

BROTHER AUSTIN. I thank you for your manifold kindness. I have received my lady grace's* alms, six

---

* Katherine, duchess of Suffolk. Bernher travelled from one place to another, secretly conveying messages or assistance to or from those who were imprisoned for the faith.

royalles,* six shillings and eightpence. I have written a letter unto her grace, but I have made no mention thereof, wherefore I desire you to render to her grace hearty thanks. Blessed be God, as for myself I want nothing, but my lady's alms come happily to relieve my poor brother's necessity whom you know they have cast and kept in prison, as I suppose you know the cause why.

Farewell, brother Austin, and take good heed, I pray you, and let my brother's case make you the more wary. Read my letter to my lady's grace. I would Mistress Wilkinson and Mistress Warcup had a copy of it; for although the letter is directed to my lady's grace alone, yet the matter thereof pertains equally to her grace, and to all good women that love God and his word, in deed and truth.

Yours in Christ,
N. RIDLEY.

LETTER XV.

To Augustine Bernher, then servant to bishop Latimer, and now a faithful minister in Christ's church; to whom, because he might not come to the prison to speak with bishop Ridley, he wrote as followeth.

BROTHER AUSTIN, you are heartily welcome to Oxford again; you have made good speed indeed, and blessed be God for his gracious goodness that all is well with you. That our dearly beloved brethren in Christ are all in good comfort, hearty in Christ's cause, and stand steadfast in the confession of his true doctrine, rejoices, I assure you, my heart in God to hear of it.

This day was doctor Croke with me, and both he and Mistress Irish, mine hostess, told me that Master Hooper 's hanged, drawn, and quartered for treason; but I did not believe them, for it is not the first tale that mine hostess hath told me of Master Hooper. And I trust the tidings that were here spread abroad since your departure, that Master Grimbold also should have been arraigned, and condemned for treason to be hanged and quartered, was not true; let me hear if there be any such thing.

* The royal was then worth fifteen shillings.

Not three days ago, there was a private warning given me from a man of God, one Lesley a glover, that we prisoners here, all three, should be shortly and suddenly conveyed into three several colleges; for what purpose and how to be ordered God knoweth. At which time, and at the earnest request of that forenamed man of God, I delivered unto him some of the things I had in hand to write out; what they are you shall know of him. Besides the things which he hath, I have some things else, which, if it please God, I would wish might come to light, if perchance any thereby might receive the light to love the truth the better, and to abhor the falsehood of antichrist.

I have written annotations upon the first book of Tonstal* more at large, but upon the second more sparingly. I would wish they might be transcribed, lest perhaps they, with me, may soon be made food for the fire.

I have also many things, but confusedly set together, of the abominable usurpation, pride, arrogance, and wickedness of the see and bishop of Rome, and altogether in Latin. If those things were written out, I would wish that Master Bradford would take them, and translate and order them as he should think might best help to open the eyes of the simple, for to see the wickedness of the synagogue of satan. But that at your last being here you cast cold water upon mine affection towards Grimbold, else methinks I could appoint where he might occupy himself to his own profit in learning which he liketh, and in no small profit which might ensue to the church of Christ in England; as, if he would take in hand to interpret Laurentius Valla, who, as he knows, is a man of singular eloquence, and his book I mean, which he made and wrote against that false feigned fable forged of Constantinus the great, and his donation and glorious exaltation of the see of Rome. And when he hath done that, let him translate a work of Eneas Sylvius, of the acts of the Council of Basle. In the which, although there are many things that savour of the pan,† and also he himself was afterwards a bishop of Rome; yet, I dare say, the papists would glory but little to see such books go forth in

---

* Bishop of Durham—his work on the Eucharist.
† Somewhat defend persecution.

English. If you will know where to have these books or treatises, you may have them both together, and many like treatises which point out the wickedness of the see of Rome, in a book set forth by a papist, called Ortuinus Gratius, entitled " Fasciculus rerum expetendarum et fugiendarum." In that book you shall find the confession of the Waldensian brethren, men of much more learning, godliness, soberness, and understanding in God's word, than I should have thought them to have been in that time, before I read their works. If such things had been set forth in our English tongue heretofore, I suppose, that surely great good might have come to Christ's church thereby.

To my good lady's grace,* and to my lady Vane, what thanks can I give, but desire almighty God to lighten, comfort, and strengthen them evermore in his ways? The other two whom you mention, I know not; but the Lord knoweth them, to whom in them all, and for all their kindness, I give most hearty thanks. Master Bradford desires that thanks should be rendered unto you for your comfortable aid, wherewith you comfort him, but you must tell him that he must bid them thank you for him, who are not bound to thank you for themselves; and if he do so, then, I think, all we prisoners of Oxford shall so stop his mouth.

Brother Austin, you for our comfort do run up and down, and who beareth your charges God knoweth. I know you must needs in so doing take much pains: I pray you take this poor token of my good will towards your charges.

Written January, 1555.

LETTER XVI.

To bishop Hooper

To my most dear brother and reverend fellow-elder in Christ, John Hooper, grace and peace.

My dearly beloved brother and fellow-elder, whom I **reverence** in the Lord, pardon me, I beseech you, that

---

* The duchess of Suffolk.

hitherto, since your captivity and mine, I have not saluted you by my letters; whereas, I do, indeed, confess, that I have received from you, such was your gentleness, two letters at sundry times; but yet, at such times as I could not be suffered to write to you again, or, if I might have written, yet I was greatly in doubt lest my letters should not safely come unto your hands.

But now, my dear brother, as I understand by your works,* which I have yet but superficially seen, that we thoroughly agree, and wholly consent together, in those things which are the grounds and substantial points of our religion, against which the world so furiously rages in these our days, howsoever, in times past, in smaller matters and circumstances of religion, your wisdom and my simplicity, I confess, have in some points varied.† Now, I say, be you assured, that even with my whole heart, God is my witness, in the bowels of Christ, I love you, and in truth for the truth's sake, which abideth in us, and, as I am persuaded, shall, by the grace of God, abide with us for evermore.

And because the world, as I perceive, brother, ceases not to play his pageant, and busily conspires against Christ our Saviour, with all possible force and power, exalting high things against the knowledge of God; let us join hands together in Christ, and if we cannot overthrow, yet to our power, and as much as in us lies, let us shake those high things, not with carnal, but with spiritual weapons. And, likewise, brother, let us prepare ourselves to the day of our dissolution, whereby, after the short time of this bodily affliction, by the grace of our Lord Jesus Christ, we shall triumph together with him in eternal glory.

I pray you, brother, salute in my name that reverend father, your fellow prisoner, Doctor Crome, by whom, since the first day that I have heard of his most godly and fatherly constancy in confessing the truth of the gospel, I have conceived great consolation and joy in the Lord. For the integrity and uprightness, the gravity and innocency, of that man, all England, I think, hath known long

---

* These were some treatises written by Hooper while in prison.
† This alludes to some difference of opinion which had subsisted between them, respecting the form and mode of consecration to the episcopal office, and which at one time arose to a painful height; but this letter shows that they were now reconciled.

ago. Blessed be God, therefore, who, in such abundance of iniquity, and decay of all godliness, hath given unto us, in his reverend old age, such a witness for the truth of his gospel. Miserable and hard-hearted is he, whom the godliness and constant confession of so worthy, so grave, and innocent a man, will not move to acknowledge and confess the truth of God.

I do not now, brother, require you to write any thing to me again, for I stand much in fear lest your letters should be intercepted before they can come to my hands. Nevertheless, know you, that it shall be great joy to me to hear of your constancy and fortitude in the Lord's quarrel. And although I have not hitherto written unto you, yet have I twice, as I could, sent unto you my mind touching the matter which in your letters you required to know, neither yet, brother, can I be otherwise persuaded. I see, methinks, many perils, whereby I am earnestly moved to counsel you not to hasten the publishing of your works, especially under the title of your own name. For I fear greatly, lest by this occasion your mouth should be stopped hereafter, and all things taken away from the rest of the prisoners, whereby otherwise, if it so pleased God, they may be able to do good to many. Farewell in the Lord, my most dear brother, and if there are any more in prison with you, for Christ's cause, I beseech you, as you may, salute them in my name; to whose prayers I do most humbly and heartily commend myself and my fellow-prisoners, concaptives in the Lord. And yet once again, and for ever in Christ, my most dear brother, farewell.

NICHOLAS RIDLEY.

LETTER XVII.

To Master Bradford.

BROTHER BRADFORD, I wish you grace, mercy, and peace in Christ our Saviour, and to all those who are with you or any where else, captives in Christ; and it heartily rejoices us to hear, that you are all in good health, and stand constantly in the confession of Christ's gospel. Know you, likewise, that we all here are, thanks be to God, in good health and comfort, watching with our lamps lighted, I trust in God, when it shall please our Master, the Bridegroom, to call us to wait upon him unto the marriage.

Now, we suppose, the day approaches apace, for we hear that the parliament is dissolved. The burgesses of Oxford are come home, and other news we hear not, but that the king* is made protector to the prince to be born, and that the bishops have full authority, *ex officio*, to inquire of heresies. Before the parliament began, it was rumoured here, that certain from the convocation-house were appointed, yea, ready to have come to Oxford, and then there was spied out one thing to lack, for want of a law to perform their intent. Now, seeing they can want no law, we cannot but look for them shortly: I trust to God's glory, let them come when they will, &c.

Brother Bradford, I marvel greatly of good Austin, where he is, for that I heard say he promised his master to have been here before this time, and he had from me that which I would be loth to lose, yea, to want when time shall be that it might do, nay, help me to do my Lord and Master Christ service. I mean my scribblings, 'Of the abominations of the Romish See and the Romish Pontiffs.' I have no copy of the same, and I look daily to be called to contend with the old serpent; and so I told him, and, I think, you also, by whose means I was more moved to let him have them. I doubt not his fidelity. I pray God he be in health and at liberty; for I have been and am anxious for him.

I have heard that Master Grimbold hath gotten his liberty: if without any blemish of Christ's glory, I am right glad thereof.† My brother-in-law is where he was, that is, in Bocardo, the common jail of the town. I have here written a letter to Master Hooper; I pray you cause it to be written to him again. Commend me to all your fellow-prisoners and our brethren in Christ. If Austin were here, I would have had more to say. The Lord grant that all be well with him, who ever preserves you and all that love our Saviour Christ in sincerity and truth. Amen.

Yours by God's grace in our Master Christ's cause unto

---

* Philip. At that time the birth of a prince was daily expected.

† Grimbold had been one of Ridley's chaplains, but turned to popery, and for some time acted as a spy among those who were in prison for religion.

the stake, and thenceforth, without all danger and peril for ever. I am sure you have heard of our new apparel, and I doubt not but London will talk of it. Sir, know you, that although this seems much thanksworthy to us in our case, yet have we not the apparel that we look for; for this in time will wear, and that which we look for, rightly done on, will endure, and is called robes of immortality.

N. RIDLEY.

LETTER XVIII.

To Master Bradford.

GRACE, peace, and mercy, &c. Although I think it is not yet three days ago since you heard from me, yet having such a messenger and so diversely enforced, I cannot but say something to you. What? shall I thank you for your golden token?* What mean you, man? Do you not know that we have food and clothing from the royal stores? I was so moved with your token, that I commanded it straightway to be taken to Bocardo, which is our common jail. I am right glad of Austin's return, for I was, as I told you, anxious for him. Blessed be God that all is well.

I have seen what he brought from you, and shortly surveyed the whole, but in such celerity, that others also might see the same before Austin's return; so that I noted nothing but a confused sum of the matter; and as yet, what the rest have done I can tell nothing at all, but it was, at the writing hereof, in their hands. To your request and Austin's earnest demand of the same, I have answered him in a brief letter, and he has replied again; but he must go without any further answer from me for this time.† I have told Austin, that I for my part, as I can and may for my slowness and dulness, will think of the matter. We are now so ordered and straitly watched, that our

---

* This token was a piece of gold sent by Bradford to relieve Ridley's brother-in-law Shipside, then prisoner in Bocardo.—*Letters of the Martyrs.*

† He here means Harry Hart, a froward free-will man, who had written a treatise against God's free election, which Bradford sent to Ridley, Cranmer, and Latimer to peruse, desiring Master Ridley to answer the same.—*Letters of the Martyrs.*

servants scarcely dare do any thing for us; so much talk and so many tales, as is said, are told of us abroad. One of us cannot easily nor shortly know the other's mind, and you know I am youngest many ways. Austin's persuasions may do more with me, in what I may do conveniently in this matter, armed with your earnest and zealous letters, than any rhetoric either of Tully or Demosthenes, I assure you thereof.

With us it is said, that Master Grimbold was adjudged to be hanged, drawn, and quartered, of whom we hear now, that he is at liberty. So we heard of late, that Master Hooper was hanged, drawn, and quartered indeed, not for heresy, but for treason; but blessed be God, we hear now that all is true alike. False tongues will not cease to lie, and mischievous hearts to imagine the worst.

Farewell in Christ, and token for token now I send you not; but know this, that, as it is told me, I have two scarlet gowns that escaped, I cannot tell how, in the spoil, whereof you shall have your part. Commend me to all our brethren, and your fellow-prisoners in the Lord.

Yours in Christ
N. Ridley.

LETTER XIX.

*To Master Bradford.**

Oh dear brother, seeing the time is now come wherein it pleases the heavenly Father, for Christ our Saviour's sake, to call upon you, and bid you to come; happy are you, that ever you were born, thus to be awake at the Lord's calling: "Well done, thou good and faithful servant; because thou hast been faithful over a few things, he shall set thee over many; enter thou into the joy of thy Lord."

O! dear brother, what meaneth this, that you are sent into your own native country? The wisdom and policy of the world may mean what it will, but I trust God will so order the matter finally, by his fatherly providence, that some great occasion of God's gracious goodness shall be

* This letter was written in answer to one from Bradford. See his letters.

plenteously poured abroad amongst his, our dear brethren in that country, by this your martyrdom.

Where the martyrs for Christ's sake shed their blood and lost their lives, what wondrous things hath Christ afterward wrought to his glory, and the confirmation of their doctrine! If it is not the place that sanctifies the man, but the holy man by Christ sanctifies the place; brother Bradford, then happy and holy shall he that place, wherein thou shalt suffer, and which shall be sprinkled over with thy ashes in Christ's cause. All thy country may rejoice of thee, that ever it brought forth such a one, who would render his life again in His cause of whom he had received it.

Brother Bradford, so long as I shall understand that thou art in thy journey, by God's grace, I shall call upon our heavenly Father for Christ's sake to set thee safely home; and then, good brother, speak you, and pray for the remnant that are to suffer for Christ's sake, according to what thou then shalt know more clearly.

We look now every day when we shall be called on, blessed be God! I think I am the weakest, many ways, of our company; and yet, I thank our Lord God and heavenly Father by Christ, that since I heard of our dear brother Rogers' departing, and stout confession of Christ and his truth, even unto the death, my heart, blessed be God, so rejoiced at it, that since that time, I say, I never felt any lumpish heaviness in my heart, as I grant I have felt sometimes before. O good brother, blessed be God in thee, and blessed be the time that ever I knew thee. Farewell, farewell.

Your brother in Christ,
N. RIDLEY.
Brother, farewell.

LETTER XX.

To Augustine Bernher.

BROTHER AUSTIN, I bless God with all my heart for his manifold merciful gifts given unto our dear brethren in Christ, especially to our dear brother Rogers, whom it pleased him to set forth first, no doubt of his gracious goodness and fatherly favour towards him. And likewise blessed be God in the rest, as Hooper, Saunders, and Taylor, whom it has pleased the Lord likewise to set in the fore front of the battle against his adversaries, and has endued them all, so far as I can hear, to stand in the confession of his truth, and to be content to lose their lives in his cause and for his gospel's sake.

And evermore and without end blessed be the same our heavenly Father for our dear and entirely beloved brother Bradford, whom now the Lord, I perceive, calls for; for I think he will no longer vouchsafe him to abide among the adulterous and wicked generation of this world. I do not doubt but that he, by those gifts of grace which the Lord hath bestowed on him plenteously, hath helped those who are gone before in their journey, that is, hath animated and encouraged them to keep the highway, and so to run that they may obtain the prize. The Lord be his comfort, whereof I do not doubt; and I thank God heartily that ever I was acquainted with him, and that ever I had such a one in my house. And yet again I bless God in our dear brother, and of this time, protomartyr Rogers,* that he was also one of my calling to be a prebendary preacher of London.

And now because Grindal is gone, the Lord, I doubt not, hath and doth know wherein he will bestow him; I trust to God it shall please him of his goodness to strengthen me to make up the trinity (three) out of Paul's church,† to suffer for Christ, whom God the Father hath anointed, the Holy Spirit beareth witness unto, and Paul and all the apostles preached. Thus fare you well. I have no paper; I was constrained thus to write.

N. RIDLEY.

LETTER XXI.

To Master Bradford.‡

DEARLY beloved brother Bradford, I had thought of late, that I had written unto you your last farewell until we should have met in the kingdom of heaven, by our

* So called because he was the first that suffered death for religion under that persecution.
† Rogers, Bradford, and Ridley.—Grindal had escaped to Germany.
‡ Bradford's execution having been suspended, many false reports were spread abroad respecting him, which Ridley notices in this letter.

dear brother Austin, and I sent it to meet you in Lancashire, whither it was said you were appointed to be sent to suffer. But now, since they have changed their purpose, and prolonged your death, I understand it is no other than once happened to Peter and Paul; who, although they were among the first that were cast into prison, and shunned peril as little as any other did, yet God would not have them put to death with the first, because he had more service to be done by their ministry, which it was his gracious pleasure they should do; so, without doubt, dear brother, I am persuaded that the same is the cause of the delay of your martyrdom.

Blessed be the Holy Trinity, the Father, the Son, and the Holy Ghost, for your threefold confession. I have read all three with great comfort and joy, and thanksgiving unto God for his manifold gifts of grace, wherewith it is manifest to the godly reader, that God assisted you mightily. And blessed be God again and again, who gave you so good a mind and remembrance of your oath once made against the bishop of Rome, lest you should be partaker of the common perjury, which almost all men are now fallen into, by bringing in again that wicked usurped power of his. Which oath was made according to the prophet, in judgment, in righteousness, and in truth, and therefore cannot be revoked without perjury, let satan roar and rage, and practise all the cruelty he can.

Oh! good Lord, that they are so busy with you about the church! It is no new thing, brother, that is happened unto you, for that was always the clamour of the wicked bishops and priests against God's true prophets: "The temple of the Lord, the temple of the Lord, the temple of the Lord:" and they said, "The law shall not depart from the priests, nor wisdom from the elders:" and yet in them, whom alone they esteemed for their priests and sages, there was neither God's law nor godly wisdom.

It is marvellous to hear what vain communications are spread abroad respecting you. It is said here, that you are pardoned your life; and when you were appointed to be banished and to go I cannot tell whither, you should say, that you had rather suffer here, than go where you could not live according to your conscience; and that this pardon should be begged for you by Bourne, the bishop of Bath, for that you saved his life.*

* Immediately after the accession of queen Mary, bishop Bourne

Again, some say, and among others mine hostess reports, that you are highly promoted, and are a great man with my lord chancellor!* This I could not believe, but denied it as a false lie; so surely was I always persuaded of your constancy. What God will do with us he knows. In the mean time, it is wonderful to behold how the wisdom of God hath infatuated the policy of the world, and scattered the crafty devices of the worldly wise. For when the state of religion was once altered, and persecution began to wax hot, no man doubted but Cranmer, Latimer, and Ridley, should have been the first to have been called to the stake. But the subtle policy of the world, setting us apart, first assaulted them by whose infirmity they thought to have more advantage, but God disappointed their subtle purpose. For whom the world esteemed weakest, praised be God, they have found most strong, sound, and valiant, in Christ's cause unto the death, to give such an onset as, I dare say, all the angels in heaven no less rejoice to behold in them, than they did in the victorious constancy of Peter, Paul, Esaias, Elias, or Jeremiah. "For greater love no man hath than to bestow his life," &c.

Good brother, have me and us all continually in your remembrance to God in your prayers, as, God willing, we shall not be forgetful of you in our prayers.

Your own in Christ,
N. RIDLEY.

LETTER XXII.

An answer to a letter written unto bishop Ridley by master West, sometime his chaplain.†

I WISH you grace in God, and love of the truth, without which, truly established in men's hearts by the mighty hand of almighty God, it is no more possible to stand by

---

was appointed to preach at Paul's Cross. In his sermon he spoke so much against the late king, Edward VI. and the Reformation, that a tumult was excited, and he would probably have suffered injury, had not Bradford stood forward and protected him.

* Bishop Gardiner.

† West had been chaplain to bishop Ridley, but turned to popery in queen Mary's reign, and, in the beginning of April, 1555, he wrote to the bishop with much earnestness and affection, urging him to

the truth in Christ in time of trouble, than it is for the wax to abide the heat of the fire.

Sir, know this, that I am, blessed be God! persuaded that this world is but transitory; and, as St. John saith, "The world passeth away, and the lust thereof." I am persuaded Christ's words are true: "Whosoever shall confess me before men, him will I confess also before my Father which is in heaven." And I believe that no earthly creature shall be saved, whom the Redeemer and Saviour of the world shall deny before his Father. The Lord grant that this may be so grafted, established, and fixed in my heart, that neither things present, nor to come, high nor low, life nor death, be able to remove me thence.

It is a goodly wish, that you wish me deeply to consider things pertaining unto God's glory: but if you had wished also, that neither fear of death, nor hope of worldly prosperity, should hinder me from maintaining God's word and his truth, which is his glory and true honour, it would have liked me well. You desire me for God's sake to remember myself; indeed, sir, now it is time so to do; for, so far as I can perceive, no less danger is before me than the loss both of my body and soul; and, I think then it is time for a man to awake, if any thing will awake him. He that will not fear Him, that threatens to cast both body and soul into everlasting fire, whom will he fear? With this fear, O Lord! fasten thou togethur our frail flesh, that we never swerve from thy laws. You say, you have made much suit for me. God grant, that you have not, in suing for my worldly deliverance, impaired and hindered the furtherance of God's word and his truth.

You have known me long indeed, in which time, it has chanced me, as you say, to mislike some things. It is true, I grant; for sudden changes, without substantial and necessary cause, and the heady setting forth of such extremities, I never loved. Confession unto the minister, who is able to instruct, correct, comfort, and inform the weak,

consider the danger he was in, not to stand against learning or in vain glory, but to return to the church of Rome, for " he must either agree or die." Ridley wrote this letter in answer: but though West was convinced he had done wrong, he wanted courage to renounce his preferments and the world. He pined away with grief and remorse, and died shortly after, even before Ridley; thus evidencing the folly of those who think to prolong their lives by sinful compliances. Gloucester Ridley considers this letter as having been written in 1555; but in Coverdale's Letters of the Martyrs it is dated 1554.

wounded, and ignorant conscience, indeed, I ever thought
might do much good in Christ's congregation, and so, I
assure you, I think even at this day.

My doctrine, and my preaching, you say, you have
heard often; and, according to your judgment, have
thought it godly, saving only for the sacrament; which,
although it was of me reverently handled, and a great deal
better than of the rest, as you say; yet in the margin you
write warily, and in this world wisely: and yet methought
all sounded not well. Sir, but that I see so many changes
in this world, and so many alterations, else, at this your
saying, I would not a little marvel. I have taken you for
my friend, and a man whom I fancied for plainness and
faithfulness, as much, I assure you, as for your learning;
and have you kept this so close in your heart from me
unto this day? Sir, I consider more things than one,
and will not say all that I think. But what need you to
care what I think, for any thing that I shall be able to
do unto you, either good or harm? You give me good
lessons, to stand in nothing against my learning, and to
beware of vain glory. Truly, sir, I herein like your counsel very well; and, by God's grace, intend to follow it
unto my life's end.

I cannot see what it will avail me to write unto those
whom you name. For this I would have you know, that
I esteem nothing available for me, which will not also
further the glory of God. And now, because I perceive
you have an entire zeal and desire for my deliverance out
of this captivity, and worldly misery, if I should not bear
you a good heart in God again, methinks I were to blame.
Sir, how nigh the day of my dissolution and departure out
of this world is at hand, I cannot tell: the Lord's will be
fulfilled, how soon soever it shall come. I know the
Lord's words must be verified on me, that I shall appear
before the incorrupt Judge, and be accountable to him for
all my former life. And although the hope of his mercy
is my sheet-anchor of eternal salvation, yet, I am persuaded, that whosoever wittingly neglects, and regards not
to clear his conscience, he cannot have peace with God,
nor a lively faith in his mercy.

Conscience, therefore, moves me, considering you were
one of my family, and one of my household, of whom then,
I think, I had especial cure, and who, above all those who
were within my house, indeed, ought to have been an

example of godliness to all the rest of my cure, not only of good life, but also in promoting of God's word to the uttermost of their power. But, alas! now when the trial separates the chaff from the corn, how small a deal* it is, God knows, which the wind does not blow away: this conscience, I say, moves me to fear, lest the lightness of my family shall be laid to my charge, for lack of more earnest and diligent instruction, which should have been done. But, blessed be God! who hath given me grace to see this my default, and to lament it from the bottom of my heart, before my departing hence.

This conscience moves me also now to require both you and my friend, Dr. Hervey, to remember your promises, made to me in times past, of the pure setting-forth and preaching of God's word and his truth. These promises, although you shall not need to fear to be charged with them of me hereafter before the world, yet look for none other (I exhort you as my friends) but to be charged with them at God's hand. This conscience, and the love that I bear you, bid me now say unto both in God's name, "Fear God, and love not the world;" for God is able to cast both body and soul into hell-fire. When his wrath shall suddenly be kindled, blessed are all they that put their trust in him. And the saying of St. John is true: "All that is in the world, as the lust of the flesh, the lust of the eyes, and the pride of life, is not of the Father, but of the world: and the world passeth away, and the lust thereof, but he that doeth the will of God abideth for ever."

For if this gift of grace, which undoubtedly is necessarily required unto eternal salvation, were truly and unfeignedly grafted, and firmly established in men's hearts, they would not be so light, or so suddenly shrink from the maintenance and confession of the truth, as it is now, alas! seen so manifestly of so many in these days. But here, peradventure, you would know of me what is the truth. Sir, God's word is the truth, as St. John saith, and that even the same that was heretofore. For, although man doth vary and change like the moon, yet God's word is stable, and abideth the same for evermore; and of Christ it is truly said, "Christ yesterday and to-day, the same is also for ever."

* Quantity.

When I was in office, all that were esteemed learned in God's word, agreed this to be a truth written in God's word, that the common prayer of the church should be had in the common tongue. You know I have conferred with many, and, I assure you, I never found man, so far as I remember, either old or new, gospeller or papist, of what judgment soever he was, in this thing to be of a contrary opinion. If then it were a truth of God's word, think you that the alteration of the world can make it an untruth? If it cannot, why then do so many men shrink from the confession and maintenance of this truth, received once of us all? For what else is it, I pray you, to confess or to deny Christ in this world, but to maintain the truth taught in God's word, or for any worldly respect to shrink from the same? This one thing have I brought for an ensample; other things are in like case, which now particularly I need not to rehearse. For he that will forsake wittingly, either for fear or gain of this world, one open truth of God's word; if he be constrained, he will assuredly forsake God and all his truth, rather than he will endanger himself to lose or to leave that which he loves better than he loves God, and the truth of his word.

I like very well your plain speaking, wherein you say, " I must either agree or die ;" and, I think, that you mean of the bodily death which is common both to the good and bad. *Sir, I know I must die, whether I agree or not.* But what folly were it then to make such an agreement, by which I could never escape this death, which is common to all, and should also incur the guilt of death and eternal damnation! Lord, grant that I may utterly abhor and detest this damnable agreement so long as I live.

And because, I dare say, you wrote from friendship unto me this short, earnest advertisement, and, I think, verily wishing me to live and not to die, therefore, bearing towards you in my heart no less love in God, than you do to me in the world, I say unto you, in the word of the Lord—and what I say to you, I say to all my friends and lovers in God—that if you do not confess and maintain to your power and knowledge, that which is grounded upon God's word, but will either, for fear or gain of the world, shrink and play the apostate, indeed you shall die the death—you know what I mean. And I beseech you all, my true friends and lovers in God, remember what I say, for this may be the last time, peradventure, that ever I shall write unto you.

From Bocardo, in Oxford, the 8th day of April, 1555.

NICHOLAS RIDLEY

LETTER XXIII.

A letter of Master Edward Grindal, then being in exile for the testimony of the truth, to Dr. Ridley, prisoner in Oxford, which we thought good to place here, for that the letter following is an answer thereof. See Coverdale's Letters of the Martyrs.

GRACE and consolation from God our Saviour, Jesus Christ.

Sir, I have often been desirous to have written to you, and to have heard from you, but the iniquity of the times has hitherto always put me out of all hope and comfort. Now at this present, God seems to offer some likelihood that these might come to your hands, which I thought to use, referring the rest to God's disposal. Your present state, not I only, who of all others am most bound, but also all others, our brethren here, do most heartily lament, as joined with the most miserable captivity that ever any church of Christ has suffered.

Notwithstanding, we give God most humble thanks, for that he hath so strengthened you and others your fellow-captives to profess a good profession before so many witnesses. And I doubt not, but He who has called you and them, not only to believe upon him, but also to suffer for him, does not leave you destitute of that unspeakable comfort which he ministers abundantly to his, in the school of the cross. May he grant that his name be glorified in you, whether it be by life or death, as may be most to his honour, and your everlasting consolation

Sir, I thought it good to advertise you somewhat of our state in these parts. We are here dispersed in divers and several places. Certain are at Zurich, good students, of either university, a number, very well treated by Master Bullinger, and the other ministers of the city. Another number of us remain at Strasburg, and take the advantage of Master Martyr's lessons, who is a very notable father

Master Scory and certain others are with him in Friesland, and have an English church there, but are not very numerous. The greatest number is at Frankfort, where I am at present; it is a very fair city, the magistrates favourable to our people, with as many other commodities, as exiles can well look for.

Here is also a church, and now God be thanked, well quieted by the prudence of Master Cox and others,* who met here for that purpose. So that now, we trust, God has provided for such as will fly forth from Babylon a resting-place, where they may truly serve him, and hear the voice of their true pastor. I suppose, in one place and another, dispersed, there are well nigh a hundred students and ministers on this side the seas. Such a Lord is God to work diversely in his, according to his unsearchable wisdom, who knows best what is in man.

The most victorious triumph is, that when in bonds for the gospel, we boldly confess our Lord. The next honour, that, withdrawing ourselves by a prudent retreat, we reserve ourselves for our Master's service. That is a public, this a private confession. The first overcomes the temporal judge; the other, content that God should judge his heart, preserves a conscience unviolated. The former shows a readier courage and intrepidity; the latter purchases his present security at the expense of great anxiety. The first, when called upon, is found already mature for glory; the latter perhaps stays for ripening. Though he who, leaving all, retires because he would not deny Christ, would also have confessed him, had his retreat been prevented. *Cyprian.*

We have also here certain copies of your answers in the Disputation: also your objections and answers to Antonius, and the treatise in English against Transubstantiation, which in time shall be translated into Latin.† It has been thought best not to print them till we see what God will do with you, lest it enhance their malicious fury, and also restrain you and others from writing hereafter,

* Some of the proceedings of Cox and his associates have been severely animadverted upon. See *The Troubles at Frankfort.*

† The account of the Disputations at Oxford are in Fox's *Acts and Monuments;* the other pieces of Ridley here mentioned will be found in the present work. The constant intercourse between the English protestants on the continent, and their brethren in England, providentially, was the means of preserving many valuable writings of the reformers. Grindal and Fox in particular were very active in seeking for them.

which should be a greater loss to the church of Christ, than forbearing these for a time. If I shall know your will to be otherwise, the same shall be followed.

Thus much I thought good to let you understand concerning these matters, and concerning the poor state of men here; who most earnestly and incessantly do cry unto God for the deliverance of his church, to behold the causes of the afflicted, and to hear the groans of his imprisoned, knowing that you, who in this state have more familiar access unto God, do not forget us. God comfort you, aid you, and assist you with his Spirit and grace, to continue his unto the end, to the glory of his name, the edification of his church, and the subversion of antichrist's kingdom. Amen. From Frankfort, the 6th May, 1555.

E. GRINDAL.

LETTER XXIV.

The Answer of Dr. Ridley.

BLESSED be God, our heavenly Father, who inclined your heart to have such a desire to write unto me, and blessed be he again, who hath heard your request, and hath brought your letters safe unto my hands: and above all this I bless him, through our Lord Jesus Christ, for the great comfort I have received by the same, of the knowledge of your state and of others, our dearly beloved brethren and countrymen in those parts beyond the sea.

Dearly beloved brother Grindal, I say to you and all the rest of our brethren in Christ with you, Rejoice in the Lord; and as ye love me and the others, my reverend fathers and fellow-captives, who, undoubtedly, are the glory of Christ, lament not our state; but I beseech you and them all to give unto our heavenly Father most hearty thanks for his endless mercies and unspeakable benefits given unto us even in the midst of all our troubles. For know, that as the weight of his cross has increased upon us, so he has not, and does not cease to multiply his mercies to strengthen us; and I trust, yea, by his grace I doubt not, but he will so do for Christ our master's sake even to the end.

To hear that you and our other brethren find in your exile favour and grace with the magistrates, ministers, and citizens at Zurich, at Frankfort, and elsewhere, greatly comforts, I dare say, all here, that do indeed love Christ and his true word. I assure you it warmed my heart to hear you name some, as Scory, Cox, &c. O that it had come in your mind to have said somewhat also of Cheke, of Turner, of Leaver, of Sampson, of Chambers, but I trust to God they are all well.

And, sir, seeing you say that there are in those parts with you so good a number of students and ministers, now, therefore, care you not for us, otherwise than to wish that God's glory may be set forth by us. For whensoever God shall call us home, as we look daily for none other, when it shall please God to say, "Come ye," blessed be God, ye are enough, through his aid, to light and set up again the lantern of his word in England.

As concerning the copies you say you have with you, I wonder they did not wander, and that they could find the way to come to you. My disputation, except you have that which I gathered myself after the disputation was done, I cannot think you have it truly.* If you have that, then you have therewith the whole manner after which I was used in the disputation.

As for the Treatise in English against Transubstantiation, I can hardly be brought to think that it would be worth while to translate it into Latin. But whatever it is I would by no means that any thing should be published in my name in either language, till you shall first be certain what God shall please to determine concerning us; and thus much unto your letters.

Now although I suppose you know a good part of our state here, for we are forthcoming, even as when ye departed, you shall understand that I was in the tower about the space of two months close prisoner, and afterwards they granted to me, without my request, the liberty of the tower, and so continued about half a year; and then, because I refused to allow† the mass with my presence, I was shut up in close prison again.

The last Lent save one it chanced, by reason of the tumult stirred up in Kent,‡ there were so many prisoners in the tower, that my lord of Canterbury, Master Latimer, Master Bradford, and I, were put altogether in one prison,

---

* It was the copy penned by Ridley's own hand, and afterwards printed in Fox's *Acts and Monuments*.

† Countenance. It has been stated that Ridley once attended mass, but this expression appears to contradict it.

‡ Wyat's insurrection.

where we remained till almost the next Easter, and then we three, Canterbury, Latimer, and I, were suddenly sent, a little before Easter, to Oxford, and were suffered to have nothing with us but what we carried upon us.

About the Whitsuntide following was our disputation at Oxford, after which all was taken from us, as pen, ink, &c. Our own servants were taken from us before, and every one had put to him a strange man, and we, each one, were appointed to be kept in several places, as we are unto this day.

Blessed be God, we three, at the writing hereof, are in good health, and in God, of good cheer. We have looked long ago to have been despatched for we were all three on one day, within a day or two of our disputations, condemned as heretics by Dr. Weston, he being the head commissioner, and since that time we remain, as we were left by him. The Lord's will be fulfilled in us, as I do not doubt but, by his grace, it shall be, to his glory and endless salvation, through Jesus Christ our Lord.

Likewise, the Lord hitherto hath preserved, above all our expectation, our dear brother, and strong champion in Christ's cause, John Bradford. He is likewise condemned, and is already delivered unto the secular power; and writs, as we have heard say, were given out for his execution, and called in again. Thus the Lord, so long as his blessed pleasure is, preserves whom he listeth, notwithstanding the wonderful raging of the world. Many, as we hear say, have suffered valiantly, confessing Christ's truth, and nothing yielding to the adversary, yea, not for the fear or pains of death.

The names of those whom I knew, and who have now suffered, are these: Farrar, the bishop of St. David's; Hooper, the bishop of Worcester; Rogers, once your fellow prebendary; Dr. Taylor, of Hadley; Mr. Sanders; and one Tomkins, a weaver; and now, this last day, Mr. Cardmaker, with another, were burnt in Smithfield, at London; and many others in Essex and Kent, whose names are written in the book of life, whom yet I do not know.

West, your old companion, and some time my officer, alas! has relented, as I have heard; but the Lord has shortened his days, for soon after he died, and is gone! Grimbold was caught by the heels, and cast into the Marshalsea, but now is at liberty again; but, I fear me, he escaped not without some becking and bowing, alas! of his knee unto Baal.

My dear friend Thomas Ridley, of the Bull-head in Cheap, who was to me the most faithful friend that I had in my trouble, is departed also unto God. My brother Shipside, that married my sister, has been almost half a year in prison for delivering, as he was accused, certain things from me: but now, thanks be to God, he is at liberty again, but so that the bishop hath taken from him his park.* Of all us three fellow captives at Oxford, I am kept most strait, and with least liberty, either because in the house where I am kept, the wife rules the husband, although he is mayor of the city, a morose and most superstitious old woman, and who thinks it for her credit that it be said of her that she guards me with the utmost caution and restraint. But the man himself, Mr. Irish, is obliging enough to every body, though to his wife something too obsequious. Though I never was married, as you know, yet from the conversation I have had with this married couple, I seem able pretty well to guess what a great misfortune and insufferable yoke it is to be linked with a bad woman in matrimony. Rightly, therefore, did the wise man say, that "A good wife is the gift of God;" again, "A virtuous woman will do her husband good." Either this, I say, is the reason, or else because the higher powers, for what cause I know not, have given command that it should be so; which, indeed, is the reason they constantly give me, whenever I complain to them of their excessive severity to me.

In Cambridge, as I hear say, all the reformations in their studies and their statutes, which were lately made, are now again cancelled and destroyed; and all things are brought back to their former confusion and old popery. All the heads of houses who favoured the gospel simplicity, or who were married, are removed, and others of the popish faction are put into their places; and so I hear are all the fellows of colleges served who refused to bend the knee to Baal Nor is it strange it should be so there, when the like is done every where else throughout the whole kingdom to all the archbishops, bishops, deans, prebendaries, parish priests, and the whole clergy. And

---

* An appointment which he held under the see of London, and of which Bonner deprived Shipside contrary to law.

to tell you much evil matter in a few words, popery reigns every where amongst us in all its ancient sway.

The Lord be merciful, and for Christ's sake pardon us our old unkindness and unthankfulness; for when he poured upon us the gifts of his manifold graces and favour, alas! we did not serve him, nor render unto him thanks, according to the same. We pastors, many of us, were too cold, and bare too much, alas! with the wicked world. Our magistrates abused to their own worldly gain, both God's gospel and the ministers of the same. The people in many places were wayward and unkind. Thus, of every side and of every sort, we have provoked God's anger and wrath to fall upon us; but blessed may he be, that hath not suffered his people to continue in those ways, which so wholly have displeased his sacred Majesty, but hath awakened them by the fatherly correction of his Son's cross, unto his glory and our endless salvation through Jesus Christ our Lord.

My daily prayer is, as God knows, and by God's grace shall be, so long as I live in this world, for you, my dear brethren, that are fled out of your own country, because you will rather forsake all worldly things than the truth of God's word. It is even the same that I used to make to God for all those churches abroad through the world, which have forsaken the kingdom of antichrist, and profess openly the purity of the gospel of Jesus Christ; that is, that God, our eternal Father, for our Saviour Christ's sake, will daily increase in you the gracious gifts of his heavenly Spirit, to the true setting forth of his glory and of his gospel; and make you to agree brotherly in the truth of the same, that there rise no root of bitterness among you that may infect that good seed which God hath sown in your hearts already. And, finally, that your life may be pure and honest according to the rule of God's word, and according to that vocation whereunto we are called by the gospel of Christ our Saviour; so that the honesty and purity of the same may provoke all that shall see or know it, to the love of your doctrine, and to love you for your honesty and virtue's sake; and so, both in the brotherly unity of your true doctrine, and also in the godly virtue of your honest life, to glorify our Father, which is in heaven.

Some great officers of our country, the lord chancellor Winchester, the earl of Arundel, and lord Paget, are upon an embassy with cardinal Pole in foreign parts, to bring about a peace (as it is reported) between the emperor, our king, and the king of France. After their return, and the queen is brought to bed, which we have long expected, and still expect every day, (and may God prosper her to the glory of his name,) we then shall expect triumphant crowns of our Lord, for our good confession, from our ancient enemy.

I most humbly and heartily commend myself to the prayers of you all, especially to you, most dear brother in Christ, and most beloved Grindal, and those of our dear brethren and beloved in the Lord, Cheke, Cox, Turner, Leaver, Sampson, Chambers, and all our brethren and countrymen who sojourn with you, and love our Lord Jesus Christ in truth.

I also recommend to your prayers my most reverend father and fellow prisoner in the Lord, Thomas Cranmer, now, indeed, most worthy of the title of the great pastor and primate; and that veteran apostle of our nation, and a true one of Christ, Hugh Latimer. Excuse, brother, the length of this letter; for I believe that from henceforth, most dear brother, you will be troubled with no more of my letters for ever.

Oxford. N. RIDLEY.

LETTER XXV.

To Mistress Glover, a woman zealous and hearty in the cause and furtherance of God's gospel.

MISTRESS GLOVER, I wish you grace and peace; and although I am not acquainted with you, yet, nevertheless, hearing that your husband, Master Glover, is in prison for God's word's sake,* and also that you are a woman hearty in God's cause; and thirdly, that old father Latimer is your uncle or near cousin, whom I do think the Lord has placed to be his standard-bearer in our age and country against his mortal foe antichrist: I am thus bold to write to you in God's behalf, to do according to the report which I heard of you; that is, that you be hearty in God's cause, and hearty to your master Christ, in furthering his cause, and setting forth his soldiers to his wars to the utmost of your power.

* He was burned at Coventry a short time before Ridley suffered.

Let no carnal, nor worldly regard of any thing, hinder
you to declare your true heart, which you are said to bear
to your master Christ, above all other things. Be hearty
now also to your husband, and declare yourself to love
him in God, as the true faithful Christian woman unto her
husband is bound to do. Now seeing that your husband,
who is set by God's ordinance to be your head, is ready
to suffer and abide in adversity by his Master's cause, and
to cleave to his head Christ; see likewise that you do
your duty accordingly, and cleave unto him your head;
suffer with him, that you may further his cause. His cause
now I understand to be Christ's cause, and therefore beware, good sister in Christ, that in no wise you hinder it.

Love so his body, and the ease and wealth thereof, that
your love may further him to the winning both of body and
soul unto everlasting life. And this love shall God allow
you; your husband shall have just cause to rejoice thereof,
and all the godly commend you therefore, and number you
for the same among the godly and holy women of God.
To your husband I have written more: and thus fare you
well now, good dear sister in our Saviour Christ.

I was the bolder to write to you, for I understood my
dearly beloved brother Austin, whom I call Faustus,
should be the carrier, a man whom I think God has appointed to do much pleasure for his servants pressed to his
wars.

Yours in Christ.
N. Ridley.

LETTER XXVI

*To a Friend that came to visit him in Prison, but could
not speak with him.*

Well-beloved, I thank you heartily for your manifold
kindness, but the Lord shall, I trust, acquit you your
meed.* Though satan rage, the Lord is strong enough to
bridle him, and to put an iron chain over his nose, when
it shall please him.

In the mean time, they that are the Lord's, will flee unto
him; and assuredly he will not forsake them that seek
him, in very deed and in truth. This bearer, my man, is
trusty; you may send your token by him. Let Nicholas

* Give you your reward.

still keep the shirts. The Lord reward that Lady Wyat, who for his sake hath thus remembered me: I do not know her personally. What can I render to Mistress Wilkinson, for all her benefits? Nothing, surely, but to desire our Lord to acquit her with his heavenly grace. If you tarry, I shall have more to say to you peradventure hereafter. Now, dearest friend, farewell in the Lord.

N. RIDLEY.

LETTER XXVII.

To a Cousin *

GOD'S Holy Spirit be with you now and ever. Amen. When I call to remembrance, beloved cousin, the state of those who for fear of trouble, or for loss of goods, will do, in the sight of the world, those things that they know and are assured are contrary to the will of God, I can do no less than lament their case, being assured that the end thereof will be so pitiful, without speedy repentance, that I tremble and fear to have it in remembrance. I would to God it lay upon some earthly burden, so that freedom of conscience might be given unto them; I write, as God knoweth, not of presumption, but only lamenting their state, whom I thought now in this dangerous time should have given both you and me comfortable instructions. But, alas, in lieu thereof, we have persuasions to follow, I lament to rehearse it, superstitious idolatry, yea, and worst of all is, they will seek to prove it by the scripture! The Lord for his mercy turn their hearts. Amen.

Yours,

N. RIDLEY.

LETTER XXVIII.

To the Queen's Majesty.†

IT may please your majesty for Christ our Saviour's sake in a matter of conscience, and now not for myself but for other poor men, to vouchsafe to hear and under-

* Gloucester Ridley supposes her to have been Mabyl, granddaughter of Lord Dacres, married to his cousin Nicholas Ridley.
† On the day previous to his martyrdom, after he had been de-

stand this mine humble supplication. Honourable Princess, in the time while I was in the ministry of the see of London, divers poor men, tenants thereof, have taken new leases of their tenantries and holdings, and some have renewed and changed their old, and therefore have paid fines and sums of money both to me and also to the chapter of Paul's, for the confirmation of the same. Now I hear say, that the bishop, who occupies the same room now,[*] will not allow the aforesaid leases, which must redound to many poor men's utter ruin and decay; wherefore this is mine humble supplication unto your honourable grace, that it may please the same, for Christ's sake, to be unto the aforesaid poor men their gracious patron and defender, either that they may enjoy their aforesaid leases and years renewed, as, when their matter shall be heard with conscience, I suppose both justice, conscience, and equity shall require; for that their leases shall be found, I trust, made without fraud or covent[†] either of their part or of mine, and also the old rents always reserved to the see, without any kind of damage thereof. Or if this will not be granted, then that it may please your gracious highness to command that the poor men may be restored to their former leases and years; and may have rendered to them again such sums of money as they paid to me and to the chapter for their leases and years so now taken from them, which concerning the fines paid to me may be easily done, if it shall please your majesty to command some portion of those goods which I left in my house, to be given unto them. I suppose that half of the value of my plate which I left in mine offices, and especially in an iron chest in my bed chamber, will go nigh to restore all such fines received; the true sums and parcels whereof are not set in their leases; and therefore if that way shall please your highness, they must be known by such ways and means as your majesty, by the advice of men of wisdom and conscience, shall appoint.

But yet, for Christ's sake I crave, and most humbly beseech your majesty, of your most gracious pity and mercy, that the former way may take place.

graded by bishop Brookes, Ridley read this letter to the bishop, and requested him to forward the petitions contained in it. Ridley then delivered it to his brother to be presented to the queen, it was dated for the day following.

[*] Bonner   [†] Deceit.

I have also a poor sister that came to me out of the north, with three fatherless children for her relief, whom I married afterwards to a servant of mine own house. She is put out of that which I did provide for them. I beseech your honourable grace, that her case may be mercifully considered, and that the rather, in contemplation that I never had of him which suffered endurance* at my entrance to the see of London, one penny of his moveable goods; for it was almost half a year after his deposition, before I did enter in that place; yea, and also, if any were left known to be his, he had license to carry it away, or for his use it did lie safe; and his officers know that I paid for the lead which I found there, when I occupied any of it to the behoof of the church or of the house. And, moreover, I had not only no part of his moveable goods, but also, as his old receiver and mine can testify, I paid for him towards his servants' common liveries and wages after his deposition £53 or £55, I cannot tell which.

In all these matters I beseech your honourable majesty to hear the advice of men of conscience, and especially the archbishop now of York, who for that he was continually in my house a year and more before mine imprisonment, I suppose he is not altogether ignorant of some part of these things; and also his grace doth know my sister, for whose succour and some relief, now unto your highness, I make most humble suit.†

N. RIDLEY.

The 16th day of October, 1555.

* Bonner. This letter shows the different treatment of the papists by King Edward, and the protestants by Queen Mary.

† Notwithstanding these godly and just requests, no justice could be had until that now of late (after queen Elizabeth's accession,) some of these shameful injuries were redressed by order of law.— *Letters of the Martyrs.*

With the godly letters of Ridley and his companions, we may contrast one written by Bonner on his restoration to the see of London. It was addressed to his cousin Thomas Shirley, and Richard and Roger Letchmore, and is too characteristic of him to be omitted.

"In most hearty wise I commend me unto you, asserting, that yesterday I was restored again to my bishopric, and replaced in the same as fully as I was at any time before I was deprived; and by the same sentence my usurper, Dr. Ridley, is utterly repulsed. So I would that ye did order all things at Kidmerley and Bushey at your pleasures; not suffering sheep's head or ship's-side, (alluding to Ridley's brother Shipside) to be any meddler therein, or to sell or carry away any thing from thence. And I trust at your coming up to the parliament, I shall so handle the said sheep's head, and the other calves' heads, that they shall perceive their sweet, shall not be without sour, sauce. This day it is looked that master Canterbury

LETTER XXIX.

To the preceding letters may be added an Extract of bishop Ridley's letter to the protector, the duke of Somerset, concerning the visitation of the University of Cambridge, which shows his faithful steadfastness for the truth, preferring it to an honourable situation to which he was appointed.

.... I perceive by your grace's letters, I have been noted by some for my barking there; and yet to bark lest God should be offended, I cannot deny, indeed it is a part of my profession, for God's word condemns the dumb dogs that will not bark and give warning of God's displeasure.

As for that which was suggested to your grace, that by my aforesaid barking I should dishonour the king's majesty, and dissuade others from the execution of the king's commission, God is my judge, that I intended, according to my duty to God and the king, to promote the maintenance and defence of his highness's royal honour and dignity If that is true, that I believe is true, which the prophet saith, the honour of the king approves just judgment. And the commissioners must needs, and I am sure will all testify, that I dissuaded no man, but contrariwise, exhorted every man, with quietness towards others, to satisfy their own conscience; desiring only that if it should otherwise be seen unto them, that I might, either by my absence or silence, satisfy mine. The which my plainness, when some took otherwise than according to my expectation, I was moved thereupon to open my mind, by my private letters, freely unto your grace......

It is a godly wish, that is wished in your grace's letters that flesh and blood, and country, might not more weigh with some men than godliness and reason; but the truth is, country, in this matter, whatsoever some men do sug-

(Cranmer) must be placed where is meet for him. He is become very humble and ready to submit himself in all things, but that will not serve. In the same predicament is Dr. Smith, my friend, and the dean of St. Paul's with others. Commend me to your bedfellows most heartily, and remember the liquor that I wrote to you for The bearer shall declare the rest, and also put you in remembrance for beeves and muttons for my house fare. And thus our blessed Lord long and well keep you all. Written in haste, this 6th of September, (1553.)

"Assuredly all your own,
"EDMUND LONDON."

gest unto your grace, shall not move me; and that your grace shall well perceive, for I shall be as ready as any other, first to expel some of my own country, if the report which is made of them can be proved.

And as for that your grace saith of flesh and blood, that is the favour or fear of mortal man,—yea, Sir, that is a matter of weight indeed, and the truth is (alas for my own feebleness) of that I am afraid; but I beseech your grace, yet once again, give me good leave, wherein here I fear my own frailty, to confess the truth.

Before God, there is no man this day (leaving the king's majesty for the honour only excepted,) whose favour or displeasure I either seek or fear so much as your grace's favour or displeasure; for both your grace's authority, and my bound duty for your grace's benefits, bind me so to do. So that if the desire of any man's favour, or fear of displeasure, should weigh more with me than godliness and reason, truly, if I may be bold to say the truth, I must needs say, that I am most in danger to offend herein, either for desire of your grace's favour, or for fear of your grace's displeasure. And yet I shall not cease (God willing) daily to pray God, so to stay and strengthen my frailty with holy fear, that I do not commit the thing, for favour or fear of any mortal man, whereby my conscience may threaten me with the loss of the favour of the living God, but that it may please him, of his gracious goodness, howsoever the world goes, to blow this in the ears of my heart, " God will send troubles upon them who seek to please men :" and thus, " It is a dreadful thing to fall into the hands of the living God :" and again, " Fear not them that kill the body."

Wherefore I most humbly beseech your grace, not to be offended with me, for renewing of this my suit unto your grace, which is, that whereunto my conscience cannot well agree, if any such thing chance in this visitation, I may, with your grace's favour, have license, either by mine absence or silence, or other like means, to keep my conscience quiet. I wish your grace, in God, honour and endless felicity. From Pembroke Hall, in Cambridge, June 1, 1549.

Your grace's humble and daily orator,
NICH. ROFFEN.

LETTER XXX.

Letter from Bishop Ridley to Sir William Cecil.

16*th Sept.* 1551.

GRACE and health.—Your preface so prettily mingled with sorrow and gladness, and the sorrowful sight that you had of the bottom of your purse, and your poor lame house, hath so affected and filled me with pity and compassion, that although indeed, I grant, I am blamed because of my fashion used towards some I may plainly seem to condemn unlawful beggary, yet you have filled mine affections so full, and have moved me so much, that you have persuaded me to grant unto you half a dozen trees, such as I may spare you, and mine officer shall appoint. I ween they must be pollards; for other, either few or none, God knoweth, I think are left of the late spoil in all my woods.

And, Sir, if you that can move men so mightily to have pity on the decay of one house, if you, I say, knew the miserable spoil that was done in the vacation time, by the king's officers, upon my woods, whereby in time past so many good houses have been builded, and hereafter might have been; also so many lame relieved, so many broken amended, so many fallen down re-edified: forsooth, I do not doubt but you were able to move the whole country to lament and mourn the lamentable case of so pitiful a decay. But, Sir, wot you what I thought, after I had refreshed my spirit with once or twice reading over of your letters? Jesus! thought I, if God had appointed this man to have been the proctor of a spiritual, that can thus move men to have pity upon a lame house; who could have passed by with a penny in his purse, but such a man could have wrung it out with words, although the passenger had been never such a cringe? And thus I wish you ever well to fare. From Fulham this 6th of Sept. 1551.[*]

Yours in Christ,
NIC. LONDON.

[*] This letter seems to be written as a gentle, though pointed rebuke, of the rapacity of the courtiers, and their eagerness to secure even small advantages to themselves at the expense of others.

LETTER XXXI.

To Sir William Cecil.

Good Mr. Cecil, I must be a suitor unto you in our good Master Christ's cause; I beseech you be good to him. The matter is, Sir, alas! he hath lain too long abroad, as you do know, without lodging, in the streets of London, both hungry, naked, and cold. Now, thanks be to Almighty God, the citizens are willing to refresh him, and to give him both meat, drink, clothing, and firing: but alas! Sir, they lack lodging for him. For in some one house, I dare say, they are fain to lodge three families under one roof. Sir, there is a wide, large, empty house of the king's majesty's, called Bridewell, that would wonderfully well serve to lodge Christ in, if he might find such good friends in the court to procure in his cause. Surely, I have such a good opinion of the king's majesty, that if Christ had such faithful and hearty friends, who would heartily speak for him, he should undoubtedly speed at the king's majesty's hands. Sir, I have promised my brethren, the citizens, to move you, because I do take you for one that feareth God, and would that Christ should lie no more abroad in the streets*.

LETTER XXXII.

A Letter sent from Dr. Ridley, late Bishop of London, (when lying in the Mayor's house of Oxford, called Mr. Irish,) unto one William Punt, who brought at that time writings from Mr. Hooper and Mr. Bradford to Dr. Ridley, Mr. Cranmer, and Mr. Latimer, to peruse, and for that he could not come to him, this letter was sent unto the said William into the town. Anno 1554.†

Brother Punt, ye do know what hath bechanced unto my brother of late; and the truth is also, that this three

---

* Gloucester Ridley does not state whether he possessed the original of this letter, nor does he mention whether he gives the whole or a part only; but it evidently refers to the application respecting the charitable foundations mentioned page 4.

† From a manuscript in the library of Emmanuel College, Cambridge

or four days I have been somewhat in a fervent heat, and felt in my body a disposition to an ague; but, thanked be God, it assuageth. I have looked for none other, nor yet do, but every hour for some to come to make a search. I have in haste read over the book, the three chapters. But mine advice is that they be not now published, lest they should be lost and no profit so might come by them; for I know no state of men, neither of high degree or low, lord, lawyer, priest, or layman, (as the world is set now,) whom I think would gladly receive them, specially of those that are learned in the Latin tongue; yea, and I fear that the setting (them) forth might be occasion to have the author of them more hardly to be handled, and so peradventure as he should be least able to do hereafter any more good either with his tongue or with his pen, which were a great pity. What this will come unto that they have gotten out by my brother-in-law's behaviour, I cannot tell; but it was not in my mind that anything should have come abroad in my name, until our bodies had been laid at rest. Commend me to all the holy prisoners in Christ, and desire them to pray for me unto our gracious Father, that as by my brother's trouble he hath somewhat increased my cross, so he will of his gracious goodness increase his gifts of grace to his glory and the furtherance of his truth. Amen.

Yours,

NICHOLAS RIDLEY.

LETTER XXXIII.*

From the Library of Emmanuel College.

WHY do you try, my dearest brother, to make an elephant of a fly? No more, I pray you, of such [folly.] By writing in this manner you at once stop my mouth, so that I can neither dare to acknowledge frankly your kindness to me and my brother, nor to thank you, lest forsooth I should seem to acquiesce in the truth of what

* This and the following letter are translated from the originals in Latin, in the library of Emmanuel College, Cambridge. They appear to have formed part of the correspondence between Ridley and Bradford, and most probably were written by Ridley, though they are without signature or address. They were first printed in the Parker Society's edition of Ridley's works.

you write, being cajoled by your mistaken compliment, or afford you an opportunity of making the same mistake hereafter.

Laying aside therefore all worldly flatteries of this nature, let us, my brother, labour diligently to contend, each one to the best of his power, to uphold the faith. Very great thanks do I render to God, through our Lord Jesus Christ, who hath suggested this thing to your mind, that what I have long been praying to God and earnestly that it might be given me, you yourself willingly and of your own accord offer me—nay, do with a most vehement entreaty demand of me; that is, the opportunity of your transcribing whatsoever little works there are of mine, undertaken with a view to defend our christian faith; and you ask me to communicate them to you, and [thus] by the very circumstance which is most gratifying to myself, you declare that you will be bound to me by a closer tie. Therefore, my brother, I willingly forward to you whatsoever I have; and a few I do possess, some written in Latin, and some in English, but all for the purpose of defending the purity of our christian religion, which Satan is now attempting with so numerous and powerful means altogether to subvert and put to the rout.

I here send you two treatises written in English, one in a bound book, and the other, in sheets not yet bound together; but in reading or transcribing from the bound book, lest your amanuensis should make any mistake, know that the introduction to that treatise is contained in 44 pages, and the annotations which precede, "*ex aug' dno reponi*" .... "*in suo loco proxime p^t lyīe 2"/,*"*

I send you here also another exhortatory epistle, written in Latin to those brethren who have embraced Christ with his cross. Lastly, I send you also those two sermons which Watson last year delivered at court before the queen during Lent; in which he appears very diligently to have laboured (as he is a man of acute parts) to impose upon the simple-minded, and to delude the unwary, that they might not acknowledge the truth, but rather embrace darkness for light, and error for truth.

---

* Some passages are uncertain, from the paper having been rubbed or torn.

These however I send you with my annotations, but not without a clue, which I know will be very evident to you when you read them.

And now, my brother, since I have thus, not without some labour, collected and reduced to order these writings such as they are, I pray you, to the end that they may be useful to me, and should I wish to lend them to others, to them also, (for it is uncertain how soon I shall have need of them,) that you will, if you wish to transcribe them, do so at your earliest convenience, and send me back my copies of them; and then you shall have whatever remaining writings I have, should you desire either to read or to transcribe them.

If I dared to send anything to my brother, who is now I think dragging out a wearisome existence in solitary confinement, I would indeed desire that he too should transcribe somewhat; but I greatly fear lest they should again surprise him in some incautious moment, and thence take occasion to exercise still greater severities upon him. I pray you, bid him be of good courage, for there is nothing whatever for him to fear. If the rumour which they are now circulating concerning Grimbald be true, I grieve much for Grimbald's sake: for the rest, I know that it matters not one jot to the cause of my brother.

Farewell, my most dear brother in the Lord.

LETTER XXXIV.

(See the note to the preceding letter.)

THAT I have so long kept silence towards you, has been caused by the somewhat diffuse labour of this my production which I now send you. Although I have been a long time in travail, nevertheless I now bring forth (alas, the folly !) a rough and shapeless lump which needs much polishing. Yet because I know you to be by no means a despiser of my labours, (by which I desire, God is my witness, to benefit as many as possible, and to hurt no one,) I have therefore determined to send it you, whatever it is, and of whatever sort it may turn out to be.

You may now inspect and judge of the whole, and if you like to transcribe anything, that also you can do.

Yet I do not now send all which I have determined to add to this treatise; but because there are not yet [incorporated] with it all those passages of scripture, with which as with a wall and trench I intend to fortify this my treatise, I have collected them to the best of my ability. After I have accomplished my intention, then I will read over again what you have previously written, and will send you back your book.

As to the book which you have given me an opportunity of reading, in which two such different writers are compared one with another, know that as I am much delighted with the genius and eloquence of the writer, so am I especially pleased with this, that I perceive the writer of that book to be a promoter of true piety and a favourer of the purity of God's word; which mind I pray God may increase and confirm in him for ever.

Farewell, most dear brother in Christ.

You will find the index of my treatise appended to the conclusion, (fol. 47,) and from its perusal you will easily see the sum of the whole treatise, and of all the matters which are discussed in it.

LETTER XXXV.

*From Augustine Bernher to Ridley.**

ALTHOUGH I am so weary as any man can be, by the reason of my journey I have had this day, yet I cannot but write two or three words to your lordship, desiring you for God's sake to pardon me because of my long absence contrary to my promise: but if you had known whereabouts I had been occupied, I am sure you would pardon me, although your lordship shall understand that I had no time at all to write out your book, the which thing truly is a great sorrow unto me. I have brought them all again, lest peradventure you should have need of them; and if so be that your goodness would let me have them for a while, I would copy them out with al' haste possible.

Good my lord, conceive nothing against me, for since my departure hence there hath been such turmoilings as never was in London, as I doubt not but your lordship hath heard of it. As yet all things go forward to the great pain of godly ministers and the perpetual shame of the people. The best tragedy to describe it would ask a great deal of time. If so be that your lordship hath not heard of the matter, I shall certify the same by my simple writing.

My lord, I pray you as you have at all times (preserved) your books, so I trust you will do forward; and if so be that God shall take your lordship out of this misery, I would by all means possible get them in print beyond the seas, where I shall have the help of learned men.

Mr. Bradford moveth to-morrow towards * * * * with my lord of Derby. I have promised him to meet him at Cambridge; therefore I pray you let me hear of you this day, for to-morrow I will be gone very early.

* From the library of Emmanuel College, Cambridge.

www.ingramcontent.com/pod-product-compliance
Lightning Source LLC
Chambersburg PA
CBHW070249230426
43664CB00014B/2455